D0655710

The Library of Pastoral Care

TITLES ALREADY PUBLISHED

Principles of Pastoral Counselling
R. S. Lee

Casework and Pastoral Care
Jean Heywood

In His Own Parish:
Pastoral Care through Parochial Visiting
Kenneth Child

Understanding the Adolescent
Michael Hare Duke

Marriage Preparation
Martin Parsons

Marriage Counselling
Kenneth Preston

Sick Call: A Book on the
Pastoral Care of the Physically Ill
Kenneth Child

Pastoral Care in Hospitals
Norman Autton

The Pastoral Care of the Mentally Ill
Norman Autton

Pastoral Care and the Drug Scene
Kenneth Leech

Caring for the Elderly
H. P. Steer

The Pastoral Care of the Dying
Norman Autton

The Pastoral Care of the Bereaved
Norman Autton

IN PREPARATION

The Pastoral Ministry to Children
Anthony Denney

Hearing Confessions
Kenneth N. Ross

God, Man, and Pastoral Care
G. B. Austin

Other volumes are planned

"A blessed companion is a book"—JERROLD

A ZOO IN MY LUGGAGE

and

ENCOUNTERS WITH ANIMALS

A ZOO IN MY LUGGAGE

and

ENCOUNTERS WITH ANIMALS

★

GERALD DURRELL

With illustrations by
RALPH THOMPSON

THE COMPANION BOOK CLUB
LONDON

*Made and printed in Great Britain
for The Companion Book Club (Odhams Press Ltd.)
by Odhams (Watford) Limited
Watford, Herts*
S.262.W

CONTENTS

★

A ZOO
IN MY
LUGGAGE

A WORD IN ADVANCE

THIS is the chronicle of a six-month trip that my wife and I made to Bafut, a mountain grassland kingdom in the British Cameroons in West Africa. Our reason for going there was, to say the least, a trifle unusual. We wanted to collect our own zoo.

Since the end of the war I had been financing and organizing expeditions to many parts of the world to collect wild animals for various zoological gardens. Bitter experience over the years had taught me that the worst and most heartbreaking part of any collecting trip came at the end when, after months of lavishing care and attention upon them, you had to part with the animals. If you are acting as mother, father, food-provider and danger eradicator to an animal, half a year is enough to build up a very real friendship with it. The creature trusts you and, what is more important, behaves naturally when you are around. Then, just when this relationship should begin to bear fruit, when you ought to be in a unique position to study the animal's habits and behaviour, you are forced to part company.

There was only one answer to this problem, as far as I was

concerned, and that was to have a zoo of my own. I could then bring my animals back knowing what type of cages they were going to inhabit, what sort of food and treatment they were going to receive (a thing which one cannot, unfortunately, be sure about with some other zoos), and secure in the knowledge that I could go on studying them to my heart's content. The zoo, of course, would have to be open to the public so that, from my point of view, it would be a sort of self-supporting laboratory in which I could keep and watch my animals.

There was another and, to my mind, more urgent reason for creating a zoo. I, like many other people, have been seriously concerned by the fact that year by year, all over the world, various species of animals are being slowly but surely exterminated in their wild state, thanks directly or indirectly to the interference of mankind. While many worthy and hardworking societies are doing their best to tackle this problem, I know a great number of animal species which, because they are small and generally of no commercial or touristic value, are not receiving adequate protection. To me the extirpation of an animal species is a criminal offence, in the same way as the destruction of anything we cannot recreate or replace, such as a Rembrandt or the Acropolis. In my opinion zoological gardens all over the world should have as one of their main objects the establishment of breeding colonies for these rare and threatened species. Then, if it is inevitable that the animal should become extinct in the wild state, at least we have not lost it completely. For many years I had wanted to start a zoo with just such an object in view, and now seemed the ideal moment to begin.

Any reasonable person smitten with an ambition of this sort would have secured the zoo first and obtained the animals afterwards. But throughout my life I have rarely if ever achieved what I wanted by tackling it in a logical fashion. So, naturally, I went and got the animals first and then set about the task of finding my zoo. This was not so easy as it might seem on the face of it, and looking back on it now I am speechless at my audacity in trying to achieve success in this way.

This, therefore, is the story of my search for a zoo, and it explains why, for some considerable time, I had a zoo in my luggage.

MAIL BY HAND

FROM my seat on the bougainvillaea-enshrouded verandah I looked out over the blue and glittering waters of the bay of Victoria, a bay dotted with innumerable forest-encrusted islands like little green, furry hats dropped carelessly on the surface. Two grey parrots flew swiftly across the sky, wolf-whistling to each other and calling "coo-eee" loudly and seductively in the brilliant blue sky. A flock of tiny canoes, like a school of black fish, moved to and fro among the islands, and dimly the cries and chatter of the fishermen came drifting across the water to me. Above, in the great palms that shaded the house, a colony of weaver-birds chattered incessantly as they busily stripped the palm fronds off to weave their basket-like nests, and behind the house, where the forest began, a tinker-bird was giving its monotonous cry, toink . . . toink . . . toink . . . like someone beating forever on a tiny anvil. The sweat was running down my spine, staining my shirt black, and the glass of beer by my side was rapidly getting warm. I was back in West Africa.

Dragging my attention away from a large, orange-headed lizard that had climbed on to the verandah rail and was busily nodding its head as if in approval of the sunshine, I turned back to my task of composing a letter.

"The Fon of Bafut,
"Fon's Palace,
"Bafut,
"Bemenda Division, British Cameroons."

I paused here for inspiration. I lit a cigarette and contemplated the sweat-marks that my fingers had left on the keys of the type-writer. I took a sip of beer and scowled at my letter. It was difficult to compose for a number of reasons.

The Fon of Bafut was a rich, clever and charming potentate who ruled over a large grassland kingdom in the mountain area of the north. Eight years previously I had spent a number of months in his country to collect the strange and rare creatures that inhabited it. The Fon had turned out to be a delightful host, and we had many fantastic parties together, for he was a great believer in enjoying life. I had marvelled at his alcoholic intake, at his immense energy and at his humour, and when I returned to England I had attempted to draw a picture of him in a book I wrote about the expedition. I had tried to show him as a shrewd and kindly man, with a great love of music, dancing, drink and other things that make life pleasant, and with an almost childlike ability for having a good time. I now wanted to revisit him in his remote and beautiful kingdom and renew our friendship; but I was a little bit worried. I had realized—too late—that the portrait I had drawn of him in my book was perhaps open to misconstruc-tion. The Fon might well have thought that the picture was that of a senile alcoholic who spent his time getting drunk amid a bevy of wives. So it was with some trepidation that I sat down to write to him and find out if I would be welcome in his kingdom. That, I reflected, was the worst of writing books. I sighed, stubbed out my cigarette and started.

"My dear friend,
"As you may have heard I have returned to the Cameroons in order to catch more animals to take back to my country. As you will remember when I was last here I came up to your country and caught most of my best animals there. Also we had a very good time together.

"Now I have returned with my wife and I would like her to meet you and see your beautiful country. May we come up to

Bafut and stay with you while we catch our animals? I would like to stay once more in your Rest House, as I did last time, if you will let me. Perhaps you would let me know?

"Yours sincerely,

"Gerald Durrell."

I sent this missive off by messenger together with two bottles of whisky which he was given strict instructions not to drink on the way. We then waited hopefully, day after day, while our mountain of luggage smouldered under tarpaulins in the sun, and the orange-headed lizards lay dozing on top of it. Within a week, the messenger returned and drew a letter out of the pocket of his tattered khaki shorts. I ripped open the envelope hastily and spread the letter on the table, where Jacquie and I craned over it.

"Fon's Palace,

"Bafut, Bemenda.

"25th January 1957.

"My good friend,

"Yours dated 23rd received with great pleasure. I was more than pleased when I read the letter sent to me by you, in the Cameroons again.

"I will be looking for you at any time you come here. How long you think to remain with me here, no objection. My Rest House is ever ready for you at any time you arrive here.

"Please pass my sincere greetings to your wife and tell her that I shall have a good chat with her when she come here.

"Yours truly,

"Fon of Bafut."

PART ONE

EN ROUTE

MAIL BY HAND

To: The Zoological Officer,
U.A.C. Manager's House,
Mamfe.

Dearest Sir,

I have once been your customer during your first tour of the Cameroons and get you different animals.

I send here one animal with my servant, I do not know the name of it. Please could you offer what price you think fit and send to me. The animal has been living in my house almost about three weeks and a half.

With love, sir.

I am,

Yrs. sincerely,
Thomas Tambic, *Hunter.*

CHAPTER ONE

THE RELUCTANT PYTHON

I HAD decided that, on the way up country to Bafut, we would make a ten-day stop at a town called Mamfe. This was at the highest navigable point of the Cross River, on the edge of an enormous tract of uninhabited country; and on the two previous occasions when I had been to the Cameroons I had found it a good collecting centre. We set off from Victoria in an impressive convoy of three lorries, Jacquie and myself in the first, our young assistant Bob in the second, and Sophie, my long-suffering secretary, in the third. The trip was hot and dusty, and we arrived at Mamfe in the brief green twilight of the third day, hungry, thirsty and covered from head to foot with a fine film of red dust. We had been told to contact the United Africa Company's manager on arrival, and so our lorries roared up the drive and screeched to a halt outside a very impressive house, ablaze with lights.

The house stood in what was certainly the best position in Mamfe. It was perched on top of a conical hill, one side of which formed part of the gorge through which the Cross River ran. From the edge of the garden, fringed with a hedge of the inevitable hibiscus bushes, you could look straight down four hundred feet into the gorge, to where a tangle of low growth and taller trees perched precariously on thirty-foot cliffs of pleated granite, thickly overgrown with wild begonias, moss and ferns. At the foot of these cliffs, round gleaming white sandbanks and strange, ribbed slabs of rocks, the river wound its way like a brown, sinuous muscle. On the opposite bank there were small patches of farmland along the edge of the river, and beyond that the forest reared up in a multitude of colours and textures, spreading endlessly back until it was turned into a dim, quivering frothy green sea by distance and heat haze.

I was, however, in no mood to admire views as I uncoiled myself from the red-hot interior of the lorry and jumped to the ground. What I wanted most in the world at that moment was a drink, a bath and a meal, in that order. Almost as urgently I wanted a wooden box to house the first animal we had acquired. This was an extremely rare creature, a baby black-footed mongoose, which I had purchased from a native in a village twenty-five miles back when we had stopped there to buy some fruit. I had been delighted that we had started the collection with such a rarity, but after struggling with her for two hours in the front seat of the lorry, my enthusiasm had begun to wane. She had wanted to investigate every nook and cranny in the cab, and fearing that she might go and get tangled up in the gears and perhaps break a leg I had imprisoned her inside my shirt. For the first half-hour she had stalked round and round my body, sniffing loudly. For the next half-hour she had made several determined attempts to dig a hole in my stomach with her exceedingly sharp claws, and on being persuaded to desist from this occupation, she had seized a large portion of my abdomen in her mouth and sucked it vigorously and hopefully, while irrigating me with an apparently unending stream of warm and pungent urine. This in no way improved my already dusty and sweaty appearance, and as I marched up the steps of the U.A.C. manager's house, with a mongoose tail dangling out of my tightly buttoned, urine-stained shirt, I looked, to say the least, slightly eccentric. Taking a deep breath and trying to seem nonchalant, I walked into the brilliantly-lit living-room, and found three people seated round a card table. They looked at me with a faint air of inquiry. "Good evening," I said, feeling rather at a loss. "My name's Durrell."

It was not, I reflected, the most telling remark made in Africa since Stanley and Livingstone met. However, a small, dark man rose from the table and came towards me, smiling charmingly, his long black hair flopping down over his forehead. He held out his hand and clasped mine, and then, ignoring my sudden appearance and my unconventional condition, he peered earnestly into my face.

"Good evening," he said. "Do you by any chance play Canasta?"

"No," I said, rather taken aback, "I'm afraid I don't."

He sighed, as if his worst fears had been realized. "A pity . . . a great pity," he said; then he cocked his head on one side and peered at me closely.

"*What* did you say your name was?" he asked.

"Durrell . . . Gerald Durrell."

"Good heavens," he exclaimed, realization dawning, "are you that animal maniac head office warned me about?"

"I expect so."

"But my dear chap, I expected you two days ago. Where have you been?"

"We would have been here two days ago if our lorry hadn't broken down with such monotonous regularity."

"These local lorries are bloody unreliable," he said, as if letting me into a secret. "Have a drink?"

"I should love one," I said fervently. "May I bring the others in? They're all waiting in the lorries."

"Yes, yes, bring 'em all in. Of course. Drinks all round."

"Thanks a lot," I said, and turned toward the door.

My host seized me by the arm and drew me back. "Tell me, dear boy," he said in a hoarse whisper, "I don't want to be personal, but is it the gin I've drunk or does your stomach *always* wriggle like that?"

"No," I said gravely. "It's not my stomach. I've got a mongoose in my shirt."

He gazed at me unblinkingly for a moment.

"Very reasonable explanation," he said at last.

"Yes," I said, "and true."

He sighed. "Well, as long as it's not the gin I don't mind *what* you keep in your shirt," he said seriously. "Bring the others in and we'll kill a noggin or two before you eat."

So we invaded John Henderson's house and within a couple of days we had turned him into what must have been the most long-suffering host on the West Coast of Africa. For a man who likes his privacy to invite four strangers to live in his house is a noble deed to start with. But when he has no liking for, and a grave mistrust of, any form of animal life, to invite four animal-collectors to stay is an action so heroic that no words can describe it. Within twenty-four hours of our arrival not only a mongoose, but a squirrel, a bushbaby and two monkeys were quartered on the verandah of John's house.

While John was getting used to the idea of having his legs embraced by a half-grown baboon every time he set foot outside his own front door, I sent messages to all my old contacts among the local hunters, gathered them together and told them the sort of creatures we were after. Then we sat back and awaited results. They were some time in coming. Then, early one afternoon, a local hunter called Agustine appeared, padding down the drive, wearing a scarlet-and-blue sarong and looking, as always, like a neat, eager, Mongolian shopwalker. He was accompanied by one of the largest West Africans I have ever seen, a great, scowling man who must have been at least six feet tall, and whose skin—in contrast to Agustine's golden bronze shade—was a deep soot black. He clumped along beside Agustine on such enormous feet that at first I thought he was suffering from elephantiasis. They stopped at the verandah steps, and while Agustine beamed cheerily, his companion glared at us in a preoccupied manner, as though endeavouring to assess our net weight for culinary purposes.

"Good morning, sah," said Agustine, giving a twist to his highly-coloured sarong to anchor it more firmly round his slim hips.

"Good morning, sah," intoned the giant, his voice sounding like the distant rumble of thunder.

"Good morning . . . you bring beef?" I inquired hopefully, though they did not appear to be carrying any animals.

"No, sah," said Agustine sorrowfully, "we no get beef. I come for ask Masa if Masa go borrow us some rope."

"Rope? What do you want rope for?"

"We done find some big boa, sah, for bush. But we no fit catch um if we no get rope, sah."

Bob, whose speciality was reptiles, sat up with a jerk.

"Boa?" he said excitedly. "What does he mean . . . boa?"

"They mean a python," I explained. One of the most confusing things about pidgin English, from the naturalist's point of view, was the number of wrong names used for various animals. Pythons were boas, leopards were tigers and so on. Bob's eyes gleamed with a fanatical light. Ever since we had boarded the ship at Southampton his conversation had been almost entirely confined to pythons, and I knew that he would not be really happy until he had added one of these reptiles to the collection.

"Where is it?" he asked, his voice quivering with ill-concealed eagerness.

" 'E dere dere for bush," said Agustine, waving a vague arm that embraced approximately five hundred square miles of forest. " 'E dere dere for some hole inside ground."

"Na big one?" I asked.

"Wah! Big?" exclaimed Agustine. " 'E big too much."

" 'E big like dis," said the giant, slapping his thigh which was about the size of a side of beef.

"We walka for bush since morning time, sah," explained Agustine. "Den we see dis boa. We run quick-quick, but we no catch lucky. Dat snake get power too much. 'E done run for some hole for ground and we no get rope so we no fit catch um."

"You done leave some man for watch dis hole," I asked, "so dis boa no go run for bush?"

"Yes, sah, we done lef' two men for dere."

I turned to Bob. "Well, here's your chance: a genuine wild python holed up in a cave. Shall we go and have a shot at it?"

"God, yes! Let's go and get it right away," exclaimed Bob.

I turned to Agustine. "We go come look dis snake, Agustine, eh?"

"Yes, sah."

"You go wait small time and we go come. First we get rope and catch net."

While Bob hurried out to our pile of equipment to fetch rope and nets, I filled a couple of bottles with water and rounded up Ben, our animal boy, who was squatting outside the back door, flirting with a damsel of voluptuous charms.

"Ben, leave that unfortunate young woman alone and get ready. We're going for bush to catch a boa."

"Yes, sah," said Ben, reluctantly leaving his girl friend. "Which side dis boa, sah?"

"Agustine say it's in a hole for ground. That's why I want you. If this hole is so small that Mr Golding and I no fit pass you will have to go for inside and catch the boa."

"Me, sah?" said Ben.

"Yes, you. All alone."

"All right," he said, grinning philosophically, "I no de fear, sah."

"You lie," I said. "You know you de fear too much."

"I no de fear, for true, sah," said Ben in a dignified manner. "I never tell Masa how I done kill bush-cow?"

"Yes, you told me twice, and I still don't believe you. Now, go to Mr Golding and get the ropes and catch nets. Hurry."

To reach the area of country in which our quarry was waiting, we had to go down the hill and cross the river by the ferry, a large, banana-shaped canoe which appeared to have been constructed about three centuries ago, and to have been deteriorating slowly ever since. It was paddled by a very old man who looked in immediate danger of dying of a heart attack, and he was accompanied by a small boy whose job it was to bale out. This was something of an unequal struggle, for the boy had a small rusty tin for the job, while the sides of the canoe were as watertight as a colander. Inevitably, by the time one reached the opposite bank one was sitting in about six inches of water. When we arrived with our equipment on the water-worn steps in the granite cliff that formed the landing-stage, we found the ferry was at the opposite shore, so while Ben, Agustine and the enormous African (whom we had christened Gargantua) lifted their voices and roared at the ferryman to return with all speed, Bob and I squatted in the shade and watched the usual crowd of Mamfe people bathing and washing in the brown waters below.

Swarms of small boys leapt shrieking off the cliffs and splashed into the water, and then shot to the surface again, their palms and the soles of their feet gleaming shell pink, their bodies like polished chocolate. The girls, more demure, bathed in their sarongs, only to emerge from the water with the cloth clinging to their bodies so tightly that it left nothing to the imagination. One small toddler, who could not have been more than five or six, made his way carefully down the cliff, his tongue protruding with concentration, carrying on his head an enormous water-jar. On reaching the edge of the water he did not pause to remove the jar from his head, or to take off his sarong. He walked straight into the water and waded slowly and determinedly out into the river until he completely disappeared; only the jar could be seen moving mysteriously along the surface of the water. At length this too vanished. There was a moment's pause, and then the jar reappeared, this time moving shorewards, and eventually, beneath it, the boy's head bobbed up. He gave a tremendous snort to expel the air from his lungs, and then struggled grimly towards the beach, the now brimming jar on his head. When he reached the shore he edged the jar carefully on to a ledge of rock, and then re-entered the water, still wearing his sarong. From some intricate fold in this garment he produced a small fragment of Lifebuoy soap, and proceeded to rub it all over himself and the sarong with complete impartiality. Presently, when he had worked up such a lather all over himself that he looked like an animated pink snowman, he ducked beneath the surface to wash off the soap, waded ashore, settled the jar once more on his head and slowly climbed the cliff and disappeared. It was the perfect example of the African application of time-and-motion study.

By this time the ferry had arrived, and Ben and Agustine were arguing hotly with its aged occupant. Instead of taking us straight across the river, they wanted him to paddle us about half a mile upstream to a large sandbank. This would save us having to walk about a mile along the bank to reach the path that led to the forest. The old man appeared to be singularly obstinate about the proposal.

"What's the matter with him, Ben?" I inquired.

"Eh! Dis na foolish man, sah," said Ben, turning to me in exasperation, " 'e no agree for take us for up de river."

"Why you no agree, my friend?" I asked the old man. "If you go take us I go pay you more money and I go dash you."

"Masa," said the old man firmly, "dis na my boat, and if I go lose um I no fit catch money again . . . I no get chop for my belly . . . I no get one-one penny."

"But how you go lose you boat?" I asked in amazement, for I knew this strip of river and there were no rapids or bad currents along it.

"Ipopo, Masa," explained the old man.

I stared at the ferryman, wondering what on earth he was

talking about. Was Ipopo perhaps some powerful local juju I had not come across before?

"Dis Ipopo," I asked soothingly, "which side 'e live?"

"Wah! Masa never see um?" asked the old man in astonishment. "'E dere dere for water close to D.O.'s house . . . 'e big like so-so motor . . . 'e de holla . . . 'e de get power too much."

"What's he talking about?" asked Bob in bewilderment.

And suddenly it dawned on me. "He's talking about the hippo herd in the river below the D.O.'s house," I explained, "but it's such a novel abbreviation of the word that he had me foxed for a moment."

"Does he think they're dangerous?"

"Apparently, though I can't think why. They were perfectly placid last time I was here."

"Well, I hope they're still placid," said Bob.

I turned to the old man again. "Listen, my friend. If you go take us for up dis water, I go pay you six shilling and I go dash you cigarette, eh? And if sometime dis ipopo go damage dis your boat I go pay for new one, you hear?"

"I hear, sah."

"You agree?"

"I agree, sah," said the old man, avarice struggling with caution. We progressed slowly upstream, squatting in half an inch of water in the belly of the canoe.

"I suppose they can't really be dangerous," said Bob casually, trailing his hand nonchalantly in the water.

"When I was here last I used to go up to within thirty feet of them in a canoe and take photographs," I said.

"Dis ipopo get strong head now, sah," said Ben tactlessly. "Two months pass dey kill three men and break two boats."

"That's a comforting thought," said Bob.

Ahead of us the brown waters were broken in many places by rocks. At any other time they would have looked exactly like rocks but now each one looked exactly like the head of a hippo, a cunning, maniacal hippo, lurking in the dark waters, awaiting our approach. Ben, presumably remembering his tale of daring with the bush-cow, attempted to whistle, but it was a feeble effort, and I noticed that he scanned the waters ahead anxiously. After all, a hippo that has developed the habit of attacking canoes gets a taste for it, like a man-eating tiger, and will go out of his way to be

unpleasant, apparently regarding it as a sport. I was not feeling in the mood for gambolling in twenty feet of murky water with half a ton of sadistic hippo.

The old man, I noticed, was keeping our craft well into the bank, twisting and turning so that we were, as far as possible, always in shallow water. The cliff here was steep, but well supplied with footholds in case of emergency, for the rocks lay folded in great layers like untidy piles of fossilized magazines, overgrown with greenery. The trees that grew on top of the cliffs spread their branches well out over the water, so that we travelled in a series of fish-like jerks up a tunnel of shade, startling the occasional kingfisher that whizzed across our bows like a vivid blue shooting-star, or a black-and-white wattled plover that flapped away upstream, tittering imbecilically to itself, with its feet grazing the water, and long yellow wattles flapping absurdly on each side of its beak.

Gradually we rounded the bend of the river, and there, about three hundred yards ahead of us on the opposite shore, lay the white bulk of the sandbank, frilled with ripples. The old man gave a grunt of relief at the sight, and started to paddle more swiftly.

"Nearly there," I said gaily, "and not a hippo in sight."

The words were hardly out of my mouth when a rock we were passing some fifteen feet away suddenly rose out of the water and gazed at us with bulbous astonished eyes, snorting out two slender fountains of spray, like a miniature whale.

Fortunately, our gallant crew resisted the impulse to leap out of the canoe *en masse* and swim for the bank. The old man drew in his breath with a sharp hiss, and dug his paddle deep into the water, so that the canoe pulled up short in a swirl and clop of bubbles. Then we sat and stared at the hippo, and the hippo sat and stared at us. Of the two, the hippo seemed the more astonished. The chubby, pinky-grey face floated on the surface of the water like a disembodied head at a séance. The great eyes stared at us with the innocent appraisal of a baby. The ears flicked back and forth, as if waving to us. The hippo sighed deeply and moved a few feet nearer, still looking at us with wide-eyed innocence. Then, suddenly, Agustine let out a shrill whoop that made us all jump and nearly upset the canoe. We shushed him furiously, while the hippo continued its scrutiny of us unabashed.

"No de fear," said Agustine in a loud voice, "na woman."

He seized the paddle from the old man's reluctant grasp, and proceeded to beat on the water with the blade, sending up a shower of spray. The hippo opened its mouth in a gigantic yawn to display a length of tooth that had to be seen to be believed. Then, suddenly, and with apparently no muscular effort, the great head sank beneath the surface. There was a moment's pause, during which we were all convinced that the beast was ploughing through the water somewhere directly beneath us, then the head rose to the surface again, this time, to our relief, about twenty yards up-river. It snorted out two more jets of spray, waggled its ears seductively and sank again, only to reappear in a moment or so still farther up-stream. The old man grunted and retrieved his paddle from Agustine.

"Agustine, why you do dat foolish ting?" I asked in what I hoped was a steady and trenchant tone of voice.

"Sah, dat ipopo no be man . . . na woman dat," Agustine explained, hurt by my lack of faith in him.

"How you know?" I demanded.

"Masa, I savvay all dis ipopo for dis water," he explained, "dis one na woman. Ef na man ipopo 'e go chop us one time. But dis woman one no get strong head like 'e husband."

"Well, thank God for the weaker sex," I said to Bob, as the old man, galvanized into activity, sent the canoe shooting diagonally across the river, so that it ground on to the sandbank in a shower of pebbles. We unloaded our gear, told the old man to wait for us and set off towards the python's lair.

The path lay at first through some old native farmland, where the giant trees had been felled and now lay rotting across the ground. Between these trunks a crop of cassava had been grown and harvested, and the ground allowed to lie fallow, so that the low growth of the forest—thorn bushes, convolvulus and other tangles —had swept into the clearing and covered everything with a cloak. There was always plenty of life to be seen in these abandoned farms, and as we pushed through the intricate web of undergrowth there were birds all around us. Beautiful little flycatchers hovered in the air, showing up powder-blue against the greenery; in the dim recesses of convolvulus-covered tree stumps robin-chats hopped perkily in search of grasshoppers, and looked startlingly like English robins; a pied crow flew up from the ground ahead and flapped heavily away, crying a harsh warning; in a thicket of thorn bushes, covered with pink flowers among which zoomed big blue bees, a kurrichane thrush treated us to a waterfall of sweet song. The path wound its way through this moist, hot, waist-high undergrowth for some time, and then quite abruptly the undergrowth ended and the path led us out on to a golden grassfield, rippling with the heat haze.

Attractive though they were to look at, these grassfields were far from comfortable to walk across. The grass was tough and spiky, growing in tussocks carefully placed to trip the unwary traveller. In places, where sheets of grey rocks were exposed to the sun, the surface, sprinkled with a million tiny mica chips, sparkled and flashed in your eyes. The sun beat down upon your neck, and its reflections rebounded off the glittering surface of the rock and hit you in the face with the impact of a blast furnace. We plodded across this sun-drenched expanse, the sweat pouring off us.

"I hope this damned reptile's had the sense to go to ground where there's some shade," I said to Bob. "You could fry an egg on these rocks."

Agustine, who had been padding eagerly ahead, his sarong turning from scarlet to wine-red as it absorbed the sweat from his body, turned and grinned at me, his face freckled with a mass of sweat-drops.

"Masa hot?" he inquired anxiously.

"Yes, hot too much," I answered, " 'e far now dis place?"

"No, sah," he said, pointing ahead, " 'e dere dere. . . . Masa never see dis man I done leave for watch?"

I followed his pointing finger and in the distance I could see an area where the rocks had been pushed up and rumpled, like bed-clothes, by some ancient volcanic upheaval, so that they formed a miniature cliff running diagonally across the grassfield. On top of this I could see the figures of two more hunters, squatting patiently in the sun. When they saw us they rose to their feet and waved ferocious-looking spears in greeting.

" 'E dere dere for hole?" yelled Agustine anxiously.

" 'E dere dere," they called back.

When we reached the base of the small cliff I could quite see why the python had chosen this spot to stand at bay. The rock face had been split into a series of shallow caves, worn smooth by wind and water, each communicating with the other, and the whole series sloping slightly upwards into the cliff, so that any-thing that lived in them would be in no danger of getting drowned in the rainy season. The mouth of each cave was about eight feet across and three feet high, which gave a snake, but not much else, room for manoeuvring. The hunters had very thoughtfully set fire to all the grass in the vicinity, in an effort to smoke the reptile out. The snake had been unaffected by this, but now we had to work in a thick layer of charcoal and feathery ash up to our ankles.

Bob and I got down on our stomachs and, shoulder to shoulder, wormed our way into the mouth of the cave to try and spot the python and map out a plan of campaign. We soon found that the cave narrowed within three or four feet of the entrance so that there was only room for one person, lying as flat as he could. After the glare of the sunshine outside, the cave seemed twice as dark as it was, and we could not see a thing. The only indication that a snake was there at all was a loud peevish hissing every time we moved. We called loudly for a torch, and when this had been unpacked and handed to us we directed its beam up the narrow passage.

Eight feet ahead of us the passage ended in a circular depres-sion in the rock, and in this the python lay coiled, shining in the torchlight as if freshly polished. It was about fifteen feet long as far as we could judge, and so fat that we pardoned Gargantua for comparing its girth with his enormous thigh. It was also in an extremely bad temper. The longer the torch beam played on it the more prolonged and shrill did its hisses become, until they rose to an eerie shriek. We crawled out into the sunlight again and sat up, both of us almost the same colour as our hunters because of the thick layer of dark ash adhering to our sweaty bodies.

"The thing is to get a noose round its neck, and then we can all pull like hell and drag it out," said Bob.

"Yes, but the job's going to be to *get* the noose round its neck. I don't fancy being wedged in that passage if it decided to come down it after one. There's no room to manoeuvre, and there's no room for anyone to help you if you do get entangled with it."

"Yes, that's a point," Bob admitted.

"There's only one thing to do," I said. "Agustine, go quick-quick and cut one fork-stick for me . . . big one . . . you hear?"

"Yes, sah," said Agustine, and whipping out his broad-bladed machete he trotted off towards the forest's edge some three hundred yards away.

"Remember," I warned Bob, "if we *do* succeed in yanking it out into the open, you can't rely on the hunters. Everyone in the Cameroons is convinced that a python is poisonous; not only do they think its bite is deadly, but they also think it can poison you with the spurs under the tail. So if we do get it out it's no good grabbing the head and expecting them to hang on to the tail. You'll have to grab one end while I grab the other, and we'll just have to hope to heaven that they co-operate in the middle."

"That's a jolly thought," said Bob, sucking his teeth meditatively.

Presently Agustine returned, carrying a long, straight sapling with a fork at one end. On to this forked end I fastened a slip knot with some fine cord which, the manufacturers had assured me, would stand a strain of three hundredweight. Then I unravelled fifty feet or so of the cord, and handed the rest of the coil to Agustine.

"No I go for inside, I go try put dis rope for 'e neck, eh? If I go catch 'e neck I go holla, and then all dis hunter man go pull one time. You hear?"

"I hear, sah."

"Now if I shout pull," I said, as I lowered myself delicately into the carpet of ash, "for Heaven's sake don't let them pull too hard. . . . I don't want the damn thing pulled on top of me."

I wriggled slowly up the cave, carrying the sapling and cord with me, the torch in my mouth. The python hissed with undiminished ferocity. Then came the delicate job of trying to

push the sapling ahead of me so that I could get the dangling noose over the snake's head. I found this impossible with the torch in my mouth, for at the slightest movement the beam swept everywhere but on to the point required. I put the torch on the ground, propped it up on some rocks with the beam playing on the snake and then, with infinite care, I edged the sapling up the cave towards the reptile. The python had, of course, coiled itself into a tight knot, with the head lying in the centre of the coils, so when I had got the sapling into position I had to force the snake to show its head. The only way of doing this was to prod the creature vigorously with the end of the sapling.

After the first prod the shining coils seemed to swell with rage, and there came echoing down the cave a hiss so shrill and so charged with malignancy that I almost dropped the sapling. Grasping the wood more firmly in my sweaty hand I prodded again, and was treated to another shrill exhalation of breath. Five times I prodded before my efforts were rewarded. The python's head appeared suddenly over the top of the coils, and swept towards the end of the sapling, the mouth wide open and gleaming pinkly in the torchlight. But the movement was so sudden that I had no chance to get the noose over its head. The snake struck three times, and each time I made ineffectual attempts to noose it. My chief difficulty was that I could not get close enough; I was working at the full stretch of my arm, and this, combined with the weight of the sapling, made my movements very clumsy. At last, dripping with sweat, my arms aching, I crawled out into the sunlight.

"It's no good," I said to Bob. "It keeps its head buried in its coils and only pops it out to strike . . . you don't get a real chance to noose it."

"Let me have a go," he said eagerly.

He seized the sapling and crawled into the cave. There was a long pause during which we could only see his large feet scrabbling and scraping for a foothold in the cave entrance. Presently he reappeared, cursing fluently.

"It's no good," he said. "We'll never get it with this."

"If they get us a forked stick like a shepherd's crook do you think you could get hold of a coil and pull it out?" I inquired.

"I think so," said Bob, "or at any rate I could probably make it uncoil so we can get a chance at the head."

So Agustine was once more despatched to the forest with minute instructions as to the sort of stick we needed, and he soon returned with a twenty-foot branch at one end of which was a fish-hook-like projection.

"If you could crawl in with me and shine the torch over my shoulder, it would help," said Bob. "If I put it on the ground, I knock it over every time I move."

So we crawled into the cave together and lay there, wedged shoulder to shoulder. While I shone the torch down the tunnel, Bob slowly edged his gigantic crook towards the snake. Slowly, so as not to disturb the snake unnecessarily, he edged the hook over the top coil of the mound, settled it in place, shuffled his body into a more comfortable position and then hauled with all his strength.

The results were immediate and confusing. To our surprise the entire bulk of the snake—after a momentary resistance—slid down the cave towards us. Exhilarated, Bob shuffled backwards (thus wedging us both more tightly in the tunnel) and hauled again. The snake slid still nearer and then started to unravel. Bob hauled again, and the snake uncoiled still farther; its head and neck appeared out of the tangle and struck at us. Wedged like a couple of outsize sardines in an undersize can we had no room to move except backwards, and so we slid backwards on our stomachs as rapidly as we could. At last, to our relief, we reached a slight widening in the passage, and this allowed us more room to manoeuvre. Bob laid hold of the sapling and pulled at it grimly. He reminded me of a lanky and earnest blackbird tugging an out-size worm from its hole. The snake slid into view, hissing madly, its coils shuddering with muscular contraction as it tried to free itself of the hook round its body. Another good heave, I calculated, and Bob would have it at the mouth of the cave. I crawled out rapidly.

"Bring dat rope," I roared to the hunters, "quick . . . quick . . . rope."

They leapt to obey as Bob appeared at the cave mouth, scrambled to his feet and stepped back for the final jerk that would drag the snake out into the open where we could fall on it. But, as he stepped back, he put his foot on a loose rock which twisted under him, and he fell flat on his back. The sapling was jerked from his hands, the snake gave a mighty heave that freed its body from the hook, and, with the smooth fluidity of water soaking into blotting paper it slid into a crack in the cave wall that did not look as though it could accommodate a mouse. As the last four feet of its length were disappearing into the bowels of the earth, Bob and I fell on it and hung on like grim death. We would feel the rippling of the powerful muscles as the snake, buried deep in the rocky cleft, struggled to break our grip on its tail. Slowly, inch by inch, the smooth scales slipped through our sweaty hands, and then, suddenly, the snake was gone. From somewhere deep in the rocks came a triumphant hiss.

Covered with ash and charcoal smears, our arms and legs scraped raw, our clothes black with sweat, Bob and I sat and glared at each other, panting for breath. We were past speech.

"Ah, 'e done run, Masa," pointed out Agustine, who seemed to have a genius for underlining the obvious.

"Dat snake 'e get power too much," observed Gargantua moodily.

"No man fit hold dat snake for inside hole," said Agustine, attempting to comfort us.

" 'E get plenty, plenty power," intoned Gargantua again, " 'e get power pass man."

In silence I handed round the cigarettes and we squatted in the carpet of ash and smoked.

"Well," I said at last, philosophically, "we did the best we could. Let's hope for better luck next time."

Bob, however, refused to be comforted. To have had the python of his dreams so close to capture and then to lose it was almost more than he could bear. He prowled around, muttering savagely to himself, as we packed up the nets and ropes, and then followed us moodily as we set off homewards.

The sun was now low in the sky, and by the time we had crossed the grassfield and entered the abandoned farmland a greenish twilight had settled on the world. Everywhere in the moist undergrowth giant glow-worms gleamed and shuddered like sapphires, and through the warm air fireflies drifted, pulsating briefly like pink pearls against the dark undergrowth. The air was full of the evening scents, wood smoke, damp earth, the sweet smell of blossom already wet with dew. An owl called in an ancient, trembling voice, and another answered it.

The river was like a moving sheet of bronze in the twilight as we scrunched our way across the milk-white sandbank. The old man and the boy were curled up asleep in the bows of the canoe. They awoke, and in silence paddled us down the dark river. On the hill top, high above us, we could see the lamps of the house shining out, and faintly, as a background to the swish and gurgle of our paddles, we could hear the gramophone playing. A drift of small white moths enveloped the canoe as it headed towards the bank. The moon, very fragile and weak, was edging its way up through the filigree of the forest behind us, and once more the owls called, sadly, longingly, in the gloom of the trees.

MAIL BY HAND

To: Mr G. Durrell,
The Zoological Department,
U.A.C. House,
Mamfe.

Dear Sir,

Here are two animals I am senting you like those animals that you should me in the pictures. Any tipe of money you want to sent to me try and rapp the money in a small piece of paper and sent it to that boy that brought animals. You know realy that a hunter always be derty so you should try to send me one bar soap.

Good greetings to you.

Yrs.,
Peter N'amabong.

CHAPTER TWO

THE BALD-HEADED BIRDS

On the opposite bank of the Cross River, eight miles through the deep forest, lay the tiny village of Eshobi. I knew both the place and its inhabitants well, for on a previous trip I had made it one of my bases for a number of months. It had been a good hunting-ground, and the Eshobi people had been good hunters, so, while we were in Mamfe, I was anxious to get in touch with the villagers and see if they could get us some specimens. As the best way of obtaining information or sending messages was via the local market, I sent for Phillip, our cook. He was an engaging character, with a wide, buck-toothed smile, and a habit of walking with a stiff military gait, and standing at attention when addressed; this argued an army training, which, in fact, he had not had. He clumped up on to the verandah and stood before me as rigid as a guardsman.

"Phillip, I want to find an Eshobi man, you hear?" I said.

"Yes, sah."

"Now, when you go for market you go find me one Eshobi man and you go bring him for here and I go give him book for take Eshobi, eh?"

"Yes, sah."

"Now, you no go forget, eh? You go find me Eshobi man one time."

"Yes, sah," said Phillip, and clumped off to the kitchen. He never wasted time on unnecessary conversation.

Two days passed without an Eshobi man putting in an appearance, and, occupied with other things, I forgot the whole matter. Then, on the fourth day, Phillip appeared, clumping down the drive triumphantly with a rather frightened looking fourteen-year-old boy in tow. The lad had obviously clad himself in his best clothes for his visit to the Metropolis of Mamfe, a fetching outfit that consisted of a tattered pair of khaki shorts, and a grubby white shirt which had obviously been made out of a sack of some sort and had across its back the mysterious but decorative message "PRODUCE OF GR" in blue lettering. On his head was perched a straw hat which, with age and wear, had attained a pleasant shade of pale silvery green. This reluctant apparition was dragged up on to the front verandah, and his captor stood smugly to attention with the air of one who has, after much practice, accomplished a particularly difficult conjuring trick. Phillip had a curious way of speaking which had taken me some time to understand, for he spoke pidgin very fast and in a sort of muted roar, a cross between a bassoon and a regimental sergeant-major, as though everyone in the world was deaf. When labouring under excitement he became almost incomprehensible.

"Who is this?" I asked, surveying the youth.

Phillip looked rather hurt. "Dis na man, sah," he roared, as if explaining something to a particularly dim-witted child. He gazed at his protégé with affection and gave the unfortunate lad a slap on the back that almost knocked him off the verandah.

"I can see it's a man," I said patiently, "but what does he want?"

Phillip frowned ferociously at the quivering youth and gave him another blow between the shoulder blades.

"Speak now," he blared, "speak now, Masa de wait."

We waited expectantly. The youth shuffled his feet, twiddled his toes in an excess of embarrassment, gave a shy, watery smile and stared at the ground. We waited patiently. Suddenly he looked up, removed his headgear, ducked his head and said: "Good morning, sah," in a faint voice.

Phillip beamed at me as if this greeting was sufficient explanation for the lad's presence. Deciding that my cook had not been designed by nature to play the part of a skilled and tactful interrogator, I took over myself.

"My friend," I said, "how dey de call you?"

"Peter, sah," he replied miserably.

"Dey de call um Peter, sah," bellowed Phillip, in case I should have been under any misapprehension.

"Well, Peter, why you come for see me?" I inquired.

"Masa, dis man your cook 'e tell me Masa want some man for carry book to Eshobi," said the youth aggrievedly.

"Ah! You be Eshobi man?" I asked, light dawning.

"Yes, sah."

"Phillip," I said, "you are a congenital idiot."

"Yes, sah," agreed Phillip, pleased with this unsolicited testimonial.

"Why you never tell me dis be Eshobi man?"

"Wah!" gasped Phillip, shocked to the depths of his sergeant-major's soul, "but I done tell Masa dis be man."

Giving Philip up as a bad job I turned back to the youth.

"Listen, my friend, you savvay for Eshobi one man dey de call Elias?"

"Yes, sah, I savvay um."

"All right. Now you go tell Elias dat I done come for Cameroon again for catch beef, eh? You go tell um I want um work hunter man again for me, eh? So you go tell um he go come for Mamfe for talk with me. You go tell um, say, dis Masa 'e live for U.A.C. Masa's house, you hear?"

"I hear, sah."

"Right, so you go walk quick-quick to Eshobi and tell Elias, eh? I go dash you dis cigarette so you get happy when you walk for bush."

He received the packet of cigarettes in his cupped hands, ducked his head and beamed at me.

"Tank you, Masa," he said.

"All right . . . go for Eshobi now. Walka good."

"Tank you, Masa," he repeated, and stuffing the packet into the pocket of his unorthodox shirt he trotted off down the drive.

Twenty-four hours later Elias arrived. He had been one of my permanent hunters when I had been in Eshobi, so I was delighted to see his fat, waddling form coming down the drive towards me, his Pithecanthropic features split into a wide grin of glad recognition. Our greetings over, he solemnly handed me a dozen eggs carefully wrapped in banana leaves, and I reciprocated with a carton of cigarettes and a hunting knife I had brought out from England for that purpose. Then we got down to the serious business of talking about beef. First he told me about all the beef he had hunted and captured in my eight years' absence, and how my various hunter friends had got on. Old N'ago had been killed by a bush-cow; Andraia had been bitten in the foot by a water beef; Samuel's gun had exploded and blown a large portion of his arm away (a good joke, this), while just recently John had killed the biggest bush-pig they had ever seen, and sold the meat for over two pounds. Then, quite suddenly, Elias said something that riveted my attention.

"Masa remember dat bird Masa like too much?" he inquired in his husky voice.

"Which bird, Elias?"

"Dat bird 'e no get bere-bere for 'e head. Last time Masa live for Mamfe I done bring um two picken dis bird."

"Dat bird who make his house with potta-potta? Dat one who get red for his head?" I asked excitedly.

"Yes, na dis one," he agreed.

"Well, what about it?" I said.

"When I hear Masa done come back for Cameroons I done go for bush for look dis bird," Elias explained. "I remember dat Masa 'e like dis bird *too much*. I look um, look um for bush for two, three days."

He paused, and looked at me, his eyes twinkling.

"Well?"

"I done find um, Masa," he said, grinning from ear to ear.

"You find um?" I could scarcely believe my luck. "Which side 'e dere . . . which side 'e live . . . how many you see . . . what kind of place. . . ?"

" 'E dere dere," Elias went on, interrupting my flow of feverish questions, "for some place 'e get big big rock. 'E live for up hill, sah. 'E get 'e house for some big rock."

"How many house you see?"

"I see three, sah. But 'e never finish one house, sah."

"What's all the excitement about?" inquired Jacquie, who had just come out on to the verandah.

"*Picathartes*," I said succinctly, and to her credit she knew exactly what I was talking about.

Picathartes was a bird that, until a few years ago, was known only from a few museum skins, and had been observed in the wild state by perhaps two Europeans. Cecil Webb, then the London Zoo's official collector, managed to catch and bring back alive the first specimen of this extraordinary bird. Six months later, when in the Cameroons, I had two adult specimens brought in to me, but these had unfortunately died on the voyage home of aspergillosis, a particularly virulent lung disease. Now Elias had found a nesting colony of them and it seemed we might, with luck, be able to get some fledglings and hand-rear them.

"Dis bird, 'e get picken for inside 'e house?" I asked Elias.

"Sometime 'e get, sah," he said doubtfully. "I never look for inside de house. I fear sometime de bird go run."

"Well," I said, turning to Jacquie, "there's only one thing to do, and that's to go to Eshobi and have a look. You and Sophie hang on here and look after the collection; I'll take Bob and spend a couple of days there after *Picathartes*. Even if they haven't got any young I would like to see the thing in its wild state."

"All right. When will you go?" asked Jacquie.

"Tomorrow, if I can arrange carriers. Give Bob a shout and tell him we're really going into the forest at last. Tell him to sort out his snake-catching equipment."

Early the next morning, when the air was still comparatively cool, eight Africans appeared outside John Henderson's house, and, after the usual bickering as to who should carry what, they loaded our bundles of equipment on to their woolly heads and we set off for Eshobi. Having crossed the river, our little cavalcade made its way across the grassfield, where our abortive python hunt occurred, and on the opposite side we plunged into the mysterious forest. The Eshobi path lay twisting and turning through the trees in a series of intricate convolutions that would have horrified a Roman road-builder. Sometimes it doubled back on itself to avoid a huge rock, or a fallen tree, and at other times it ran as straight as a rod through all such obstacles, so that our carriers were forced to stop and form a human chain to lift the loads over a tree trunk, or lower them down a small cliff.

I had warned Bob that we would see little, if any, wild life on the way, but this did not prevent him from attacking every rotten tree trunk we passed, in the hopes of unearthing some rare beast from inside it. I am so tired of hearing and reading about the dangerous and evil tropical forest, teeming with wild beasts. In the first place it is about as dangerous as the New Forest in mid-summer, and in the second place it does not teem with wild life; every bush is *not* aquiver with some savage creature waiting to pounce. The animals are there, of course, but they very sensibly keep out of your way. I defy anyone to walk through the forest to Eshobi, and, at the end of it, be able to count on the fingers of both hands the "wild beasts" he has seen. How I wish these descriptions were true. How I wish that every bush did contain some "savage denizen of the forest" lurking in ambush. A collector's job would be so much easier.

The only wild creatures at all common along the Eshobi path were butterflies and these, obviously not having read the right books, showed a strong disinclination to attack us. Whenever the path dipped into a small valley, a tiny stream would lie at the bottom, and on the damp, shady banks alongside the clear waters the butterflies would be sitting in groups, their wings opening and closing slowly, so that from a distance areas of the stream banks took on an opalescent quality, changing from flame red to white, from sky blue to mauve and purple, as the insects—in a sort of trance—seemed to be applauding the cool shade with their wings. The brown, muscular legs of the carriers would tramp through them unseeingly, and suddenly we would be waist-high in a swirling merry-go-round of colour as the butterflies dipped and wheeled around us and then, when we had passed, settled again on the dark soil which was as rich and moist as a fruit cake, and just as fragrant.

One vast and ancient tree marked the half-way point on the Eshobi road, a tree so tangled in a web of lianas as to be almost invisible. This was a resting place, and the carriers, grunting and exhaling their breath sharply through their front teeth in a sort of exhausted whistle, lowered their loads to the ground and squatted beside them, the sweat glistening on their bodies. I handed round cigarettes and we sat and enjoyed them quietly: in the dim, cathedral-like gloom of the forest there was no breeze, and the smoke rose in straight, swaying blue columns into the air. The only sounds were the incessant, circular saw songs of the great green cicadas clinging to every tree, and, in the distance, the drunken honking of a flock of hornbills.

As we smoked we watched some of the little brown forest skinks hunting among the roots of the trees around us. These little lizards always looked neat and shining, as though they had been cast in chocolate and had just that second stepped out of the mould, gleaming and immaculate. They moved slowly and deliberately, as if they were afraid of getting their beautiful skins dirty. They peered from side to side with bright eyes as they slid through their world of brown, dead leaves, forests of tiny toadstools and lawns of moss that padded the stones like a carpet. Their prey was the immense population of tiny creatures that inhabited the forest floor, the small black beetles hurrying along like undertakers late for a funeral, the slow, smooth-sliding slugs, weaving a silver filigree of slime over the leaves, and the small, nut-brown crickets who squatted in the shadows waving their immensely long antennae to and fro, like amateur fishermen on the banks of a stream.

Among the dark, damp hollows between the buttress roots of the great tree under which we sat there were small clusters of an insect which had never failed to fascinate me. They looked like a small daddy-longlegs in repose, but with opaque, misty-white wings. They sat there in groups of about ten, trembling their wings gently, and moving their fragile legs up and down, like restive horses. When disturbed they all took to the air and started a combined operation which was quite extraordinary to watch. They rose about eight inches above the ground, formed a circle in an area that could be covered by a saucer and then began to fly round and round very rapidly, some going up and over, as it were, while the others swept round and round like a wheel. The effect from a distance was rather weird, for they resembled a whirling ball of shimmering misty white, changing its shape slightly at intervals, but always maintaining exactly the same position in the air. They flew so fast, and their bodies were so slender, that all you could see was this shimmer of frosty wings. I am afraid that this aerial display intrigued me so much that I used to go out of my way, when walking in the forest, to find groups of these insects and disturb them so that they would dance for me.

Eventually, we reached Eshobi at mid-day, and I found it had changed little from the days when I had been there eight years before. There was still the same straggle of dusty thatched huts in two uneven rows, with a wide area of dusty path lying between them that served as the village high street, a playground for children and dogs and a scratching ground for the scrawny fowls. Elias came waddling down this path to greet us, picking his way carefully through the sprawling mass of babies and livestock, followed by a small boy carrying two large green coconuts on his head.

"Welcome, Masa, you done come?" he called huskily.

"Iseeya, Elias," I replied.

He grinned at us delightedly, as the carriers, still grunting and whistling, deposited our equipment all over the village street.

"Maso go drink dis coconut?" Elias asked hopefully, waving his machete about.

"Yes, we like um too much," I said, regarding the huge nuts thirstily.

Elias bustled into activity. From the nearest hut were brought two dilapidated chairs, and Bob and I were seated in a small patch of shade in the centre of the village street, surrounded by a crowd of politely silent but deeply fascinated Eshobites. With quick, accurate strokes of his machete Elias stripped away the thick husk from the coconut. When the tips of the nuts were exposed he gave each of them a swift slice with the end of his machete-blade, and then handed them to us, each neatly trepanned so that we could drink the cool, sweet juice inside. In each nut there was about two and a half glassfuls of this thirst-quenching, hygienically-sealed nectar, and we savoured every mouthful.

After the rest, our next job was to get the camp in order. Two hundreds yards from the village there was a small stream, and on its banks we chose an area that would not be too difficult to clear. A group of men armed with machetes set to work to cut down all the small bushes and saplings, while another group followed behind with short-handled, broad-bladed hoes, in an effort to level the red earth. At length, after the usual African uproar of insults, accusations of stupidity, sit-down strikes and minor brawls, the area had been worked over so that it resembled a badly ploughed field, and we could get the tents up. While a meal was being prepared we went down to the stream and washed the dirt and sweat from our bodies in the icy waters, watching the pink-and-brown crabs waving their pincers to us from among the rocks, and feeling the tiny, brilliant blue-and-red fish nibbling gently at our feet. We wended our way back to camp, feeling refreshed, and found some sort of organization reigning. When we had eaten, Elias came and squatted in the shade of our lean-to tent, and we discussed hunting plans.

"What time we go look dis bird, Elias?"

"Eh, Masa savvay now 'e be hot too much. For dis time dis bird 'e go look for chop for bush. For evening time when it get cold 'e go for dis 'e house for work, and den we go see um."

"All right, then you go come back for four o'clock time, you hear? Then we go look dis bird, eh?"

"Yes, sah," said Elias, rising to his feet.

"And if you no speak true, if we never see dis bird, if you've been funning me I go shoot you, bushman, you hear?"

"Eh!" he exclaimed, chuckling, "I never fun with Masa, for true, sah."

"All right, we go see you, eh?"

"Yes, sah," he said, as he twisted his sarong round his ample hips and padded off towards the village.

At four o'clock the sun had dipped behind the tallest of the forest trees, and the air had the warm, drowsy stillness of evening. Elias returned, wearing, in place of his gaudy sarong, a scrap of dirty cloth twisted round his loins. He waved his machete nonchalantly.

"I done come, Masa," he proclaimed. "Masa ready?"

"Yes," I said, shouldering my field-glasses and collecting-bag. "Let's go, hunter man."

Elias led us down the dusty main street of the village, and then branched off abruptly down a narrow alley-way between the huts. This led us into a small patch of farmland, full of feathery cassava bushes and dusty banana plants. Presently, the path dipped across a small stream and then wound its way into the forest. Before we had left the village street Elias had pointed out a hill to me which he said was the home of *Picathartes,* and although it had looked near enough to the village, I knew better than to believe it. The Cameroon forest is like the Looking-glass Garden. Your objective seems to loom over you, but as you walk towards it, it appears to shift position. At times, like Alice, you are forced to walk in the opposite direction in order to get there.

And so it was with this hill. The path, instead of making straight for it, seemed to weave to and fro through the forest in the most haphazard fashion, until I began to feel I must have been looking at the wrong hill when Elias had pointed it out to me. At that moment, however, the path started to climb in a determined manner, and it was obvious that we had reached the base of the hill. Elias left the path and plunged into the undergrowth on one side, hacking his way through the overhanging lianas and thorn-bushes with his machete, hissing softly through his teeth, his feet spreading out in the soft leaf mould without a sound. In a very short time we were plodding up a slope so steep that, on occasions, Elias' feet were on a level with my eyes.

Most hills and mountains in the Cameroons are of a curious and exhausting construction. Created by ancient volcanic eruption, they had been pushed skywards viciously by the massive underground forces, and this has formed them in a peculiar way. They are curiously geometrical, some perfect isosceles triangles, some acute angles, some cones and some box-shaped. They reared up in such a bewildering variety of shapes that it would have been no surprise to see a cluster of them demonstrating one of the more spiky and incomprehensible of Euclid's theorems.

The hill whose sides we were now assaulting reared up in an almost perfect cone. After you had been climbing for a bit you began to gain the impression that it was much steeper than it had first appeared, and within a quarter of an hour you were convinced that the surface sloped at the rate of one in one. Elias went up it as though it were a level macadam road, ducking and weaving skilfully between the branches and overhanging undergrowth, while Bob and I, sweating and panting, struggled along behind, sometimes on all fours, in an effort to keep pace with him. Then, to our relief, just below the crest of the hill, the ground flattened out into a wide ledge, and through the tangle of trees we could see, ahead of us, a fifty-foot cliff of granite, patched with ferns and begonias, with a tumbled mass of giant, water-smoothed boulders at its base.

"Dis na de place, Masa," said Elias, stopping and lowering his fat bottom on to a rock.

"Good," said Bob and I in unison, and sat down to regain our breath.

When we had rested, Elias led us along through the maze of boulders to a place where the cliff face sloped outwards, overhanging the rocks below. We moved some little way along under this overhang, and then Elias stopped suddenly.

"Dere de house, Masa," he said, his fine teeth gleaming in a grin of pride. He was pointing up at the rock face, and I saw, ten feet above us, the nest of a *Picathartes*.

At first glance it resembled a huge swallow's nest, made out of reddish-brown mud and tiny rootlets. At the base of the nest longer roots and grass stalks had been woven into the earth so that they hung down in a sort of beard; whether this was just untidy workmanship on the part of the bird, or whether it was done for reasons of camouflage, was difficult to judge. Certainly the trailing beard of roots and grass did disguise the nest, for, at first sight, it resembled nothing more than a tussock of grass and mud that had become attached to the gnarled, water-ribbed surface of the cliff. The whole nest was about the size of a football and this position under the overhang of the cliff nicely protected it from any rain.

Our first task was to discover if the nest contained anything. Luckily a tall, slender sapling was growing opposite, so we shinned up this in turn and peered into the inside of the nest. To our annoyance it was empty, though ready to receive eggs, for it had been lined with fine roots woven into a springy mat. We moved a little way along the cliff and soon came upon two more nests, one complete like the first one, and one half finished. But there was no sign of young or eggs.

"If we go hide, small time dat bird go come, sah," said Elias.

"Are you sure?" I asked doubtfully.

"Yes, sah, for true, sah."

"All right, we'll wait small time."

Elias took us to a place where a cave had been scooped out of the cliff, its mouth almost blocked by an enormous boulder, and we crouched down behind this natural screen. We had a clear view of the cliff-face where the nests hung, while we ourselves were in shadow and almost hidden by the wall of stone in front of us. We settled down to wait.

The forest was getting gloomy now, for the sun was well down. The sky through the tangle of leaves and lianas above our heads was green flecked with gold, like the flanks of an enormous dragon seen between the trees. Now the very special evening noises had started. In the distance we could hear the rhythmic crash of a troupe of mona monkeys on their way to bed, leaping from tree to

tree, with a sound like great surf on a rocky shore, punctuated by occasional cries of "Oink . . . Oink . . ." from some member of the troupe. They passed somewhere below us along the base of the hill, but the undergrowth was too thick for us to see them. Following them came the usual retinue of hornbills, their wings making fantastically loud whooping noises as they flew from tree to tree. Two of them crashed into the branches above us and sat there silhouetted against the green sky, carrying on a long and complicated conversation, ducking and swaying their heads, great beaks gaping, whining and honking hysterically at each other. Their fantastic heads, with the great beaks and sausage-shaped casques lying on top, bobbing and mowing against the sky, looked like some weird devil-masks from a Ceylonese dance.

The perpetual insect orchestra had increased a thousandfold with the approach of darkness, and the valley below us seemed to vibrate with their song. Somewhere a tree-frog started up, a long, trilling note, followed by a pause, as though he were boring a hole through a tree with a miniature pneumatic drill, and had to pause now and then to let it cool. Suddenly I heard a new noise. It was a sound I had never heard before and I glanced inquiringly at Elias. He had stiffened, and was peering into the gloomy net of lianas and leaves around us.

"Na whatee dat?" I whispered.

"Na de bird, sah."

The first cry had been quite far down the hill, but now came another cry, much closer. It was a curious noise which can only be described, rather inadequately, as similar to the sudden sharp yap of a pekinese, but much more flute-like and plaintive. Again it came, and again, but we still could not see the bird, though we strained our eyes in the gloom.

"D'you think it's *Picathartes*?" whispered Bob.

"I don't know. . . . It's a noise I haven't heard before."

There was a pause, and then suddenly the cry was repeated, very near now, and we lay motionless behind our rock. Not far in front of our position grew a thirty-foot sapling, bent under the weight of a liana as thick as a bell-rope that hung in loops around it, its main stem hidden in the foliage of some nearby tree. While the rest of the area we could see was gloomy and ill-defined, this sapling, lovingly entwined by its killer liana, was lit by the last rays of the setting sun, so that the whole setting was rather like a meticulous backcloth. And, as though a curtain had gone up on this miniature stage, a real live *Picathartes* suddenly appeared before us.

I say suddenly and I mean it. Animals and birds in a tropical forest generally approach so quietly that they appear before you suddenly, unexpectedly, as if dropped there by magic. The thick liana fell in a huge loop from the top of the sapling, and on this loop the bird materialized, swaying gently on its perch, its head cocked on one side as if listening. Seeing any wild animal in its natural surroundings is a thrill, but to watch something that you know is a great rarity, something that you know has only been seen by a handful of people before you, gives the whole thing an added excitement and spice. So Bob and I lay there staring at the bird with the ardent, avid expressions of a couple of philatelists who have just discovered a penny black in a child's stamp album.

The *Picathartes* was about the size of a jackdaw, but its body had the plump, sleek lines of a blackbird. Its legs were long and powerful, and its eyes large and obviously keen. The breast was a delicate creamy-buff and the back and long tail a beautiful slate grey, pale and powdery-looking. The edge of the wing was black and this acted as a dividing-line that showed up wonderfully the breast and back colours. But it was the bird's head that caught the attention and held it. It was completely bare of feathers: the forehead and top of the head were a vivid sky blue, the back a bright rose-madder pink, while the sides of the head and the cheeks were black. Normally a bald-headed bird looks rather revolting, as if it were suffering from some unpleasant and incurable disease, but *Picathartes* looked splendid with its tricoloured head, as if wearing a crown.

After the bird had perched on the liana for a minute or so it flew down on to the ground, and proceeded to work its way to and fro among the rocks in a series of prodigious leaps, quite extraordinary to watch. They were not ordinary bird-like hops, for *Picathartes* was projected into the air as if those powerful legs were springs. It disappeared from view among the rocks, and we heard it call. It was answered almost at once from the top of the cliff, and looking up we could see another *Picathartes* on a branch above us, peering down at the nests on the cliff-face. Suddenly it spiralled downwards and alighted on the edge of one of the nests, paused a moment to look about, and then leaned forward to tidy up a hairlike rootlet that had become disarranged. Then the bird leaped into the air—there was no other way to describe it—and swooped down the hill into the gloomy forest. The other emerged from among the rocks and flew after it, and in a short time we heard them calling to each other plaintively among the trees.

"Ah," said Elias, rising and stretching himself, " 'e done go."

" 'E no go come back?" I asked, pummelling my leg, which had gone to sleep.

"No, sah. 'E done go for inside bush, for some big stick where 'e go sleep. Tomorrow 'e go come back for work dis 'e house."

"Well, we might as well go back to Eshobi then."

Our progress down the hill was a much speedier affair than our ascent. It was now so dark under the canopy of trees that we frequently missed our footing and slid for considerable distances on our backsides, clutching desperately at trees and roots as we passed in an effort to slow down. Eventually we emerged in the Eshobi high street bruised, scratched and covered with leaf-mould. I was filled with elation at having seen a live *Picathartes*, but, at the same time, depressed by the thought that we could not hope to get any of the youngsters. It was obviously useless hanging around in Eshobi, so I decided we would set off again for Mamfe the next day, and try to do a little collecting as we passed through the forest. One of the most successful ways of collecting animals in the Cameroons is to smoke out hollow trees, and on our way to Eshobi I had noticed several huge trees with hollow insides, which I thought might well repay investigation.

Early the next morning we packed up our equipment, and sent the carriers off with it. Then, accompanied by Elias and three other Eshobi hunters, Bob and I followed at a more leisurely pace.

The first tree was three miles into the forest, lying fairly close to the edge of the Eshobi road. It was a hundred and fifty feet high, and the greater part of its trunk was as hollow as a drum. There is quite an art to smoking out a hollow tree. It is a prolonged and sometimes complicated process. Before going to all the trouble of smoking a tree the first thing to do, if possible, is to ascertain whether or not there is anything inside worth smoking out. If the tree has a large hole at the base of the trunk, as most of them do, this is a relatively simple matter. You simply stick your head inside and get somebody to beat the trunk with a stick. If there are any animals inside you will hear them moving about uneasily after the reverberations have died away, and even if you can't hear them you can be assured of their presence by the shower of powdery rotten wood that will come cascading down the trunk. Having discovered that there is something inside the tree the next job is to scan the top part of the trunk with fieldglasses and try and spot all exit holes, which then have to be covered with nets. When this has been done, a man is stationed up the tree to retrieve any creature that gets caught up there, the holes at the base of the trunk are stopped. You then light a fire, and this is the really tricky part of the operation, for the inside of these trees is generally dry and tinder-like, and if you are not careful you can set the whole thing ablaze. So first of all you kindle a small bright blaze with dry twigs, moss and leaves, and when this is well alight you care-fully cover it with ever-increasing quantities of green leaves, so that the fire no longer blazes but sends up a sullen column of pungent smoke, which is sucked up the hollow barrel of the tree exactly as if it were a chimney. After this anything can happen and generally does, for these hollow trees often contain a weird variety of inhabitants, ranging from spitting cobras to civet cats, from bats to giant snails; half the charm and excitement of smoking out a tree is that you are never quite sure what is going to appear next.

The first tree we smoked was not a wild success. All we got was a handful of leaf-nosed bats with extraordinary gargoyle-like faces, three giant millipedes that looked like Frankfurter sausages with a fringe of legs underneath and a small grey dormouse which bit one of the hunters in the thumb and escaped. So we removed the nets, put out the fire and proceeded on our way. The next hollow tree was considerably taller and of tremendous girth. At its base was an enormous split in the trunk shaped like a church door, and four of us could stand comfortably in the gloomy interior of the trunk. Peering up the hollow barrel of the trunk and beating on the wood with a machete we were rewarded by vague scuffling noises from above, and a shower of powdery rotten wood fell on our upturned faces and into our eyes. Obviously the tree contained something. Our chief problem was to get a hunter to the top of the tree to cover the exit holes, for the trunk swept up about a hundred and twenty feet into the sky as smooth as a walking-stick. Eventually, we joined all three of our rope-ladders together, and tied a strong, light rope to one end. Then, weighting the rope end, we hurled it up into the forest canopy until our arms ached, until at last it fell over a branch and we could haul the ladders up into the sky and secure them. So, when the nets were fixed in position at the top and bottom of the tree, we lit the fire at the base of the trunk and stood back to await results.

Generally one had to wait four or five minutes for the smoke to percolate to every part of the tree before one got any response, but in this particular case the results were almost immediate. The first beasts to appear were those nauseating-looking creatures called whip-scorpions. They cover, with their long angular legs, the area of a soup plate, and they look like a nightmare spider that has been run over by a steamroller and reduced to a paper-like thickness. This enables them to slide in and out of crevices that would allow access to no other beast, in a most unnerving manner. Apart from this they could glide about over the surface of the wood as though it were ice, and at a speed that was quite incredible. It was this speedy and silent movement, combined with such a forest of legs, that made them so repulsive, and made one instinctively shy away from them, even though one knew they were harmless. So, when the first one appeared magically out of a crack and scuttled over my bare arm as I leant against the tree, it produced an extra-ordinary demoralizing effect, to say the least.

I had only just recovered from this when all the other inhabitants of the tree started to vacate in a body. Five fat grey bats flapped out into the nets, where they hung chittering madly and screwing up their faces in rage. They were quickly joined by two green forest squirrels with pale fawn rings round their eyes, who uttered shrill grunts of rage as they rolled about in the meshes of the nets while we tried to disentangle them without getting bitten. They were followed by six grey dormice, two large greeny rats with orange noses and behinds, and a slender green tree-snake with enormous eyes, who slid calmly through the meshes of the nets with a slightly affronted air, and disappeared into the under-growth before anyone could do anything sensible about catching him. The noise and confusion was incredible: Africans danced about through the billowing smoke, shouting instructions of which nobody took the slightest notice, getting bitten with shrill yells of agony, stepping on each other's feet, wielding machetes and sticks with gay abandon and complete disregard for safety. The man posted in the top of the tree was having fun on his own, and was shouting and yelling and leaping about in the branches with such vigour that I expected to see him crash to the forest floor at any moment. Our eyes streamed, our lungs were filled with smoke, but the collecting bags filled up with a wiggling, jumping cargo of creatures.

Eventually the last of the tree's inhabitants had appeared, the smoke had died down and we could pause for a cigarette and to examine each other's honourable wounds. As we were doing this the man at the top of the tree lowered down two collecting bags on the end of long strings, before preparing to return to earth himself. I took the bags gingerly, not knowing what the contents were, and inquired of the stalwart at the top of the tree how he had fared.

"What you get for dis bag?" I inquired.

"Beef, Masa," he replied intelligently.

"I know it's beef, bushman, but what kind of beef you get?"

"Eh! I no savvay how Masa call um. 'E so so rat, but 'e get wing. Dere be one beef for inside 'e get eye big big like man, sah."

I was suddenly filled with an inner excitement.

"'E get hand like rat or like monkey?" I shouted.

"Like monkey, sah."

"What is it?" asked Bob with interest, as I fumbled with the string round the neck of the bags.

"I'm not sure, but I think it's a bushbaby . . . if it is it can only be one of two kinds, and both of them are rare."

I got the string off the neck of the bag after what seemed an interminable struggle, and cautiously opened it. Regarding me from inside it was a small, neat grey face with huge ears folded back like fans against the side of the head, and two enormous golden eyes, that looked at me with the horror-stricken expression of an elderly spinster who had discovered a man in the bathroom cupboard. The creature had large, human-looking hands, with long, slender bony fingers. Each of these, except the forefinger, was tipped with a small, flat nail that looked as though it had been delicately manicured, while the forefinger possessed a curved claw that looked thoroughly out of place on such a human hand.

"What is it?" asked Bob in hushed tones, seeing that I was gazing at the creature with an expression of bliss on my face.

"This," I said ecstatically, "is a beast I have tried to get every time I've been to the Cameroons. *Euoticus elegantulus,* or better known as a needle-clawed lemur or bushbaby. They're extremely rare, and if we succeed in getting this one back to England it will be the first ever to be brought back to Europe."

"Gosh," said Bob, suitably impressed.

I showed the little beast to Elias.

"You savvay dis beef, Elias?"

"Yes, sah, I savvay um."

"Dis kind of beef I want *too much*. If you go get me more I go pay you one one pound. You hear."

"I hear, sah. But Masa savvay dis kind of beef 'e come out for night time. For dis kind of beef you go look um with hunter light."

"Yes, but you tell all people of Eshobi I go pay one one pound for dis beef, you hear?"

"Yes, sah. I go tell um."

"And now," I said to Bob, carefully tying up the bag with the precious beef inside, "let's get back to Mamfe quick and get this into a decent cage where we can see it."

So we packed up the equipment and set off at a brisk pace through the forest towards Mamfe, pausing frequently to open the bag and make sure that the precious specimen had got enough air, and had not been spirited away by some frightful juju. We reached Mamfe at lunch-time and burst into the house, calling to Jacquie and Sophie to come and see our prize. I opened the bag cautiously and *Euoticus* edged its head out and surveyed us all in turn, with its enormous, staring eyes.

"Oh, isn't it *sweet*," said Jacquie.

"Isn't it a *dear*?" said Sophie.

"Yes," I said proudly, "it a . . ."

"What shall we call it?" asked Jacquie.

"We'll have to think of a good name for it," said Sophie.

"It's an extremely rare . . ." I began.

"How about Bubbles?" suggested Sophie.

"No, it doesn't look like a Bubbles," said Jacquie surveying it critically.

"It's an *Euoticus* . . ."

"How about Moony?"

"No one has ever taken it back . . ."

"No, it doesn't look like a Moony either."

"No European zoo has ever . . ."

"What about Fluffykins?" asked Sophie.

I shuddered.

"If you must give it a name call it Bug-eyes," I said.

"Oh, yes!" said Jacquie, "that suits it."

"Good," I said, "I am relieved to know that we have successfully christened it. Now what about a cage for it?"

"Oh, we've got one here," said Jacquie. "Don't worry about that."

We eased the animal into the cage, and it squatted on the floor glaring at us with unabated horror.

"Isn't it sweet?" Jacquie repeated.

"Is 'o a poppet?" gurgled Sophie.

I sighed. It seemed that, in spite of all my careful training, both my wife and my secretary relapsed into the most revolting fubsy attitude when faced with anything fluffy.

"Well," I said resignedly, "supposing you feed 'oos poppet? This poppet's going inside to get an itsy-bitsy slug of gin."

PART TWO

BACK TO BAFUT

MAIL BY HAND

My good friend,
I am glad that you have arrive once more to Bafut. I welcome you. When you are calm from your journeys come and see me.
Your good friend,
Fon of Bafut.

CHAPTER THREE

THE FON'S BEEF

ON our return from Eshobi, Jacquie and I loaded up our lorry with the cages of animals we had obtained to date, and set out for Bafut, leaving Bob and Sophie in Mamfe for a little longer to try and obtain some more of the rain-forest animals.

The journey from Mamfe to the highlands was long and tedious, but never failed to fascinate me. To begin with, the road ran through the thick forest of the valley in which Mamfe lay. The lorry roared and bumped its way along the red road between gigantic trees, each festooned with creepers and lianas, through which flew small flocks of hornbills, honking wildly, or pairs of jade-green touracos with magenta wings flashing as they flew. On the dead trees by the side of the road the lizards, orange, blue and black, vied with the pigmy kingfishers over the spiders, locusts and other succulent tit-bits to be found amongst the purple and white convolvulus flowers. At the bottom of each tiny valley ran a small stream, spanned by a creaking wooden bridge, and as the lorry roared across, great clouds of butterflies rose from the damp earth at the sides of the water and swirled briefly round the bonnet. After a couple of hours the road started to climb, at first almost imperceptibly, in a series of great swinging loops through the forest, and here and there by the side of the road you

58

could see the giant tree-ferns like green fountains spouting miraculously out of the low growth. As one climbed higher, the forest gave way to occasional patches of grassland bleached white by the sun.

Then, gradually, as though we were shedding a thick green coat, the forest started to drop away and the grassland took its place. The gay lizards ran sun-drunk across the road, and flocks of minute finches burst from the undergrowth and drifted across in front of us, their crimson feathering making them look like showers of sparks from some gigantic bonfire. The lorry roared and shuddered, steam blowing up from the radiator, as it made the final violent effort and reached the top of the escarpment. Behind lay the Mamfe forest, in a million shades of green, and before us was the grassland, hundreds of miles of rolling mountains, lying in folds to the farthest dim horizons, gold and green, stroked by cloud shadows, remote and beautiful in the sun. The driver eased the lorry on to the top of the hill and brought it to a shuddering halt that made the red dust swirl up in a waterspout that enveloped us and our belongings. He smiled the wide, happy smile of a man who has accomplished something of importance.

"Why we stop?" I inquired.

"I go piss," explained the driver frankly, as he disappeared into the long grass at the side of the road.

Jacquie and I uncoiled ourselves from the red-hot interior of the cab and walked round to the back of the lorry to see how our creatures were faring. Phillip, seated stiff and upright on a tarpaulin, turned to us a face bright red with dust. His trilby, which had been a very delicate pearl grey when we started, was also bright red. He sneezed violently into a green handkerchief, and surveyed me reproachfully.

"Dust *too much*, sah," he roared at me, in case the fact had escaped my observation. As Jacquie and I were almost as dusty in the front of the lorry, I was not inclined to be sympathetic.

"How are the animals?" I said.

" 'E well, sah. But dis bush-hog, sah, 'e get strong head *too much.*"

"Why, what the matter with it?"

" 'E done tief dis ma pillow," said Phillip indignantly.

I peered into Ticky, the black-footed mongoose's cage. She had whiled away the tedium of the journey by pushing her paw through the bars and gradually dragging in with her the small pillow which was part of our cook's bedding. She was sitting on the remains, looking very smug and pleased with herself, surrounded by snow-drifts of feathers.

"Never mind," I said consolingly, "I'll buy you a new one. But you go watch your other things, eh? Sometimes she go tief them as well."

"Yes, sah, I go watch um," said Phillip, casting a black look at the feather-smothered Ticky.

So we drove on through the green, gold and white grassland, under a blue sky veined with fine wisps of wind-woven white cloud, like frail twists of sheep's wool blowing across the sky. Everything in this landscape seemed to be the work of the wind. The great outcrops of grey rocks were carved and ribbed by it into fantastic shapes; the long grass was curved over into frozen waves by it; the small trees had been bent, carunculated and distorted by it. And the whole landscape throbbed and sang with the wind, hissing softly in the grass, making the small trees creak and whine, hooting and blaring round the towering cornices of rock.

So we drove on towards Bafut, and towards the end of the day the sky became pale gold. Then, as the sun sank behind the farthest rim of mountains, the world was enveloped in the cool green twilight, and in the dusk the lorry roared round the last bend and drew up at the hub of Bafut, the compound of the Fon. To the left lay the vast courtyard, and behind it the clusters of huts in which lived the Fon's wives and children. Dominating them all was the great hut in which dwelt the spirit of his father, and a great many other lesser spirits, looming like a monstrous, time-blackened beehive against the jade night sky. To the right of the road, perched on top of a tall bank, was the Fon's Rest House, like a two-storey Italian villa, stone-built and with a neatly tiled roof. Shoe-box shaped, both lower and upper storeys were surrounded by wide verandahs, festooned with bougainvillaea covered with pink and brick-red flowers.

Tiredly we climbed out of the lorry and supervised the unloading of the animals and their installation on the top-storey verandah. Then the rest of the equipment was off-loaded and stored, and while we made vague attempts to wash some of the red dust off our bodies, Phillip seized the remains of his bedding, his box full of cooking utensils and food and marched off to the kitchen quarters in a stiff, brisk way, like a military patrol going to quell a small but irritating insurrection. By the time we had fed the animals he had reappeared with an astonishingly good meal and having eaten it we fell into bed and slept like the dead.

The next morning, in the cool dawn light, we went to pay our respects to our host, the Fon. We made our way across the great courtyard and plunged into the maze of tiny squares and alleyways formed by the huts of the Fon's wives. Presently, we found ourselves in a small courtyard shaded by an immense guava tree, and there was the Fon's own villa, small, neat, built of stone and tiled with a wide verandah running along one side. And there, at the top of the steps running up to the verandah, stood my friend the Fon of Bafut.

He stood there, tall and slender, wearing a plain white robe embroidered with blue. On his head was a small skull-cap in the same colours. His face was split by the joyous, mischievous grin I knew so well and he was holding out one enormous slender hand in greeting.

"My friend, Iseeya," I called, hurrying up the stairs to him.

"Welcome, welcome . . . you done come . . . welcome," he exclaimed, seizing my hand in his huge palm and draping a long arm round my shoulders and patting me affectionately.

"You well, my friend?" I asked, peering up into his face.

"I well, I well," he said grinning.

It seemed to me an understatement: he looked positively blooming. He had been well into his seventies when I had last met him, eight years before, and he appeared to have weathered the intervening years better than I had. I introduced Jacquie, and was quietly amused by the contrast. The Fon, six foot three inches, and appearing taller because of his robes, towered beamingly over Jacquie's five-foot-one-inch, and her hand was as lost as a child's in the depths of his great dusky paw.

"Come, we go for inside," he said, and clutching our hands led us into his villa.

The interior was as I remembered it, a cool, pleasant room with leopard skins on the floor, and wooden sofas, beautifully carved, piled high with cushions. We sat down, and one of the Fon's wives came forward carrying a tray with glasses and drinks on it. The Fon splashed Scotch into three glasses with a liberal hand, and passed them round, beaming at us. I surveyed the four inches of neat spirit in the bottom of my glass and sighed. I could see that the Fon had not, in my absence, joined the Temperance movement, whatever else he had done.

"Chirri-ho!" said the Fon, and downed half the contents of his glass at a gulp. Jacquie and I sipped ours more sedately.

"My friend," I said, "I happy too much I see you again."

"Wah! Happy?" said the Fon. "I get happy for see you. When dey done tell me you come for Cameroon again I get happy too much."

I sipped my drink cautiously.

"Some man done tell me that you get angry for me because I done write dat book about dis happy time we done have together before. So I de fear for come back to Bafut," I said.

The Fon scowled.

"Which kind of man tell you dis ting?" he inquired furiously.

"Some European done tell me."

"Ah! European," said the Fon shrugging, as if surprised that I should believe anything told to me by a white person, "Na lies dis."

"Good," I said, greatly relieved. "If I think you get angry for me my heart no go be happy."

"No, no, I no get angry for you," said the Fon, splashing another large measure of Scotch into my glass before I could stop him. "Dis book you done write . . . I like um foine . . . you done make my name go for all de world . . . every kind of people 'e know my name . . . na foine ting dis."

Once again I realized I had underestimated the Fon's abilities. He had obviously realized that any publicity is better than none. "Look um," he went on, "plenty plenty people come here for Bafut, all different different people, dey all show me dis your book 'e get my name for inside . . . na foine ting dis."

"Yes, na fine thing," I agreed, rather shaken. I had had no idea that I had unwittingly turned the Fon into a sort of Literary Lion.

"Dat time I done go for Nigeria," he said, pensively holding the bottle of Scotch up to the light. "Dat time I done go for Lagos to meet dat Queen woman, all dis European dere 'e get dis your book. Plenty plenty people dey ask me for write dis ma name for inside dis your book."

I gazed at him open-mouthed; the idea of the Fon in Lagos

sitting and autographing copies of my book rendered me speechless.

"Did you like the Queen?" asked Jacquie.

"Wah! Like? I like um too much. No foine woman dat. Na small small woman, same same for you. But 'e get power, time no dere. Wah! Dat woman get power *plenty*."

"Did you like Nigeria?" I asked.

"I no like," said the Fon firmly. " 'E hot too much. Sun, sun, sun, I shweat, I shweat. But dis Queen woman she get plenty power . . . she walka walka she never shweat. Na foine woman dis."

He chuckled reminiscently, and absent-mindedly poured us all out another drink.

"I done give dis Queen," he went on, "dis teeth for elephant. You savvay um?"

"Yes, I savvay um," I said, remembering the magnificent carved tusk the Cameroons had presented to Her Majesty.

"I done give dis teeth for all dis people of Cameroon," he explained. "Dis Queen she sit for some chair an' I go softly softly for give her dis teeth. She take um. Den all dis European dere dey say it no be good ting for show your arse for dis Queen woman, so all de people walka walka backwards. I walka walka backwards. Wah! Na step dere, eh? I de fear I de fall, but I walka walka softly and I never fall . . . but I de fear too much."

He chuckled over the memory of himself backing down the steps in front of the Queen until his eyes filled with tears.

"Nigeria no be good place," he said, "hot too much . . . I shweat."

At the mention of sweat I saw his eyes fasten on the whisky bottle, so I rose hurriedly to my feet and said that we really ought to be going, as we had a lot of unpacking to do. The Fon walked out into the sunlit courtyard with us, and, holding our hands, peered earnestly down into our faces.

"For evening time you go come back," he said. "We go drink, eh?"

"Yes, for evening time we go come," I assured him.

He beamed down at Jacquie.

"For evening time I go show you what kind of happy time we get for Bafut," he said.

"Good," said Jacquie, smiling bravely.

The Fon waved his hands in elegant dismissal, and then turned and made his way back into his villa, while we trudged over to the Rest House.

"I don't think I could face any breakfast after that Scotch," said Jacquie.

"But that wasn't drinking," I protested. "That was just a sort of mild apéritif to start the day. You wait until tonight."

"Tonight I shan't drink . . . I'll leave it to you two," said Jacquie firmly. "I shall have one drink and that's all."

After breakfast, while we were attending to the animals, I happened to glance over the verandah rail and noticed on the road below a small group of men approaching the house. When they drew nearer I saw that each of them was carrying either a raffia basket or a calabash with the neck stuffed with green leaves. I could hardly believe that they were bringing animals as soon as this, for generally it takes anything up to a week for the news to get around and for the hunters to start bringing in the stuff. But as I watched them with bated breath they turned off the road and started to climb the long flight of steps up to the verandah, chattering and laughing among themselves. Then, when they reached the top step they fell silent, and carefully laid their offerings on the ground.

"Iseeya, my friends," I said.

"Morning, Masa," they chorused, grinning.

"Na whatee all dis ting?"

"Na beef, sah," they said.

"But how you savvay dat I done come for Bafut for buy beef?" I asked, greatly puzzled.

"Eh, Masa, de Fon 'e done tell us," said one of the hunters.

"Good lord, if the Fon's been spreading the news before we arrived we'll be inundated in next to no time," said Jacquie.

"We're pretty well inundated now," I said, surveying the group of containers at my feet, "and we haven't even unpacked the cages yet. Oh, well, I suppose we'll manage. Let's see what they've got."

I bent down, picked up a raffia bag and held it aloft.

"Which man bring dis?" I asked.

"Na me, sah."

"Na whatee dere for inside?"

"Na squill-lill, sah."

"What," inquired Jacquie, as I started to unravel the strings on the bag, "is a squill-lill?"

"I haven't the faintest idea," I replied.

"Well, hadn't you better ask?" suggested Jacquie practically. "For all you know it might be a cobra or something."

"Yes, that's a point," I agreed, pausing.

I turned to the hunter who was watching me anxiously.

"Na whatee dis beef squill-lill?"

"Na small beef, sah."

"Na bad beef? 'E go chop man?"

"No, sah, at all. Dis one na squill-lill small, sah . . . na picken."

Fortified with this knowledge I opened the bag and peered into its depths. At the bottom, squirming and twitching in a nest of grass, lay a tiny squirrel about three and a half inches long. It couldn't have been more than a few days old, for it was still covered in the neat, shining plush-like fur of an infant, and it was still blind. I lifted it out carefully, and it lay in my hand making faint squeaking noises like something out of a Christmas cracker, pink mouth open in an O like a choirboy's, minute paws making paddling motions against my fingers. I waited patiently for the flood of anthropomorphism to die down from my wife.

"Well," I said, "if you want it, keep it. But I warn you it will be hell to feed. The only reason I can see for trying is because it's a baby black-eared, and they're quite rare."

"Oh, it'll be all right," said Jacquie optimistically. "It's strong and that's half the battle."

I sighed. I remembered the innumerable baby squirrels I had struggled with in various parts of the world, and how each one had seemed more imbecile and more bent on self-destruction than the last. I turned to the hunter. "Dis beef, my friend. Na fine beef dis, I like um too much. But 'e be picken, eh? Sometime 'e go die-o, eh?"

"Yes, sah," agreed the hunter gloomily.

"So I go pay you two shilling now, and I go give you book. You go come back for two week time, eh, and if dis picken 'e alive I go pay you five shilling more, eh? You agree?"

"Yes, sah, I agree," said the hunter, grinning delightedly.

I paid him the two shillings, and then wrote out a promissory note for the other five shillings, and watched him tuck it carefully into a fold of his sarong.

"You no go lose um," I said. "If you go lose um I no go pay you."

"No, Masa, I no go lose um," he assured me, grinning.

"You know, it's the most beautiful colour," said Jacquie, peering at the squirrel in her cupped hands. On that point I agreed with her. The diminutive head was bright orange, with a neat black rim behind each ear, as though its mother had not washed it properly. The body was brindled green on the back and pale yellow on the tummy, while the ridiculous tail was darkish green above and flame orange below.

"What shall I call it?" asked Jacquie.

I glanced at the quivering scrap, still doing choral practice in her palm.

"Call it what the hunter called it: Squill-lill Small," I suggested. So Squill-lill Small she became, later to be abbreviated to Small for convenience.

While engaged in this problem of nomenclature I had been busy untying another raffia basket, without having taken the precaution of asking the hunter what it contained. So, when I incautiously opened it, a small, pointed, rat-like face appeared, bit me sharply on the finger, uttered a piercing shriek of rage and disappeared into the depths of the basket again.

"What on earth was that?" asked Jacquie, as I sucked my finger and cursed, while all the hunters chorused "Sorry, sah, sorry, sah," as though they had been collectively responsible for my stupidity.

"That fiendish little darling is a pigmy mongoose," I said. "For their size they're probably the fiercest creatures in Bafut, and they've got the most penetrating scream of any small animal I know, except a marmoset."

"What are we going to keep it in?"

"We'll have to unpack some cages. I'll leave it in the bag until I've dealt with the rest of the stuff," I said, carefully tying the bag up again.

"It's nice to have two different species of mongoose," said Jacquie.

"Yes," I agreed, sucking my finger. "Delightful."

The rest of the containers, when examined, yielded nothing more exciting than three common toads, a small green viper and four weaver-birds which I did not want. So, having disposed of them and the hunters, I turned my attention to the task of housing the pigmy mongoose. One of the worst things you can do on a collecting trip is to be unprepared with your caging. I had made this mistake on my first expedition; although we had taken a lot of various equipment, I had failed to include any ready-made cages, thinking there would be plenty of time to build them on the spot. The result was that the first flood of animals caught us unprepared and by the time we had struggled night and day to house them all adequately, the second wave of creatures had arrived and we were back where we started. At one point I had as many as six different creatures tied to my camp-bed on strings. After this experience I have always taken the precaution of bringing some collapsible cages with me on a trip so that, whatever else happens, I am certain I can accommodate at least the first forty or fifty specimens.

I now erected one of our specially built cages, filled it with dry banana leaves and eased the pigmy mongoose into it without getting bitten. It stood in the centre of the cage, regarding me with small, bright eyes, one dainty paw held up, and proceeded to utter shriek upon shriek of fury until our ears throbbed. The noise was so penetrating and painful that, in desperation, I threw a large lump of meat into the cage. The pigmy leaped on it, shook it vigorously to make sure it was dead and then carried it off to a corner where it settled down to eat. Though it still continued to shriek at us, the sounds were now mercifully muffled by the food. I placed the cage next to the one occupied by Ticky, the black-footed mongoose, and sat down to watch.

At a casual glance no one would think that the two animals were even remotely related. The black-footed mongoose, although still only a baby, measured two feet in length and stood about eight inches in height. She had a blunt, rather dog-like face with dark, round and somewhat protruberant eyes. Her body, head and tail were a rich creamy-white, while her slender legs were a rich brown that was almost black. She was sleek, sinuous and svelte and reminded me of a soft-skinned Parisienne *belle-amie* clad in nothing more than two pairs of black silk stockings. In contrast the pigmy mongoose looked anything but Parisienne. It measured, including tail, about ten inches in length. It had a tiny, sharply pointed face with a small, circular pink nose and a pair of small, glittering, sherry-coloured eyes. The fur, which was rather long and thick, was a deep chocolate brown with a faint ginger tinge here and there.

Ticky, who was very much the *grande dame*, peered out of her cage at the newcomer with something akin to horror on her face, watching it fascinated as it shrieked and grumbled over its gory hunk of meat. Ticky was herself a very dainty and fastidious feeder and would never had dreamt of behaving in this uncouth way, yelling and screaming with your mouth full and generally carrying on as though you had never had a square meal in your life. She watched the pigmy for a moment or so and then gave a sniff of scorn, turned round elegantly two or three times and then lay down and went to sleep. The pigmy, undeterred by this comment on its behaviour, continued to champ and shrill over the last bloody remnants of its food. When the last morsel had been gulped down, and the ground around carefully inspected for any bits that might have been overlooked, it sat down and scratched itself vigorously for a while and then curled up and went to sleep as well. When we woke it up about an hour later to record its voice for posterity, it produced such screams of rage and indignation that we were forced to move the microphone to the other end of the verandah. But by the time evening came we had not only successfully recorded the pigmy mongoose but Ticky as well, and had unpacked ninety per cent of our equipment into the bargain. So we bathed, changed and dined feeling well satisfied with ourselves.

After dinner we armed ourselves with a bottle of whisky and an abundant supply of cigarettes and, taking our pressure-lamp, we set off for the Fon's house. The air was warm and drowsy, full of the scents of wood smoke and sun-baked earth. Crickets tinkled and trilled in the grass verges of the road and in the gloomy fruit-trees around the Fon's great courtyard we could hear the fruit bats honking and flapping their wings among the branches. In the courtyard a group of the Fon's children were standing in a circle clapping their hands and chanting in some sort of game, and away through the trees in the distance a small drum throbbed like an irregular heart beat. We made our way through the maze of wives' huts, each lit by the red glow of a cooking fire, each heavy with the smell of roasting yams, frying plantain, stewing meat or the sharp, pungent reek of dried salt fish. We came presently to the Fon's villa and he was waiting on the steps to greet us, looming large in the gloom, his robe swishing as he shook our hands.

"Welcome, welcome," he said, beaming, "come, we go for inside."

"I done bring some whisky for make our heart happy," I said, flourishing the bottle as we entered the house.

"Wah! Good, good," said the Fon, chuckling. "Dis whisky na foine ting for make man happy."

He was wearing a wonderful scarlet-and-yellow robe that glowed like a tiger skin in the soft lamplight, and one slender wrist carried a thick, beautifully carved ivory bracelet. We sat down and waited in silence while the solemn ritual of the pouring of the first drink was observed. Then, when each of us was clutching half a tumbler full of neat whisky, the Fon turned to us, giving his wide, mischievous grin.

"Chirri-ho!" he said raising his glass, "tonight we go have happy time." And so began what we were to refer to later as The Evening of the Hangover.

As the level in the whisky bottle fell the Fon told us once again about his trip to Nigeria, how hot it had been and how much he had "shweated." His praise for the Queen knew no bounds, for, as he pointed out, here was he in his own country feeling the heat and yet the Queen could do twice the amount of work and still manage to look cool and charming. I found his lavish and perfectly genuine praise rather extraordinary, for the Fon belonged to a society where women are considered to be nothing more than rather useful beasts of burden.

"You like musica?" inquired the Fon of Jacquie, when the subject of the Nigerian tour was exhausted.

"Yes," said Jacquie, "I like it very much."

The Fon beamed at her.

"You remember dis my musica?" he asked me.

"Yes, I remember. You get musica time no dere, my friend."

The Fon gave a prolonged crow of amusement.

"You done write about dis my musica inside dis your book, eh?"

"Yes, that's right."

"And," said the Fon, coming to the point, "you done write about dis dancing an' dis happy time we done have, eh?"

"Yes . . . all dis dance we done do na fine one."

"You like we go show dis your wife what kind of dance we get here for Bafut?" he inquired, pointing a long forefinger at me.

"Yes, I like too much."

"Foine, foine . . . come, we go for dancing house," he said, rising to his feet majestically, and stifling a belch with one slender hand. Two of his wives, who had been sitting quietly in the background, rushed forward and seized the tray of drinks and scuttled ahead of us, as the Fon led us out of his house and across the compound towards his dancing house.

The dancing house was a great, square building, not unlike the average village hall, but with an earth floor and very few and very small windows. At one end of the building stood a line of wickerwork armchairs, which constituted a sort of Royal enclosure, and on the wall above these were framed photographs of various members of the Royal family. As we entered the dancing hall the assembled wives, about forty or fifty of them, uttered the usual greeting, a strange, shrill ululation, caused by yelling loudly and clapping their hands rapidly over their mouths at the same time. The noise was deafening. All the petty councillors there in their brilliant robes clapped their hands as well, and thus added to the general racket. Nearly deafened by this greeting, Jacquie and I were installed in two chairs, one on each side of the Fon, the table of drinks was placed in front of us, and the Fon, leaning back in his chair, surveyed us both with a wide and happy grin.

"Now we go have happy time," he said, and leaning forward poured out half a tumblerful of Scotch each from the depths of a virgin bottle that had just been broached.

"Chirri-ho," said the Fon.

"Chin-chin," I said absent-mindedly.

"Na whatee dat?" inquired the Fon with interest.

"What?" I asked, puzzled.

"Dis ting you say."

"Oh, you mean chin-chin?"

"Yes, yes, dis one."

"It's something you say when you drink."

"Na same same for Chirri-ho?" asked the Fon, intrigued.

"Yes, na same same."

He sat silent for a moment, his lips moving, obviously comparing the respective merits of the two toasts. Then he raised his glass again.

"Shin-shin," said the Fon.

"Chirri-ho!" I responded, and the Fon lay back in his chair and went off into a paroxysm of mirth.

By now the band had arrived. It was composed of four youths and two of the Fon's wives and the instruments consisted of three drums, two flutes and a calabash filled with dried maize that gave off a pleasant rustling noise similar to a marimba. They got themselves organized in the corner of the dancing house, and then gave a few experimental rolls on the drums, watching the Fon expectantly. The Fon, having recovered from the joke, barked out an imperious order and two of his wives placed a small table in the centre of the dance floor and put a pressure lamp on it. The drums gave another expectant roll.

"My friend," said the Fon, "you remember when you done come for Bafut before you done teach me European dance, eh?"

"Yes," I said, "I remember."

This referred to one of the Fon's parties when, having partaken liberally of the Fon's hospitality, I had proceeded to show him, his councillors and wives how to do the conga. It had been a riotous success, but in the eight years that had passed I had supposed that the Fon would have forgotten about it.

"I go show you," said the Fon, his eyes gleaming. He barked out another order and about twenty of his wives shuffled out on to the dance floor and formed a circle round the table, each one holding firmly to the waist of the one in front. Then they assumed a strange, crouching position, rather like runners at the start of a race, and waited.

"What are they going to do?" whispered Jacquie.

I watched them with an unholy glee. "I do believe," I said dreamily, "that he's been making them dance the conga ever since I left, and we're now going to have a demonstration."

The Fon lifted a large hand and the band launched itself with enthusiasm into a Bafut tune that had the unmistakable conga rhythm. The Fon's wives, still in their strange crouching position, proceeded to circle round the lamp, kicking their black legs out on the sixth beat, their brows furrowed in concentration. The effect was delightful.

"My friend," I said, touched by the demonstration, "dis na fine ting you do."

"Wonderful," agreed Jacquie enthusiastically, "they dance very fine."

"Dis na de dance you done teach me," explained the Fon.

"Yes, I remember."

He turned to Jacquie, chuckling. "Dis man your husband 'e get plenty power . . . we dance, we dance, we drink. . . . Wah! We done have happy time."

The band came to an uneven halt, and the Fon's wives, smiling shyly at our applause, rose from their crouching position and returned to their former places along the wall. The Fon barked an order and a large calabash of palm wine was brought in and distributed among the dancers, each getting their share poured into their cupped hands. Stimulated by this sight the Fon filled all our glasses again.

"Yes," he went on, reminiscently, "dis man your husband get plenty power for dance and drink."

"I no get power now," I said, "I be old man now."

"No, no, my friend," said the Fon laughing, "I be old, you be young."

"You look more young now den for the other time I done come to Bafut," I said, and really meant it.

"That's because you've got plenty wives," said Jacquie.

"Wah! No!" said the Fon, shocked. "Dis ma wives tire me too much."

He glared moodily at the array of females standing along the wall, and sipped his drink. "Dis ma wife dey humbug me too much," he went on.

"My husband says I humbug him," said Jacquie.

"Your husband catch lucky. 'E only get one wife, I get plenty," said the Fon, "an' dey de humbug me time no dere."

"But wives are very useful," said Jacquie.

The Fon regarded her sceptically.

"If you don't have wives you can't have *babies* . . . men can't have babies," said Jacquie practically.

The Fon was so overcome with mirth at this remark I thought he might have a stroke. He lay back in his chair and laughed until he cried. Presently he sat up, wiping his eyes, still shaking with gusts of laughter. "Dis woman your wife get brain," he said, still chuckling, and poured Jacquie out an extra large Scotch to celebrate her intelligence. "You be good wife for me," he said, patting her on the head affectionately. "Shin-shin."

The band now returned, wiping their mouths from some mysterous errand outside the dancing house and, apparently well fortified, launched themselves into one of my favourite Bafut tunes, the Butterfly dance. This was a pleasant, lilting little tune and the Fon's wives again took the floor and did the delightful dance that accompanied it. They danced in a row with minute but complicated hand and feet movements, and then the two that formed the head of the line joined hands, while the one at the farther end of the line whirled up and then fell backwards, to be caught and thrown upright again by the two with linked hands. As the dance progressed and the music got faster and faster the one representing the butterfly whirled more and more rapidly, and the ones with linked hands catapulted her upright again with more and more enthusiasm. Then, when the dance reached its feverish climax, the Fon rose majestically to his feet, amid screams of delight from the audience, and joined the end of the row of dancing wives. He started to whirl down the line, his scarlet and yellow robe turning into a blur of colour, loudly singing the words of the song.

"I dance, I dance, and no one can stop me," he carolled merrily, "but I must take care not to fall to the ground like the butterfly."

He went whirling down the line of wives like a top, his voice booming out above theirs.

"I hope to God they don't drop him," I said to Jacquie, eyeing the two short, fat wives who, with linked hands, were waiting rather nervously at the head of the line to receive their lord and master.

The Fon performed one last mighty gyration and hurled himself backwards at his wives, who caught him neatly enough but reeled under the shock. As the Fon landed he spread his arms wide so that for a moment his wives were invisible under the flowing sleeves of his robes and he lay there looking very like a gigantic, multicoloured butterfly. He beamed at us, lolling across his wives' arms, his skull-cap slightly askew, and then his wives with an effort bounced him back to his feet again. Grinning and panting he made his way back to us and hurled himself into his chair.

"My friend, na fine dance dis," I said in admiration. "You get power time no dere."

"Yes," agreed Jacquie, who had also been impressed by this display, "you get plenty power."

"Na good dance dis, na foine one," said the Fon, chuckling, and automatically pouring us all out another drink.

"You get another dance here Bafut I like too much," I said. "Dis one where you dance with dat beer-beer for horse."

"Ah, yes, yes, I savvay um," said the Fon. "Dat one where we go dance with dis tail for horshe."

"That's right. Sometime, my friend, you go show dis dance for my wife?"

"Yes, yes, my friend," he said. He leant forward and gave an order and a wife scuttled out of the dancing hall. The Fon turned and smiled at Jacquie.

"Small time dey go bring dis tail for horshe an' den we go dance," he said.

Presently the wife returned carrying a large bundle of white, silky horses' tails, each about two feet long, fitted into handles beautifully woven out of leather thongs. The Fon's tail was a particularly long and luxuriant one, and the thongs that had been used to make the handle were dyed blue, red and gold. The Fon swished it experimentally through the air with languid, graceful movements of his wrist, and the hair rippled and floated like a cloud of smoke before him. Twenty of the Fon's wives, each armed with a switch, took the floor and formed a circle. The Fon walked over and stood in the centre of the circle; he gave a wave of his horse's tail, the band struck up and the dance was on.

Of all the Bafut dances this horsetail dance was undoubtedly the most sensuous and beautiful. The rhythm was peculiar, the small drums keeping up a sharp, staccato beat, while beneath them the big drums rumbled and muttered and the bamboo flutes squeaked and twittered with a tune that seemed to have nothing to do with the drums and yet emerged with it perfectly. To this tune the Fon's wives gyrated slowly round in a clockwise direction, their feet performing minute but formalized steps, while they waved the horse's tails gently to and fro across their faces. The Fon, meanwhile, danced round the inside of the circle in an anti-clockwise direction, bobbing, stamping and twisting in a curiously stiff, unjointed sort of way, while his hand with incredibly supple wrist movements kept his horse's tail weaving through the air in a series of lovely and complicated movements. The effect was odd and almost indescribable: one minute the dancers resembled a bed of white seaweed, moved and rippled by sea movement, and the next minute the Fon would stamp and twist, stiff-legged, like some strange bird with white plumes, absorbed in a ritual dance of courtship among his circle of hens. Watching this slow pavane and the graceful movements of the tails had a curious hypnotic effect, so that even when the dance ended with a roll of drums one could still see the white tails weaving and merging before your eyes.

The Fon moved gracefully across the floor towards us, twirling his horse's tail negligently, and sank into his seat. He beamed breathlessly at Jacquie.

"You like dis ma dance?" he asked.

"It was *beautiful*," she said. "I liked it very much."

"Good, good," said the Fon, well pleased. He leaned forward and inspected the whisky bottle hopefully, but it was obviously empty. Tactfully I refrained from mentioning that I had some more over at the Rest House. The Fon surveyed the bottle gloomily.

"Whisky done finish," he pointed out.

"Yes," I said unhelpfully.

"Well," said the Fon, undaunted, "we go drink gin."

My heart sank, for I had hoped that we could now move on to something innocuous like beer to quell the effects of so much neat alcohol. The Fon roared at one of his wives and she ran off and soon reappeared with a bottle of gin and one of bitters. The Fon's idea of gin-drinking was to pour out half a tumblerful and then colour it a deep brown with bitters. The result was guaranteed to slay an elephant at twenty paces. Jacquie, on seeing this cocktail the Fon concocted for me, hastily begged to be excused, saying that she couldn't drink gin on doctor's orders. The Fon, though obviously having the lowest possible opinion of a medical man who could even suggest such a thing, accepted with good grace.

The band started up again and everyone poured on to the floor and started to dance, singly and in couples. As the rhythm of the tune allowed it, Jacquie and I got up and did a swift foxtrot round the floor, the Fon roaring encouragement and his wives hooting with pleasure.

"Foine, foine," shouted the Fon as we swept past.

"Thank you my friend," I shouted back, steering Jacquie carefully through what looked like a flower-bed of councillors in their multicoloured robes.

"I do wish you wouldn't tread on my feet," said Jacquie plaintively.

"Sorry. My compass bearings are never at their best at this hour of night."

"So I notice," said Jacquie acidly.

"Why don't you dance with the Fon?" I inquired.

"I did think of it, but I wasn't sure whether it was the right thing for a mere woman to ask him."

"I think he'd be tickled pink. Ask him for the next dance," I suggested.

"What can we dance?" asked Jacquie.

"Teach him something he can add to his Latin American repertoire," I said. "How about a rumba?"

"I think a samba would be easier to learn at this hour of

night," said Jacquie. So, when the dance ended we made our way back to where the Fon was sitting, topping up my glass.

"My friend," I said, "you remember dis European dance I done teach you when I done come for Bafut before?"

"Yes, yes, na foine one," he replied, beaming.

"Well, my wife like to dance with you and teach you other European dance. You agree?"

"Wah!" bellowed the Fon in delight, "foine, foine. Dis your wife go teach me. Foine, foine, I agree."

Eventually we discovered a tune that the band could play that had a vague samba rhythm and Jacquie and the Fon rose to their feet, watched breathlessly by everyone in the room.

The contrast between the Fon's six-foot-three and Jacquie's five-foot-one made me choke over my drink as they took the floor. Very rapidly Jacquie showed him the simple, basic steps of the samba, and to my surprise the Fon mastered them without trouble. Then he seized Jacquie in his arms and they were off. The delightful thing from my point of view was that as he clasped Jacquie tightly to his bosom she was almost completely hidden by his flowing robes; indeed, at some points in the dance you could not see her at all and it looked as though the Fon, having mysteriously grown another pair of feet, was dancing round by himself. There was something else about the dance that struck me as curious, but I could not pin it down for some time. Then I suddenly realized that Jacquie was leading the Fon. They danced past, both grinning at me, obviously hugely enjoying themselves.

"You dance fine, my friend," I shouted. "My wife done teach you fine."

"Yes, yes," roared the Fon over the top of Jacquie's head. "Na foine dance dis. Your wife na good wife for me."

Eventually, after half an hour's dancing, they returned to their chairs, hot and exhausted. The Fon took a large gulp of neat gin to restore himself, and then leaned across to me.

"Dis your wife na foine," he said in a hoarse whisper, presumably thinking that praise might turn Jacquie's head. "She dance foine. She done teach me foine. I go give her mimbo . . . special mimbo I go give her."

I turned to Jacquie who, unaware of her fate, was sitting fanning herself.

"You've certainly made a hit with our host," I said.

"He's a dear old boy," said Jacquie, "and he dances awfully well . . . did you see how he picked up that samba in next to no time?"

"Yes," I said, "and he was so delighted with your teaching that he's going to reward you."

Jacquie looked at me suspiciously. "How's he going to reward me?" she asked.

"You're now going to receive a calabash of special mimbo ... palm wine."

"Oh God, and I can't stand the stuff," said Jacquie in horror.

"Never mind. Take a glassful, taste it, tell him it's the finest you've ever had, and then ask if he will allow you to share it with his wives."

Five calabashes were brought, the neck of each plugged with green leaves, and the Fon solemnly tasted them all before making up his mind which was the best vintage. Then a glass was filled and passed to Jacquie. Summoning up all her social graces she took a mouthful, rolled it round her mouth, swallowed and allowed a look of intense satisfaction to appear on her face.

"This is very fine mimbo," she proclaimed in delighted astonishment, with the air of one who has just been presented with a glass of Napoleon brandy. The Fon beamed. Jacquie took another sip, as he watched her closely. An even more delighted expression appeared on her face.

"This is the best mimbo I've ever tasted," said Jacquie.

"Ha! Good!" said the Fon, with pleasure. "Dis na foine mimbo. Na fresh one."

"Will you let your wives drink with me?" asked Jacquie.

"Yes, yes," said the Fon with a lordly wave of his hand, and so the wives shuffled forward, grinning shyly, and Jacquie hastily poured the remains of the mimbo into their pink palms.

At this point, the level of the gin bottle having fallen alarmingly, I suddenly glanced at my watch and saw, with horror, that in two and a half hours it would be dawn. So, pleading heavy work on the morrow, I broke up the party. The Fon insisted on accompanying us to the foot of the steps that led up to the Rest House, preceded by the band. Here he embraced us fondly.

"Good night, my friend," he said shaking my hand.

"Good night," I replied. "Thank you. You done give us happy time."

"Yes," said Jacquie, "thank you very much."

"Wah!" said the Fon, patting her on the head, "we done dance foine. You be good wife for me, eh?"

We watched him as he wended his way across the great court-yard, tall and graceful in his robes, the boy trotting beside him carrying the lamp that cast a pool of golden light about him. They disappeared into the tangle of huts, and the twittering of the flutes and the bang of the drums became fainter and died away, until all we could hear was the calls of crickets and tree frogs and the faint honking cries of the fruit bats. Somewhere in the distance the first cock crowed, huskily and sleepily, as we crept under our mosquito nets.

MAIL BY HAND

My good friend,
  Good morning to you all.
  Your note to me received and contents well understood.
  I am a beat relief from that cough but not much.
  I agree for you to hire my landrover as from today on weekly payments. I will also want to bring to your notice that the landrover will be under your charge as from today, but any time I am called for a meeting at Ndop, Bemenda or elsewhere, or any urgent matter, I shall inform you to allow me the motor for the day.
  I want to remind you of the last trip which you hired the landrover and settlement had not yet been made.

Your good friend,
Fon of Bafut.

CHAPTER FOUR

BEEF IN BOXES

As soon as Bob and Sophie had joined us in Bafut we set about the task of organizing our already large and ever-growing collection. The great, shady verandah that ran round the upstairs rooms of the Fon's Rest House was divided into three: one section for reptiles, one for birds and one for mammals. Thus each of us had a particular section to look after and whoever finished first lent a hand with somebody else's group. First thing in the morning we would all wander to and fro along the verandah in our pyjamas carefully looking at each animal to make sure it was all right. It is only by this day-to-day routine of careful watching that you can get to know your animals so well that you detect the slightest sign of illness, when to anyone else the animal would appear to be perfectly healthy and normal. Then we cleaned and fed all the delicate animals that could not wait (such as the sunbirds who had to have their nectar as soon as it was light, and the baby creatures that needed their early morning bottles) and then we paused for breakfast. It was during mealtime that we compared notes on our charges. This mealtime conversation would have put any normal mortal off his food, for it was mainly concerned with the bowel movements of our creatures; with wild animals, diarrhœa or constipation is often a good indication as to whether you are feeding it correctly, and it can also be the first (and sometimes the only) symptom of an illness.

On any collecting trip acquiring the animals is, as a rule, the simplest part of the job. As soon as the local people discover that you are willing to buy live wild creatures the stuff comes pouring in; ninety per cent is, of course, the commoner species, but they do bring an occasional rarity. If you want the really rare stuff you generally have to go out and find it yourself, but while you are devoting your time to this you can be sure that all the common local fauna will be brought in to you. So one might almost say that getting the animals is easy: the really hard part is keeping them once you have got them.

The chief difficulty you have to contend with when you have got a newly caught animal is not so much the shock it might be suffering from capture, but the fact that the capture forces it to exist in close proximity to a creature it regards as an enemy of the worst possible sort: yourself. On many occasions an animal may take to captivity beautifully, but can never reconcile itself to the intimate terms on which it has to exist with man. This is the first great barrier to break down and you can only do it by patience and kindness. For month after month an animal may snap and snarl at you every time you approach its cage, until you begin to despair of ever making a favourable impression on it. Then, one day, sometimes without any preliminary warning, it will trot forward and take food from your hand, or allow you to tickle it behind the ears. At such moments you feel that all the waiting in the world was justified.

Feeding, of course, is one of your main problems. Not only must you have a fairly extensive knowledge of what each species eats in the wild state, but you have to work out a suitable substitute if the natural food is unavailable, and then teach your specimen to eat it. You also have to cater for their individual likes and dislikes, which vary enormously. I have known a rodent which, refusing all normal rodent food—such as fruit, bread, vegetables—live for three days on an exclusive diet of spaghetti. I have had a group of five monkeys, of the same age and species, who displayed the most weird idiosyncrasies. Out of the five, two had a passion for hard-boiled eggs, while the other three were frightened of the strange white shapes and would not touch them, actually screaming in fear if you introduced such a fearsome object as a hard-boiled egg in to their cage. These five monkeys all adored orange but, whereas four would carefully peel their fruit and throw away the skin, the fifth would peel his orange equally carefully and then throw away the orange and eat the peel. When you have a collection of several hundred creatures all displaying such curious characteristics you are sometimes nearly driven mad in your efforts to satisfy their desires, and so keep them healthy and happy.

But of all the irritating and frustrating tasks that you have to undertake during a collecting trip, the hand-rearing of baby animals is undoubtedly the worst. To begin with, they are generally stupid over taking a bottle and there is nothing quite so unattractive as struggling with a baby animal in a sea of luke-warm milk. Secondly, they have to be kept warm, especially at night, and this means (unless you take them to bed with you, which is often the answer) you have to get up several times during the night to replenish hot-water bottles. After a hard day's work, to drag yourself out of bed at three in the morning to fill hot-water bottles is an occupation that soon loses its charm. Thirdly, all baby animals have extremely delicate stomachs and you must watch them like a hawk to make sure that the milk you are giving them is not too rich or too weak; if too rich, they can develop intestinal troubles which may lead to nephritis, which will prob-ably kill them, and if too weak, it can lead to loss of weight and condition, which leaves the animal open to all sorts of fatal complaints.

Contrary to my gloomy prognostications, the baby black-eared squirrel, Squill-lill Small (Small to her friends) proved an exemplary baby. During the day she lay twitching in a bed of cotton-wool balanced on a hot-water bottle in the bottom of a deep biscuit-tin; at night the tin was placed by our beds under the rays of a Tilley infra-red heater. Almost immediately we were made aware of the fact that Small had a will of her own. For such a tiny animal she could produce an extraordinary volume of noise, her cry being a loud and rapid series of "chucks" that sounded like a cheap alarm clock going off. Within the first twenty-four hours she had learnt when to expect her feeds and if we were as much as five minutes late she would trill and chuck incessantly until we arrived with the food. Then came the day when Small's eyes opened for the first time and she could take a look at her foster parents and the world in general. This, however, presented a new problem. We happened that day to be a bit late with her food. We had rather dawdled over our own lunch, deep in a discussion about some problem or other, and we had, I regret to say, forgotten all about Small. Suddenly I heard a faint scuffling behind me and, turning round, I saw Small squatting in the doorway of the dining-room looking, to say the least, extremely indignant. As soon as she saw us she went off like an alarm clock and hurrying across the floor hauled herself, panting, up Jacquie's chair and then leapt to her shoulder, where she sat flicking her tail up and down and shouting indignantly into Jacquie's ear. Now this, for a baby squirrel, was quite a feat. To begin with, as I say, her eyes had only just opened. Yet she had succeeded in climbing out of her tin and finding her way out of our bedroom (piled high with camera equipment and film); she had made her way down the full length of the verandah, running the gauntlet of any number of cages filled with potentially dangerous beasts, and eventually located us (presumably by sound) in the diningroom which was at the extreme end of the verandah. She had covered seventy yards over unknown territory, through innumerable dangers, in order to tell us she was hungry. Needless to say, she got her due of praise and, what was more important from her point of view, she got her lunch.

As soon as Small's eyes opened she grew rapidly and soon developed into one of the loveliest squirrels I have ever seen. Her orange head and neat, black-rimmed ears nicely set off her large dark eyes, and her fat body developed a rich moss green tinge against which the two lines of white spots that decorated her sides stood out like cats'-eyes on a dark road. But her tail was her best feature. Long and thick, green above and vivid orange below, it was a beautiful sight. She liked to sit with it curved over her back, the tip actually hanging over her nose, and then she would flick it gently in an undulating movement so that the whole thing looked like a candle flame in a draught.

Even when she was quite grown-up, Small slept in her biscuittin by our bed. She awoke early in the morning and, uttering her loud cry, she leaped from the tin on to one of our beds and crawled under the bed-clothes with us. Having spent ten minutes or so investigating our semi-comatose bodies, she jumped to the floor and went to explore the verandah. From these expeditions she would frequently return with some treasure she had found (such as a bit of rotten banana, or a dry leaf, or a bougainvillaea flower) and store it somewhere in our beds, getting most indignant if we hurled the offering out on to the floor. This continued for some months, until the day when I decided that Small would have to occupy a cage like the rest of the animals; I awoke one morning in excruciating agony to find her trying to stuff a peanut into my ear. Having found such a delicacy on the verandah she obviously thought that simply to cache it in my bed was not safe enough, but my ear provided an ideal hiding-place.

Bug-eyes, the needle-clawed lemur we had captured near Eshobi, was another baby, although she was fully weaned when we found her. She had become tame in a short space of time and very rapidly became one of our favourites. For her size she had enormous hands and feet, with long, attenuated fingers, and to see her dancing around her cage on her hind legs, her immense hands held up as though in horror, her eyes almost popping out of her head, as she pursued a moth or butterfly we had introduced, was a delightfully comic spectacle. Once she had caught it she sat there with it clasped tightly in her pink hand and regarded it with a wild, wide-eyed stare, as if amazed that such a creature should suddenly appear in the palm of her hand. Then she stuffed it into her mouth and continued to sit with what appeared to be a fluttering moustache of butterfly wing decorating her face, over which her huge eyes peered in astonishment.

It was Bug-eyes who first showed me an extraordinary habit that bushbabies have, a habit which to my shame I had never noticed before, in spite of the fact that I had kept innumerable bushbabies. I was watching her one morning when she had popped out of her nesting box for a feed of mealworms and a quick wash and brush up. She had, as I said before, large ears which were as delicate as flower petals. They were so fine that they were almost transparent and, presumably to prevent them from becoming torn or damaged in the wild state, she had the power of folding them back against the sides of her head like the furled sails of a yacht. Her ears were terribly important to her as you could tell by watching her. The slightest sound, however faint, would be picked up and her ears would twitch and turn towards it like radar. Now I had always noticed that she spent a lot of time cleaning and rubbing her ears with her hands, but on this particular morning I watched the whole process from start to finish and was considerably startled by what I saw. She began

by sitting on a branch, staring dreamily into space while she daintily cleaned her tail, parting the hair carefully and making sure there were no snags or tangles, reminding me of a little girl plaiting her hair. Then she put one of her outsize, puppet-like hands beneath her and deposited in the palm a drop of urine. With an air of concentration, she rubbed her hands together and proceeded to anoint her ears with the urine, rather after the manner of a man rubbing brilliantine into his hair. Then she got another drop of urine and rubbed it carefully over the soles of her

87

feet and the palms of her hands, while I sat and watched her in amazement.

I watched her do this three days in succession before I was satisfied that I was not imagining things, for it seemed to me to be one of the weirdest animal habits I had ever encountered. I can only conclude that the reason for it was this: unless the skin of the ears, so extremely delicate and thin, were kept moistened it must inevitably get dry and perhaps crack, which would have been fatal for an animal that relied so much on hearing. The same would apply to the delicate skin on the soles of her feet and hands, but here the urine would also provide an additional advantage. The soles of feet and hands were slightly cupped, so that as the creature leapt from bough to bough the hands and feet acted almost like the suckers on the toes of a tree-frog. Now, moistened with urine, these "suckers" became twice as efficient. When, later on in the trip, we obtained a great number of Demidoff's bushbabies (the smallest of the tribe, each being the size of a large mouse) I noticed that they all had the same habit.

This is, to my mind, the best part of a collecting trip, the close daily contact with the animals that allows you to observe, learn and record. Every day, and almost at every moment of the day, something new and interesting was happening somewhere in the collection. The following diary entries show fairly well how each day bristled with new tasks and interesting observations:

February 14: Two patas monkeys brought in; both had severe infestation of jiggers in toes and fingers. Had to lance them, extract jiggers and as precaution against infection injected penicillin. Baby civet did her first adult "display," making the mane of hair on her back stand up when I approached her cage suddenly. She accompanied this action with several loud sniffs, much deeper and more penetrating than her normal sniffing round food. Large brow-leaf toad brought in with extraordinary eye trouble. What appears to be a large malignant growth, situated behind the eyeball, had blinded the creature and then grown outwards, so that the toad looked as though it was wearing a large balloon over one eye. It did not appear to be suffering so am not attempting to remove the growth. So much for animals being happy and carefree in the wild state.

February 20: At last, after much trial and error, Bob has discovered what the hairy frogs eat: snails. We had previously tried young mice and rats, baby birds, eggs, beetles and their larvæ, locusts, all without success. Snails they devour avidly, so we have high hopes of getting the frogs back alive. Have had an outbreak of what appears to be nephritis among the Demidoff's bushbabies. Two discovered this morning drenched in urine as though they had been dipped. Have weakened the milk they get; it may be too strong. Also organized more insect food for them. The five baby Demidoff's are still thriving on their Complan milk, which is curious as this is incredibly rich, and if ordinary dried milk affects the adults one would have thought Complan would have had a similar effect on the babies.

March 16: Two nice cobras brought in, one about six feet long and the other about two feet. Both fed straight away. Best item today was female pigmy mongoose and two babies. The babies are still blind and an extraordinary pale fawn in contrast to the dark brown mother. Have removed babies to hand-rear them as felt sure female would either neglect or kill them if they were put with her.

March 17: Young pigmy mongooses flatly refuse to feed from bottle or from fountain-pen filler. In view of this (since their chances seemed slim) put them into cage with female. To my surprise she has accepted them and is suckling them well. Most unusual. Had two broken leg jobs today: Woodford's owl which had been caught in a gin-trap and a young hawk with a green-stick fracture. I don't think the owl will regain use of leg for all the ligaments appear to be torn, and the bone badly splintered. Hawk's leg should be O.K. as it's a young bird. Both are feeding well. Demidoff's make a faint mewing hiss when disturbed at night, the only sound I have heard them make apart from their bat-like twittering when fighting. Clawed toads have started to call at night: very faint "peep-peep" noise, rather like someone flicking the edge of a glass gently with finger-nail.

April 2: Young male chimp, about two years old, brought in today. Was in a terrible mess. Had been caught in one of the wire noose-traps they use for antelopes, and had damaged its left hand and arm. The palm of the hand and the wrist were split right open and badly infected with gangrene. The animal was very weak, not being able to sit up, and the colour of the skin was a curious yellowish grey. Attended to wound and injected penicillin. Drove it in to Bemenda for the Dept. of Agriculture's vet to have a look at, as did not like skin colour or curious lethargy in spite of stimulants. He took blood test and diagnosed sleeping-sickness. Have done all we can but the animal appears to be sinking fast. He seems pathetically grateful for anything you do for him.

April 3: Chimp died. They are a "protected" animal and yet up here, as in other parts of the Cameroons, they are killed and eaten regularly. Big rhinoceros viper fed for first time: small rat. One of the green forest squirrels appears to be developing a bald patch on his back: presume lack of vitamins so am increasing his Abidec. As we now get good supply of weaver-bird's eggs each day all the squirrels are getting them, in addition to their normal diet. The brush-tail porcupines, when disturbed at night, beat rapid tattoo with their hind-feet (like a wild rabbit) then swing their backside round to face danger and rustle bunch of quills on end of tail, producing a sound reminiscent of rattlesnake.

April 5: Have found simple, rapid way of sexing pottos. Nice young male brought in today. Although external genitalia in both sexes is remarkably similar to a superficial glance, have discovered that simplest way is to smell them. The testicles of the male give out a faint, sweet odour, like pear drops, when the animal is handled.

We were not the only ones interested in the animals. Many of the local people had never seen some of the creatures we had acquired, and many called and asked for permission to look round the collection. One day the Headmaster of the local Mission School called and asked if he could bring his entire school of two-hundred-odd boys to see the collection. I was glad to agree to this, for I feel that if you can, by showing live animals, arouse people's interest in their local fauna and its preservation you are doing something worthwhile. So, on the appointed date, the boys came marching down the road in a double column, shepherded by five masters. In the road below the Rest House the boys were divided up into groups of twenty and then brought up in turn by a master. Jacquie, Sophie, Bob and I took up stations at various points in the collection to answer any queries. The boys behaved in a model fashion; there was no pushing or shoving, no skylarking. They wended their way from cage to cage, absorbed and fascinated, uttering amazed cries of "Wah!" at each new wonder and clicking their fingers in delight. Finally, when the last group had been led round, the Headmaster grouped all the boys at the bottom of the steps and then turned to me, beaming.

"Sir," he said, "we are very grateful to you for allowing us to see your zoological collections. May I ask if you would be kind enough to answer some of the boys' questions?"

"Yes, with pleasure," I said, taking up my stand on the steps above the crowd.

"Boys," roared the Head, "Mr Durrell has kindly say that he will answer any questions. Now who has a question?"

The sea of black faces below me screwed themselves up in thought, tongues protruded, toes wiggled in the dust. Then, slowly at first, but with increasing speed as they lost their embarrassment, they shot questions at me, all of which were extremely intelligent and sensible. There was, I noticed, one small boy in the front of the crowd who had, throughout the proceedings, fixed me with a basilisk eye. His brow was furrowed with concentration, and he stood stiffly at attention. At last, when the supply of questions started to peter out, he suddenly summoned up all his courage, and shot his hand up.

"Yes, Uano, what is your question?" asked the Head, smiling down fondly at the boy.

The boy took a deep breath and then fired his question at me rapidly. "Please, sah, can Mr Durrell tell us why he take so many photographs of the Fon's wives?"

The smile vanished from the Head's face and he threw me a look of chagrin.

"That is not a zoological question, Uano," he pointed out severely.

"But please, sah, why?" repeated the child stubbornly.

The Head scowled ferociously. "That is *not* a zoological question," he thundered. "Mr Durrell only said he would answer zoological questions. The matter of the Fon's wives is not zoological."

"Well, loosely speaking it could be called biological, Head-master, couldn't it?" I asked, coming to the lad's rescue.

"But, sir, they shouldn't ask you questions like that," said the Head, mopping his face.

"Well, I don't mind answering. The reason is that, in my country, everyone is very interested to know how people in other parts of the world live and what they look like. I can tell them, of course, but it's not the same as if they see a photograph. With a photograph they know exactly what everything is like."

"There . . ." said the Headmaster, running a finger round the inside of his collar. "There, Mr Durrell has answered your question. Now, he is a very busy man so there is no more time for further questions. Kindly get into line."

The boys formed themselves once more into two orderly lines, while the Headmaster shook my hand and earnestly assured me that they were all most grateful. Then he turned once more to the boys.

"Now, to show our appreciation to Mr Durrell I want three hearty cheers."

Two hundred young lungs boomed out the hearty cheers. Then the boys at the head of the line produced from bags they were carrying several bamboo flutes and two small drums. The Headmaster waved his hand and they started to walk off down the road, led by the school band playing, of all things, "Men of Harlech." The Head followed them mopping his face, and the dark looks he kept darting at young Uano's back did not augur well for the boy's prospects when he got back to the classroom.

That evening the Fon came over for a drink and, after we had shown him the new additions to the collection, we sat on the verandah and I told him about Uano's zoological question. The Fon laughed and laughed, particularly at the embarrassment of the Headmaster. "Why you never tell um," he inquired, wiping his eyes, "why you never tell um dat you take dis photo of dis ma wife for show all Europeans for your country dat Bafut women be beautiful?"

"Dis boy na picken," I said solemnly. "I think sometime he be too small to understand dis woman palaver."

"Na true, na true," said the Fon, chuckling, "'e be picken. 'E catch lucky, 'e no get women for humbug him."

"They tell me, my friend," I said, trying to steer the conversation away from the pros and cons of married life, "they tell me tomorrow you go for N'dop. Na so?"

"Na so," said the Fon, "I go for two days, for Court. I go come back for morning time tomorrow tomorrow."

"Well," I said, raising my glass, "safe journey, my friend."

The following morning, clad in splendid yellow and black robes and wearing a curious hat, heavily embroidered, with long, drooping ear flaps, the Fon took his seat in the front of his new Land-Rover. Into the back went the necessities of travel: three bottles of Scotch, his favourite wife and three council members. He waved vigorously to us until the vehicle rounded the corner and was lost from sight.

That evening, having finished the last chores of the day, I went out on to the front verandah for a breath of air. In the great courtyard below I noticed large numbers of the Fon's children assembling. Curiously I watched them. They grouped themselves in a huge circle in the centre of the compound and, after much discussion and argument, they started to sing and clap their hands rhythmically, accompanied by a seven-year-old who stood in the centre of the circle beating a drum. Standing like this they lifted up their young voices and sang some of the most beautiful and haunting of the Bafut songs. This, I could tell, was not just an ordinary gathering of children; they had assembled there for some definite purpose, but what they were celebrating (unless it was their father's departure) I could not think. I stood there watching them for a long time and then John, our houseboy, appeared at my elbow in his unnervingly silent way.

"Dinner ready, sah," he said.

"Thank you, John. Tell me, why all dis picken sing for the Fon's compound?"

John smiled shyly. "Because de Fon done go for N'dop, sah."

"Yes, but why they sing?"

"If the Fon no be here, sah, each night dis picken must for sing inside de Fon's compound. So dey keep dis his compound warm."

This, I thought, was a delightful idea. I peered down at the circle of children, singing lustily in the gloomy wastes of the great courtyard, to keep their father's compound warm.

"Why they never dance?" I asked.

"Dey never get light, sah."

"Take them the pressure light from the bedroom. Tell them I send it so that I can help keep the Fon's compound warm."

"Yes, sah," said John. He hurried off to fetch the light and presently I saw it cast a golden pool round the circle of children. There was a pause in the singing, while John delivered my message, and then came a series of delighted shrieks and echoing up to me the shrill voices crying, "Tank you, Masa, tank you."

As we sat down to dinner the children were singing like larks, and stamping and weaving their way round the lamp, their shadows long and attenuated, thrown halfway across the courtyard by the softly hissing lamp in their midst.

MAIL BY HAND

My good friend,
 Would you like to come and have a drink with us this evening at eight o'clock?
> Your friend,
> Gerald Durrell.

My good friend,
 Expect me a 7.30 p.m. Thanks.
> Your good friend,
> Fon of Bafut.

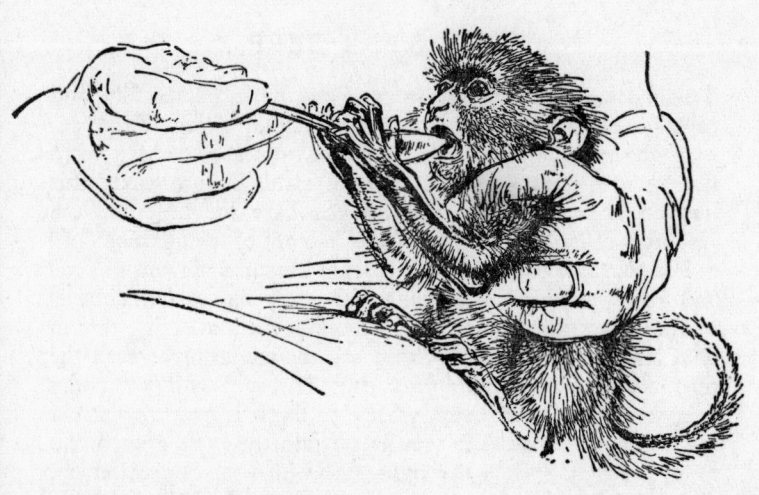

CHAPTER FIVE

FILM STAR BEEF

THERE are several different ways of making an animal film, and probably one of the best methods is to employ a team of cameramen who spend about two years in some tropical part of the world filming the animals in their natural state. Unfortunately this method is expensive, and unless you have the time and the resources of Hollywood behind you it is out of the question.

For someone like myself, with only a limited amount of time and money to spend in a country, the only way to film animals is under controlled conditions. The difficulties of trying to film wild animals in a tropical forest are enough to make even the most ardent photographer grow pale. To begin with you hardly ever see a wild animal and, when you do, it is generally only a momentary glimpse as it scuttles off into the undergrowth. To be in the right spot at the right time with your camera set up, your exposure correct and an animal in front of you in a suitable setting, engaged in some interesting and filmable action, would be almost a miracle. So, the only way round this is to catch your animal first and establish it in captivity. Once it has lost some of its fear of human beings you can begin work. Inside a huge netting "room" you create a scene which is as much like the animal's natural habitat as possible, and yet which is—photographically speaking—suitable. That is to say, it must not have too many holes in which a shy creature can hide, your undergrowth must not be so thick that you get awkward patches of shade, and so on. Then you introduce your animal to the set, and allow it time to settle down, which may be anything from an hour to a couple of days.

It is essential, of course, to have a good knowledge of the animal's habits, and to know how it will react under certain circumstances. For example, a hungry pouched rat, if released in an appropriate setting and finding a lavish selection of forest fruits on the ground, will promptly proceed to stuff as many of them into his immense cheek pouches as they will hold, so that in the end he looks as though he is suffering from a particularly virulent attack of mumps. If you don't want to end up with nothing more exciting than a series of pictures of some creature wandering aimlessly to and fro amid bushes and grass, you must provide the circumstances which will allow it to display some interesting habit or action. However, even when you have reached this stage you still require two other things: patience and luck. An animal— even a tame one—cannot be told what to do like a human actor. Sometimes a creature which has performed a certain action day after day for weeks will, when faced with a camera, develop an acute attack of stage fright, and refuse to perform. When you have spent hours in the hot sun getting everything ready, to be treated to this sort of display of temperament makes you feel positively homicidal.

A prize example of the difficulties of animal photography was, I think, the day we attempted to photograph the water chevrotain. These delightful little antelopes are about the size of a fox-terrier, with a rich chestnut coat handsomely marked with streaks and spots of white. Small and dainty, the water chevrotain is extremely photogenic. There are several interesting points about the chevrotain, one of which is its adaptation to a semi-aquatic life in the wild state. It spends most of its time wading and swimming in streams in the forest and can even swim for considerable distances under water. The second curious thing is that it has a passion for snails and beetles, and such carnivorous habits in an antelope are most unusual. The third notable characteristic is its extraordinary placidity and tameness: I have known a chevrotain, an hour after capture, take food from my

hand and allow me to tickle its ears for all the world as if it had been born in captivity.

Our water chevrotain was no exception; she was ridiculously tame, adored having her head and tummy scratched and would engulf, with every sign of satisfaction, any quantity of snails and beetles you cared to provide. Apart from this she spent her spare time trying to bathe in her water bowl, into which she could just jam—with considerable effort—the extreme rear end of her body.

So, to display her carnivorous and aquatic habits, I designed a set embracing a section of river bank. The undergrowth was carefully placed so that it would show off her perfect adaptive coloration to the best advantage. One morning, when the sky was free from cloud and the sun was in the right place, we carried the chevrotain cage out to the set and prepared to release her.

"The only thing I'm afraid of," I said to Jacquie, "is that I'm not going to get sufficient movement out of her. You know how quiet she is . . . she'll probably walk into the middle of the set and refuse to move."

"Well, if we offer her a snail or something from the other side I should think she'll walk across," said Jacquie.

"As long as she doesn't just stand there, like a cow in a field. I want to get *some* movement out of her," I said.

I got considerably more movement out of her than I anticipated. The moment the slide of her cage was lifted she stepped out daintily and paused with one slender hoof raised. I started the camera and awaited her next move. Her next move was somewhat unexpected. She shot across my carefully prepared set like a rocket, went right through the netting wall as if it had not been there and disappeared into the undergrowth in the middle distance before any of us could make a move to stop her. Our reactions were slow, because this was the last thing we had expected, but as I saw my precious chevrotain disappearing from view I uttered such a wail of anguish that everyone, including Phillip the cook, dropped whatever they were doing and assembled on the scene like magic.

"Water beef done run," I yelled. "I go give ten shillings to the man who go catch um."

The effect of this lavish offer was immediate. A wedge of Africans descended on to the patch of undergrowth into which the antelope had disappeared, like a swarm of hungry locusts. Within five minutes Phillip, uttering a roar of triumph like a sergeant-major, emerged from the bushes clutching to his bosom the kicking, struggling antelope. When we replaced her in her cage she stood quite quietly, gazing at us with limpid eyes as if astonished at all the fuss. She licked my hand in a friendly fashion, and when tickled behind the ears went off into her usual trance-like state, with half-closed eyes. We spent the rest of the day trying to film the wretched creature. She behaved beautifully in her box, splashing in a bowl of water to show how aquatic she was, eating beetles and snails to show how carnivorous she was, but the moment she was released into the film set she fled towards the horizon as if she had a brace of leopards on her tail. At the end of the day, hot and exhausted, I had exposed fifty feet of film, all of which showed her standing stock still outside her box, preparatory to dashing away. Sadly we carried her cage back to the Rest House, while she lay placidly on her banana-leaf bed and munched beetles. It was the last time we tried to photograph the water chevrotain.

Another creature that caused me untold anguish in the photographic field was a young Woodford's owl called, with singular lack of originality, Woody. Woodfords are very lovely owls, with a rich chocolate plumage splashed and blotched with white, and possessing what must be the most beautiful eyes in the whole of the owl family. They are large, dark and liquid, with heavy lids of a delicate pinky-mauve. These they raise and lower over their eyes in what seems to be slow motion, like an ancient film actress considering whether to make a comeback. This seductive fluttering of eyelids is accompanied by loud clickings of the beak like castanets. When excited the eyelid fluttering becomes very pronounced and the birds sway from side to side on the perch, as if about to start a hula-hula, and then they suddenly spread their wings and stand there clicking their beaks at you, looking like a tombstone angel of the more fiercely religious variety. Woody would perform all these actions perfectly inside his cage and would, moreover, perform them to order when shown a succulent tit-bit like a small mouse. I felt sure that, if he was provided with a suitable background, I could get his display on film with the minimum of trouble.

So, in the netting room I used for bird photography I set to and created what looked like a forest tree, heavily overgrown with creepers and other parasites, using green leaves and a blue sky as background. Then I carried Woody out and placed him on the branch in the midst of this wealth of foliage. The action I wanted him to perform was a simple and natural one not calculated to tax even the brain of an owl. With a little co-operation on his part the whole thing could have been over in ten minutes. He sat on the branch regarding us with wide-eyed horror, while I took up my position behind the camera. Just as I pressed the button he blinked his eyes once, very rapidly, and then, as if overcome with disgust at our appearance, he very firmly turned his back on us. Trying to remember that patience was the first requisite of an animal photographer, I wiped the sweat from my eyes, walked up to the branch, turned him round and walked back to the camera. By the time I had reached it Woody once more had his back towards us. I thought that maybe the light was too strong, so several members of the staff were sent to cut branches and these were rigged up so that the bird was sheltered from the direct rays of the sun. But still he persisted in keeping his back to us. It was obvious that, if I wanted to photograph him, I would have to rearrange my set so that it faced

the opposite way. After considerable labour about a ton of under-growth was carefully shifted and rearranged so that Woody was now facing the way he obviously preferred.

During this labour, while we sweated with massive branches and coils of creepers, he sat there regarding us in surprise. He generously allowed me to get the camera set up in the right position (a complicated job, for I was now shooting almost directly into the sun) and then he calmly turned his back on it. I could have strangled him. By this time ominous black clouds were rolling up, preparatory to obscuring the sun, and so further attempts at photography were impossible. I packed up the camera and then walked to the branch, murder in my heart, to collect my star. As I approached he turned round, clicked his beak delightedly, executed a rapid hula-hula and then spread his wings and bowed to me, with the mock-shy air of an actor taking his seventeenth curtain call.

Of course not all our stars caused us trouble. In fact, one of the best sequences I managed to get on film was accomplished with the minimum of fuss and in record time. And yet, on the face of it, one would have thought that it was a much more difficult object to achieve than getting an owl to spread his wings. Simply, I wanted to get some shots of an egg-eating snake robbing a nest. Egg-eating snakes measure about two feet in length and are very slender. Coloured a pinkish-brown, mottled with darker mark-ings, they have strange, protuberant eyes of a pale silvery colour with fine vertical pupils like a cat's. The curious point about them is that three inches from the throat (internally, of course) the vertebræ protrude, hanging down like stalactites. The reptile engulfs an egg, whole, and this passes down its body until it lies directly under these vertebræ. Then the snake contracts its muscles and the spikes penetrate the egg and break it; the yolk and white are absorbed and the broken shell, now a flattened pellet, is regurgitated. The whole process is quite extraordinary and had never, as far as I knew, been recorded on film.

We had, at that time, six egg-eating snakes, all of which were, to my delight, identical in size and coloration. The local children did a brisk trade in bringing us weaver-birds' eggs to feed this troupe of reptiles, for they seemed capable of eating any number we cared to put in their cage. In fact, the mere introduction of an egg into the cage changed them from a somnolent pile of snakes to a writhing bundle, each endeavouring to get at the egg first. But, although they behaved so beautifully in the cage, after my experiences with Woody and the water chevrotain, I was inclined to be a bit pessimistic. However, I created a suitable set (a flowering bush in the branches of which was placed a small nest) and collected a dozen small blue eggs as props. Then the snakes were kept without their normal quota of eggs for three days, to make sure they all had good appetites. This, incidentally, did not hurt them at all, for all snakes can endure considerable fasts, which with some of the bigger constrictors run into months or years. However, when my stars had got what I hoped was a good edge to their appetites, we started work.

The snakes' cage was carried out to the film set, five lovely blue eggs were placed in the nest and then one of the reptiles was placed gently in the branches of the bush, just above the nest. I started the camera and waited.

The snake lay flaccidly across the branches seeming a little dazed by the sunlight after the cool dimness of its box. In a moment its tongue started to flicker in and out, and it turned its head from side to side in an interested manner. Then with smooth fluidity it started to trickle through the branches towards the nest. Slowly it drew closer and closer, and when it reached the rim of the nest, it peered over the edge and down at the eggs with its fierce silvery eyes. Its tongue flicked again as if it were smelling the eggs and it nosed them gently like a dog with a pile of biscuits. Then it pulled itself a little farther into the nest, turned its head sideways, opened its mouth wide and started to engulf one of the eggs. All snakes have a jaw so constructed that they can dislocate the hinge, which enables them to swallow a prey that, at first sight, looks too big to pass through their mouths. The egg-eater was no exception and he neatly dislocated his jaws and the skin of his throat stretched until each scale stood out individually and you could see the blue of the egg shining through the fine, taut skin as the egg was forced slowly down his throat. When the egg was about an inch down his body he paused for a moment's meditation and then swung himself out of the nest and into the branches. Here, as he made his way along, he rubbed the great swelling in his body that the egg had created against the branches so that the egg was forced farther and farther down.

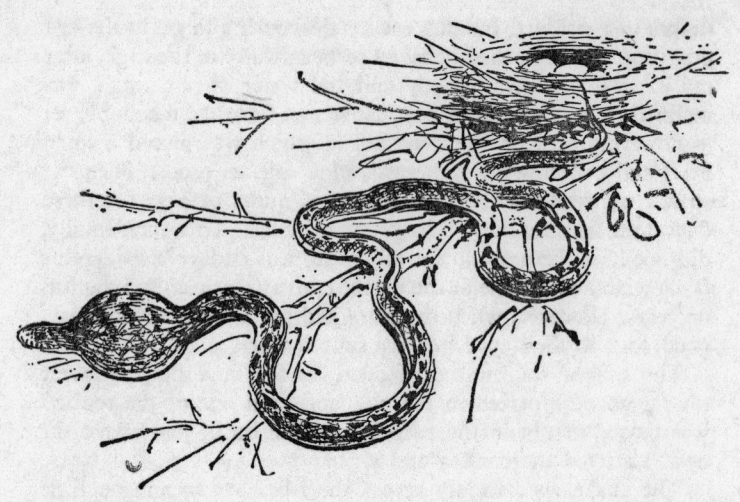

Elated with this success we returned the snake to his box so that he could digest his meal in comfort, and I shifted the camera's position and put on my big lenses for close-up work. We put another egg into the nest to replace the one taken, and then got out another egg-eater. This was the beauty of having all the snakes of the same size and coloration: as the first snake would not look at another egg until he had digested the first, he could not be used in the close-up shots. But the new one was identical and as hungry as a hunter, and so without any trouble whatsoever I got all the close-up shots I needed as he glided rapidly down to the nest and took an egg. I did the whole thing all over again with two other snakes and on the finished film these four separate sequences were intercut and no one, seeing the finished product, could tell that they were seeing four different snakes.

All the Bafutians, including the Fon, were fascinated by our filming activities, since not long before they had seen their very first cinema. A mobile ciné van had come out to Bafut and shown them a colour film of the Coronation and they had been terribly thrilled with it. In fact it was still a subject of grave discussion when we were there, nearly a year and a half later. Thinking that the Fon and his council would be interested to learn more about filming, I invited them to come across one morning and attend a filming session and they accepted with delight.

"What are you going to film?" asked Jacquie.

"Well, it doesn't really matter, so long as it's innocuous," I said.

"Why innocuous?" asked Sophie.

"I don't want to take any risks. . . . If I got the Fon bitten by something I would hardly be *persona grata,* would I?"

"Good God, no, that would never do," said Bob. "What sort of thing did you have in mind?"

"Well, I want to get some shots of those pouched rats, so we might as well use them. They can't hurt a fly."

So the following morning we got everything ready. The film set, representing a bit of forest floor, had been constructed on a Dexion stand, one of our specially made nylon tarpaulins had been erected nearby, under which the Fon and his court could sit, and beneath it were placed a table of drinks and some chairs. Then we sent a message over to the Fon that we were ready for him.

We watched him and his council approaching across the great courtyard and they were a wonderful spectacle. First came the Fon, in handsome blue and white robes, his favourite wife trotting along beside him, shading him from the sun with an enormous orange and red umbrella. Behind him walked the council members in their fluttering robes of green, red, orange, scarlet, white and yellow. Around this phalanx of colour some forty-odd of the Fon's children skipped and scuttled about like little black beetles round a huge, multicoloured caterpillar. Slowly the procession made its way round the Rest House and arrived at our improvised film studio.

"Morning, my friend," called the Fon, grinning. "We done come for see dis cinema."

"Welcome, my friend," I replied. "You like first we go have drink together?"

"Wah! Yes, I like," said the Fon, lowering himself cautiously into one of our camp chairs.

I poured out the drinks, and as we sipped them I explained the mysteries of ciné photography to the Fon, showing him how the camera worked, what the film itself looked like and explaining how each little picture was of a separate movement.

"Dis filum you take, when we go see um?" asked the Fon, when he had mastered the basic principles of photography.

"I have to take um for my country before it get ready," I said sadly, "so I no fit show you until I go come back for the Cameroons."

"Ah, good," said the Fon, "so when you go come back for dis ma country we go have happy time and you go show me dis your filum."

We had another drink to celebrate the thought of my impending return to Bafut.

By this time everything was ready to show the Fon how one set about making a sequence. Sophie, as continuity girl, wearing trousers, shirt, sun-glasses and an outsize straw hat, was perched precariously on a small camp-stool, her pad and pencil at the ready to make notes of each shot I took. Near her Jacquie, a battery of still cameras slung round her, was crouched by the side of the recording machine. Near the set, Bob stood in the role of dramatic coach, armed with a twig, and the box in which our stars were squeaking vociferously. I set up the camera, took up my position behind it and gave the signal for action. The Fon and councillors watched silent and absorbed as Bob gently tipped the two pouched rats out on to the set, and then guided them into the right positions with his twig. I started the camera and at the sound of its high-pitched humming a chorus of appreciative "Ahs" ran through the audience behind me. It was just at that moment that a small boy carrying a calabash wandered into the compound and, oblivious of the crowd, walked up to Bob and held up his offering. I was fully absorbed in peering through the viewfinder of the camera and so I paid little attention to the ensuing conversation that Bob had with the child.

"Na whatee dis?" asked Bob, taking the calabash, which had its neck plugged with green leaves.

"Beef," said the child succinctly.

Instead of inquiring more closely into the nature of the beef, Bob pulled out the plug of leaves blocking the neck of the calabash. The result surprised not only him but everyone else as well. Six feet of agile and extremely angry green mamba shot out of the calabash like a jack-in-the-box and fell to the ground.

"Mind your feet!" Bob shouted warningly.

I removed my eye from the viewfinder of the camera to be

treated to the somewhat disturbing sight of the green mamba sliding determinedly through the legs of the tripod towards me. I leaped upwards and backwards with an airy grace that only a prima ballerina treading heavily on a tin-tack could have emulated. Immediately pandemonium broke loose. The snake slid past me and made for Sophie at considerable speed. Sophie took one look and decided that discretion was the better part of valour. Seizing her pencil, pad and, for some obscure reason, her camp stool too, she ran like a hare towards the massed ranks of the councillors. Unfortunately this was the way the snake wanted to go as well, so he followed hotly on her trail. The councillors took one look at Sophie, apparently leading the snake into their midst, and did not hesitate for a moment. As one man, they turned and fled. Only the Fon remained, rooted to his chair, so wedged behind the table of drinks that he could not move. "Get a stick," I yelled to Bob and ran after the snake. I knew, of course, that the snake would not deliberately attack anyone. It was merely trying to put the greatest possible distance between itself and us. But when you have fifty panic-stricken Africans, all bare-footed, running madly in all directions, accompanied by a frightened and deadly snake, an accident is possible. The scene now, according to Jacquie, was fantastic. The council members were running across the compound, pursued by Sophie, who was pursued by the snake, who was pursued by me, who, in turn, was being pursued by Bob with a stick. The mamba had, to my relief, by-passed the Fon. Since the wave of battle had missed him the Fon sat there and did nothing more constructive than help himself to a quick drink to soothe his shattered nerves.

At last Bob and I managed to corner the mamba against the Rest House steps. Then we held it down with a stick, picked it up and popped it into one of our capacious snake-bags. I returned to the Fon, and found the council members drifting back from various points of the compass to join their monarch. If in any other part of the world you had to put to flight a cluster of dignitaries by introducing a snake into their midst, you would have had to suffer endless recriminations, sulks, wounded dignity and other exhausting displays of human nature. But not so with the Africans. The Fon sat in his chair, beaming. The councillors chattered and laughed as they approached, clicking their fingers at the danger that was past, making fun of each other for running so fast, and generally thoroughly enjoying the humorous side of the situation.

"You done hold um, my friend?" asked the Fon, generously pouring me out a large dollop of my own whisky.

"Yes," I said, taking the drink gratefully, "we done hold um."

The Fon leaned across and grinned at me mischievously. "You see how all dis ma people run?" he asked.

"Yes, they run time no dere," I agreed.

"They de fear," explained the Fon.

"Yes. Na bad snake dat."

"Na true, na true," agreed the Fon, "all dis small small man de fear dis snake too much."

"Yes."

"I never fear dis snake," said the Fon. "All dis ma people dey de run . . . dey de fear too much . . . but I never run."

"No, my friend, na true . . . you never run."

"I no de fear dis snake," said the Fon in case I had missed the point.

"Na true. But dis snake 'e de fear you."

" 'E de fear me?" asked the Fon, puzzled.

"Yes, dis snake no fit bite you . . . na bad snake, but he no fit kill Fon of Bafut."

The Fon laughed uproariously at this piece of blatant flattery, and then, remembering the way his councillors had fled, he laughed again, and the councillors joined him. At length, still reeling with merriment at the incident, they left us and we could hear their chatter and hilarious laughter long after they had disappeared. This is the only occasion when I have known a green mamba to pull off a diplomatic *coup d'état*.

MAIL BY HAND

My good friend,

Good morning to you all. I received your note, but sorry my sickness is still going on as it was yesterday.

I was sorry for I failed coming to drink with you, due to the sickness.

I was grateful for the bottle of whiskey and the medicine which you sent to me. I used the medicine yesterday evening and today morning, but no improvement yet. The thing which is giving me trouble is cough, if you can get some medicine for it, kindly send it to me through bearer.

I think that whiskey will also help, but I do not know yet. Please send me some gin if any.

I am lying on bed.

Yours good friend,
Fon of Bafut.

CHAPTER SIX

BEEF WITH HAND LIKE MAN

OF all the animals one finds on a collecting trip the ones that fascinate me most are, I think, members of the monkey tribe. They are delightfully child-like, with their quick intelligence, their uninhibited habits, their rowdy, eager live-for-the-moment attitude towards life, and their rather pathetic faith in you when they have accepted you as a foster-parent.

In the Cameroons, monkeys are one of the staple items of diet, and, as there are no enforced laws covering the number that are shot or the season at which they are shot, it is natural that a vast quantity of females carrying young are slaughtered. The mother falls from the trees with the baby still clinging tightly to her body, and in most cases the infant is unhurt. Generally the baby is then killed and eaten with the mother; occasionally the hunter will take it back to his village, keep it until it is adult and then eat it. But when there is an animal collector in the vicinity, of course, all these orphans end up with him, for he is generally willing to pay much more than the market price for the living animal. So, at the end of two or three months in a place like the Cameroons you generally find that you are playing foster-parent to a host of monkeys of all shapes and ages.

In Bafut, towards the end of the trip, we had seventeen monkeys (not counting apes and the more primitive members of the tribe, such as pottos and bushbabies) and they caused us endless amusement. Probably the most colourful were the patas, slender monkeys about the size of a terrier, with bright gingery red fur, soot-black faces and white shirt-fronts. In the wild state these monkeys live in the grasslands, rather than the forest, walking about like dogs in large family groups, assiduously searching the grass roots and rotten logs for insects or birds' nests, turning over stones to get worms, scorpions, spiders and other delicacies. Periodically they will stand up on their hind-legs to peer over the grass or, if the grass is too tall, they will leap straight up in the air as though they are on springs. Then, if they see anything that smacks of danger they utter loud cries of "proup . . . proup . . . proup" and canter away through the grass, with a swinging stride like little red racehorses.

Our four patas lived in a large cage together, and when they were not carefully grooming each other's fur with expressions of intense concentration on their sad, black faces, they were indulging in weird sorts of Oriental dances. Patas are the only monkeys I know that really do dance. Most monkeys will, during an exuberant game, twirl round and round or jump up and down, but patas have worked out special dance sequences for themselves and, moreover, have quite an extensive repertoire. They would start by bouncing up and down on all fours like a rubber ball, all four feet leaving the ground simultaneously, getting faster and faster and higher and higher, until they were leaping almost two feet in to the air. Then they would stop and start a new series of "steps". Keeping their back legs and hindquarters quite still they would swing the front of their body from side to side like a pendulum, twisting their heads from left to right as they did so. When they had done this twenty or thirty times they would launch into a new variation, which consisted of standing up stiff and straight on their hind legs, arms stretched above their heads, faces peering up at the roof of their cage, and then staggering round and round in circles until they were so dizzy that they fell backwards. This whole dance would be accompanied by a little song, the lyric of which went like this: "Waaaaow . . . waaaaow

. . . proup . . . proup . . . waaaaow . . . proup," which was considerably more attractive and comprehensible than the average popular song sung by the average popular crooner.

The patas, of course, adored live food of any description and they felt their day was incomplete if they did not have a handful of grasshoppers apiece, or some birds' eggs, or a brace of juicy, hairy spiders. But for them the caviare of life was the larva of the palm beetle. Palm beetles are an oval insect about two inches in length, which are very common in the Cameroons. They lay their eggs in rotting tree-trunks, but show a marked preference for the soft, fibrous interior of the palm trees. Here, in a moist, soft bed of food, the egg hatches out and the grub soon grows into a livid white, maggot-like creature about three inches long and as thick as your thumb. These fat, twitching grubs were considered by the patas to be the Food of the Gods, and the shrieks of delight that would greet my appearance with a tinful of them would be almost deafening. The curious thing was that, although they adored eating the larvæ, they were really scared of them. After I had emptied the grubs on the floor of the cage, the patas would squat round the pile, still screaming with pleasure, and keep touching the delicacies with trembling, tentative fingers. If the grubs moved, they would hastily withdraw their hands and wipe them hurriedly on their fur. At last one of them would grab a fat larva and, screwing up his face and closing his eyes tightly, he would stuff the end into his mouth and bite hard. The larva, of course, would respond to this unkind decapitation with a frantic dying wriggle and the patas would drop it hastily, wipe his hands again and, still sitting with tightly closed eyes and screwed-up face, would munch on the morsel he had bitten off. They reminded me of débutantes being introduced to their first fresh oysters.

Unwittingly one day—under the impression that I was doing them a kindness—I caused pandemonium in the patas cage. An army of local children kept us supplied with live food for the animals and they would arrive just after dawn with calabashes full of snails, birds' eggs, beetle-larvæ, grasshoppers, spiders, tiny hairless rats and other strange food that our animals enjoyed. On this particular morning one lad had brought in, as well as his normal offering of snails and palm beetle larvæ, the larvæ of two Goliath beetles. Goliath beetles are the biggest beetles in the world—an adult measures six inches in length and four inches

across the back—so it goes without saying that the larvæ were monsters. They were also about six inches long, and as thick as my wrist. They were the same horrid unhealthy white as the palm beetle larvæ, but they were much fatter, and their skin was wrinkled and folded and tucked like an eiderdown. They had flat, nut-brown heads the size of a shilling, with great curved jaws that could give you quite a pinch if you handled them incautiously. I was very pleased with these monstrous, bloated maggots, for I felt that, since the patas liked palm beetle larvæ so much, their delight would know no bounds when they set eyes on these gigantic tit-bits. So I put the Goliath larvæ in the usual tin with the other grubs and went to give them to the patas as a light snack before they had their breakfast.

As soon as they saw the familiar tin on the horizon the patas started to dance up and down excitedly, crying, "proup . . . proup". As I was opening the door they sat down in a circle, their little black faces wearing a worried expression, their hands held out beseechingly. I pushed the tin through the door and tipped it up so that the two Goliath larvæ fell on to the floor of the cage with a soggy thud, where they lay unmoving. To say that the patas were surprised is an understatement; they uttered faint squeaks of astonishment and shuffled backwards on their bottoms, surveying these barrage-balloons of larvæ with a horrified mistrust. They watched them narrowly for a minute or so, but as there was no sign of movement from the larvæ, they gradually became braver, and shuffled closer to examine this curious phenomenon more minutely. Then, having studied the grubs from every possible angle, one of the monkeys, greatly daring, put out a hand and prodded a grub with a tentative forefinger. The grub, who had been lying on his back in a sort of trance, woke up at once, gave a convulsive wriggle and rolled over majestically on to his tummy. The effect of this movement on the patas was tremendous. Uttering wild screams of fear they fled in a body to the farthest corner of the cage, where they indulged in a disgracefully cowardly scrimmage, vaguely reminiscent of the Eton wall-game, each one doing his best to get into the extreme corner of the cage, behind all his companions. Then the grub, after pondering for a few seconds, started to drag his bloated body laboriously across the floor towards them. At this the patas showed such symptoms of collective hysteria that I was forced to intervene and remove the grubs. I put them in Ticky the black-footed mongoose's cage, and she, who was not afraid of anything, disposed of them in four snaps and two gulps. But the poor patas were in a twittering state of nerves for the rest of the day and ever after that, when they saw me coming with the beetle larvæ tin, they would retreat hurriedly to the back of the cage until they were sure that the tin contained nothing more harmful or horrifying than palm-beetle larvæ.

One of our favourite characters in the monkey collection was a half-grown female baboon called Georgina. She was a creature of tremendous personality and with a wicked sense of humour. She had been hand-reared by an African who had kept her as a sort of pet-cum-watchdog, and we had purchased her for the magnificent sum of ten shillings. Georgina was, of course, perfectly tame and wore a belt round her waist, to which was attached a long rope; and every day she was taken out and tied to one of the trees in the compound below the Rest House. For the first couple of days we tied her up fairly near the gate leading into the compound, through which came a steady stream of hunters, old ladies selling eggs and hordes of children with insects and snails for sale. We thought that this constant procession of humanity would keep Georgina occupied and amused. It certainly did, but not in the way we intended. She very soon discovered that she could go to the end of her rope and crouch down out of sight behind the hibiscus hedge, just near the gate. Then, when some poor unsuspecting African came into the compound, she would leap out of her ambush, embrace him round the legs while at the same time uttering such a blood-curdling scream as to make even the staunchest nerves falter and break.

Her first successful ambuscade was perpetrated on an old hunter who, clad in his best robe, was bringing a calabash full of rats to us. He had approached the Rest House slowly and with great dignity, as befitted one who was bringing such rare creatures for sale, but his aristocratic poise was rudely shattered as he came through the gate. Feeling his legs seized in Georgina's iron grasp, and hearing her terrifying scream, he dropped his calabash of rats, which promptly broke so that they all escaped, leaped straight up in the air with a roar of fright and fled down the road in a very undignified manner and at a speed quite remarkable for one of his age. It cost me three packets of cigarettes and considerable tact to soothe his ruffled feelings. Georgina, meanwhile, sat there looking as if butter would not melt in her mouth and, as I scolded her, merely raised her eyebrows, displaying her pale pinkish eyelids in an expression of innocent astonishment.

Her next victim was a handsome sixteen-year-old girl who had brought a calabash full of snails. The girl, however, was almost as quick in her reactions as Georgina. She saw the baboon out of the corner of her eye, just as Georgina made her leap. The girl sprang away with a squeak of fear and Georgina, instead of getting a grip on her legs, merely managed to fasten on to the trailing corner of her sarong. The baboon gave a sharp tug and the sarong came away in her hairy paw, leaving the unfortunate damsel as naked as the day she was born. Georgina, screaming with excitement, immediately put the sarong over her head like a shawl and sat chattering happily to herself, while the poor girl, overcome with embarrassment, backed into the hibiscus hedge endeavouring to cover all the vital portions of her anatomy with her hands. Bob, who happened to witness this incident with me, needed no encouragement whatever to volunteer to go down into the compound, retrieve the sarong and return it to the damsel.

So far Georgina had had the best of these skirmishes, but the next morning she overplayed her hand. A dear old lady, weighing about fourteen stone, came waddling and wheezing up to the Rest House gate, balancing carefully on her head a kerosene tin full of groundnut oil, which she was hoping to sell to Phillip the cook. Phillip, having spotted the old lady, rushed out of the kitchen to warn her about Georgina, but he arrived on the scene too late. Georgina leapt from behind the hedge with the stealth of a leopard and threw her arms round the old lady's fat legs, uttering her frightening war-cry as she did so. The poor old lady was far too fat to jump and run as the other victims had, so she remained rooted to the spot, uttering screams that for quality and quantity closely rivalled the sounds Georgina was producing. While they indulged in this cacophonous duet, the kerosene tin wobbled precariously on the old lady's head. Phillip came clumping across the compound on his enormous feet, roaring hoarse instructions to the old lady, none of which she appeared to obey or even hear. When he reached the scene of the battle, Phillip, in his excitement, did a very silly thing. Instead of confining his attention to the tin on the old lady's head, he concentrated on her other end, and seizing Georgina attempted to pull her away. Georgina, however, was not going to be deprived of such a plump and prosperous victim so easily and, screaming indignantly, she clung on like a limpet. Phillip, holding the baboon round the waist, tugged with all his might. The old lady's vast bulk quivered like a mighty tree on the point of falling and the kerosene tin on her head gave up the unequal struggle with the laws of gravity and fell to the ground with a crash. A wave of oil leapt into the air as the tin struck the ground and covered the three protagonists in a golden, glutinous waterfall. Georgina, startled by this new, cowardly and possibly dangerous form of warfare, gave a grunt of fright, let go of the old lady's legs and retreated to the full stretch of her rope, where she sat down and endeavoured to rid her fur of the sticky oil. Phillip stood there looking as though he was slowly melting from the waist down, and the front of the old lady's sarong was equally sodden.

"Wah!" roared Phillip, ferociously, "you *stupid* woman, why you throw dis oil for ground?"

"Foolish man," screamed the old lady, equally indignant, "dis beef come for bite me, how I go do?"

"Dis monkey no go bite you, blurry fool, na tame one," roared Phillip, "and now look dis my clothes done spoil . . . na your fault dis."

"No be my fault, no be my fault," screeched the old lady, her impressive bulk quivering like a dusky volcano, "na your own fault, bushman, an' all my dress do spoil, all dis my oil done throw for ground."

"Blurry foolish woman," blared Phillip, "you be bushwoman, you done throw dis oil for ground for no cause . . . all dis my clothes done ruin."

He stamped his large foot in irritation with the unfortunate result that it landed in the pool of oil and splashed over the front of the old lady's already dripping sarong. Giving a scream like a descending bomb the old lady stood there quivering as if she would burst. Then she found her voice. She only uttered one word, but I knew that this was the time to intervene.

"Ibo!" she hissed malevolently.

Phillip reeled before this insult. The Ibos are a Nigerian tribe whom the Cameroonians regard with horror and loathing, and to call someone in the Cameroons an Ibo is the deadliest insult you can offer. Before Phillip could collect his wits and do something violent to the old lady, I intervened. I soothed the good lady, gave her compensation for her sarong and lost oil, and then somewhat mollified the still simmering Phillip by promising to give him a new pair of shorts, socks and a shirt out of my own wardrobe. Then I untied the glutinous Georgina, and removed her to a place where she could not perform any more expensive attacks on the local population.

But Georgina had not finished yet. Unfortunately I tied her up under the lower verandah, close to a room which we used as a bathroom. In it was a large, circular red plastic bowl which was prepared each evening so that we could wash the sweat and dirt of the day's work from our bodies. The difficulty of bathing in this plastic bowl was that it was a shade too small. To recline in the warm water and enjoy it you were forced to leave your feet and legs outside, as it were, resting on a wooden box. As the bowl was slippery it generally required a considerable effort to rise from this reclining position to reach the soap or the towel or some other necessity. This bath was not the most comfortable in the world, but it was the best we could do in the circumstances.

Sophie adored her bath, and would spend far longer than anyone else over it, lying back luxuriously in the warm water, smoking a cigarette and reading a book by the light of a tiny hurricane lantern. On this particular night her ablutions were not so prolonged. The battle of the bathroom commenced with one of the staff coming and saying, in the conspiratorial manner they always seemed to adopt, "Barf ready, madam." Sophie got her book and her tin of cigarettes and wandered down to the bathroom. She found it already occupied by Georgina, who had discovered that the length of her rope and the position in which I had tied her allowed her access to this interesting room. She was sitting by the bath dipping the towel in the water, uttering little throaty cries of satisfaction. Sophie shooed her out, called for a new towel and then, closing the door, she undressed and lowered herself into the warm water.

Unfortunately, as she soon discovered, Sophie had not shut the door properly. Georgina had never seen anyone bathe before and she was not going to let such a unique opportunity pass without taking full advantage of it. She hurled herself against the door and threw it wide open. Sophie now found herself in a predicament: she was so tightly wedged in the bath that she could not get out and shut the door without considerable difficulty, and yet to lie there with the door open was out of the question. With a great effort she leaned out of the bath and reached for her clothes which she had fortunately placed near by. Georgina, seeing this, decided that it represented the beginnings of a promising game and jumping forward she clasped Sophie's clothes to her hairy bosom and ran outside with them. This left only the towel. Struggling out of the bath Sophie draped herself in this inadequate covering and, after making sure that no one was around, went outside to try and retrieve her garments. Georgina, finding that Sophie was entering into the spirit of the game, gave a chattering cry of delight and as Sophie made a dart at her she ran back into the bathroom and hurriedly put Sophie's clothes in the bath. Taking Sophie's cry of horror to be encouragement she then seized the tin of cigarettes and put that in the bath too, presumably to see if it would float. It sank, and forty-odd cigarettes floated dismally to the surface. Then, in order to leave no stone unturned in her efforts to give Sophie pleasure, Georgina tipped all the water out of the bath. Attracted by the uproar I appeared on the scene just in time to see Georgina leap nimbly into the bath and start to jump up and down on the mass of sodden cigarettes and clothes rather after the manner of a wine-treader. It took some considerable time to remove the excited baboon, get Sophie fresh bath water, cigarettes and clothing, by which time the dinner was cold. So Georgina was responsible for a really exhilarating evening.

But of all our monkey family, it was the apes, I think, that gave us the most pleasure and amusement. The first one we obtained was a baby male who arrived one morning, reclining in the arms of a hunter, with such an expression of sneering aristocracy on his small, wrinkled face that one got the impression he was employing the hunter to carry him about, in the manner of an Eastern potentate. He sat quietly on the Rest House steps watching us with intelligent, scornful brown eyes, while the hunter and I bargained over him, rather as though this sordid wrangling over money was acutely distasteful to a chimpanzee of his upbringing and background. When the bargain had been struck and the filthy lucre had changed hands, this simian aristocrat took my hand condescendingly and walked into our living-room, peering about him with an air of ill-concealed disgust, like a duke visiting the kitchen of a sick retainer, determined to be democratic however unsavoury the task. He sat on the table and accepted our humble offering of a banana with the air of one who is weary of the honours that have been bestowed upon him throughout life. Then and there we decided that he must have a name befitting such a blue-blooded primate, so we christened him Cholmondely St John, pronounced, of course, Chumley Sinjun. Later, when we got to know him better, he allowed us to become quite familiar with him and call him Chum, or sometimes, in moments of stress, "you bloody ape", but this latter term always made us feel as though we were committing *lèse-majesté*.

We built Chumley a cage (to which he took grave exception) and only allowed him out at set times during the day, when we could keep an eye on him. First thing in the morning, for example, he was let out of his cage, and accompanied a member of the staff into our bedroom with the morning tea. He would gallop across the floor and leap into bed with me, give me a wet and hurried kiss as greeting and then, with grunts and staccato cries of "Ah! Ah!" he would watch the tea tray put in position and examine it carefully to make sure that his cup (a large tin one for durability) was there. Then he would sit back and watch me carefully while I put milk, tea and sugar (five spoons) into his mug, and then take it from me with twitching, excited hands, bury his face in it and with a noise like a very large bath running out, start to drink. He would not even pause for breath, but the mug would be lifted higher and higher, until it was upside down over his face. Then there was a long pause as he waited for the delicious, semi-melted sugar to slide down into his open mouth. Having made quite sure that there was no sugar left at the bottom, he would sigh deeply, belch in a reflective manner and hand the mug back to me in the vague hopes that I would refill it. Having made quite sure that this wish was not going to be fulfilled, he would watch me drink my tea, and then set about the task of entertaining me.

There were several games he had invented for my benefit and all of them were exhausting to take part in at that hour of the morning. To begin with he would prowl down to the end of the bed and squat there, giving me surreptitious glances to make sure I was watching. Then he would insert a cold hand under the bedclothes and grab my toes. I was then supposed to lean forward with a roar of pretended rage, and he would leap off the bed and run to the other side of the room, watching me over his shoulder with a wicked expression of delight in his brown eyes. When I tired of this game I would pretend to be asleep, and he would then walk slowly and cautiously down the bed and peer into my face for a few seconds. Then he would shoot out a long arm, pull a handful of my hair and rush down to the bottom of the bed before I could catch him. If I did succeed in grabbing him, I would put my hands round his neck and tickle his collar bones, while he wriggled and squirmed, opening his mouth wide and drawing back his lips to display a vast acreage of pink gum and white teeth, giggling hysterically like a child.

Our second acquisition was a large five-year-old chimp called Minnie. A Dutch farmer turned up one day and said that he was willing to sell us Minnie, as he was soon due to go on leave and did not want to leave the animal to the tender mercies of his staff. We could have Minnie if we went and fetched her. As the Dutchman's farm was fifty miles away at a place called Santa, we arranged to go there in the Fon's Land-Rover, see the chimp and, if she proved healthy, buy her and bring her back to Bafut. So, taking a large crate with us, we set off very early one morning, thinking we would be back with the chimp in time for a late lunch.

To reach Santa we had to drive out of the valley in which Bafut lay, climb the great Bemenda escarpment (an almost sheer three-hundred-foot cliff) and then drive on into the range of mountains that lay beyond it. The landscape was white with heavy morning mist which, waiting for the sun to drag it into the sky in great toppling columns, lay placidly in the valleys like pools of milk, out of which rose the peaks of hills and escarpments like strange islands in a pallid sea. As we moved higher into the mountains we drove more slowly, for here the slight dawn wind, in frail spasmodic gusts, rolled and pushed these great banks of mist so that they swirled and poured across the road like enormous pale amoebas, and we would suddenly round a corner and find ourselves deep in the belly of a mist bank, visibility cut down to a few yards. At one point, as we edged our way through a bank of mist, there appeared in front of us what seemed, at first sight, to be a pair of elephant tusks. We shuddered to a halt, and out of the mist loomed a herd of the long-horned Fulani cattle which surrounded us in a tight wedge, peering through the Land-Rover windows with serious interest. They were huge, beautiful beasts of a dark chocolate brown, with enormous melting eyes and a massive spread of white horns, sometimes as much as five feet from tip to tip. They pressed closely around us, their warm breath pouring from their nostrils in white clouds, the sweet cattle smell of their bodies heavy in the cold air, while the guide cow's bell tinkled pleasantly with each movement of her head. We sat and surveyed each other for a few minutes and then there was a sharp whistle and a harsh cry as the herdsman appeared out of the mist, a typical Fulani, tall and slender with fine-boned features and a straight nose, somewhat resembling an ancient Egyptian mural.

"Iseeya, my friend," I called.

"Morning, Masa," he answered, grinning and slapping the dewy flank of an enormous cow.

"Na your cow dis?"

"Yes, sah, na ma own."

"Which side you take um?"

"For Bemenda, sah, for market."

"You fit move um so we go pass?"

"Yes, sah, yes, sah, I go move um," he grinned and with loud shouts he urged the cows onwards into the mist, dancing from one to the other and beating a light tattoo on their flanks with his bamboo walking-stick. The great beasts moved off into the mist, giving deep, contented bellows, the guide cow's bell tinkling pleasantly.

"Thank you, my friend, walka good," I called after the tall herdsman.

"Tank you, Masa, tank you," came his voice out of the mist, against a background of deep, bassoon-like cow calls.

By the time we reached Santa the sun was up and the mountains had changed to golden-green, their flanks still striped here and there with tenacious streaks of mist. We reached the Dutchman's house to find that he had been unexpectedly called away. However, Minnie was there and she was the purpose of our visit. She lived, we discovered, in a large circular enclosure that the Dutchman had built for her, surrounded by a tallish wall and furnished simply but effectively with four dead trees, planted upright in cement, and a small wooden house with a swing door. One gained access to this enclosure by lowering a form of drawbridge in the wall which allowed one to cross the dry moat that surrounded Minnie's abode.

Minnie was a large, well-built chimp about three feet six in height, and she sat in the branches of one of her trees and surveyed us with an amiable if slightly vacuous expression. We regarded each other silently for about ten minutes, while I endeavoured to assess her personality. Although the Dutchman had assured me that she was perfectly tame, I had had enough experience to know that even the tamest chimp, if it takes a dislike to you, can be a nasty creature to have a rough and tumble with, and Minnie, though not very tall, had an impressive bulk.

Presently I lowered the drawbridge and went into the enclosure, armed with a large bunch of bananas with which I hoped to purchase my escape if my estimation of her character was faulty. I sat on the ground, the bananas on my lap, and waited for Minnie to make the first overtures. She sat in the tree watching me with interest, thoughtfully slapping her rotund tummy with her large hands. Then, having decided that I was harmless, she climbed down from the tree and loped over to where I sat. She squatted down about a yard away and held out a hand to me. Solemnly I shook it. Then I, in turn, held out a banana which she accepted and ate, with small grunts of satisfaction.

Within half an hour she had eaten all the bananas and we had established some sort of friendship: that is to say, we played pat-a-cake, we chased each other round her compound and in and out of her hut, and we climbed one of the trees together. At this point I thought it was a suitable moment to introduce the crate into the compound. We carried it in, placed it on the grass with its lid and allowed Minnie plenty of time to examine it and decide it to be harmless. The problem now was to get Minnie into the crate without, firstly, frightening her too much and, secondly, getting bitten. As she had never in her life been confined in a box or small cage I could see that the whole operation presented difficulties, especially as her owner was not there to lend his authority to the manœuvre.

So, for three and a half hours I endeavoured, by example, to show Minnie that the crate was harmless. I sat in it, lay in it, jumped about on top of it, even crawled round with it on my back like a curiously shaped tortoise. Minnie enjoyed my efforts to amuse her immensely, but she still treated the crate with a

certain reserve. The trouble was that I realized I should only have one opportunity to trap her, for if I messed it up the first time and she realized what I was trying to do, no amount of coaxing or cajoling would induce her to come anywhere near the crate. Slowly but surely she had to be lured to the crate so that I could tip it over on top of her. So, after another three-quarters of an hour of concentrated and exhausting effort, I had got her to sit in front of the upturned crate and take bananas from inside it. Then came the great moment.

I baited the box with a particularly succulent bunch of bananas and then sat myself behind it, eating a banana myself and looking around the landscape nonchalantly, as though nothing could be farther from my mind than the thought of trapping chimpanzees. Minnie edged forward, darting surreptitious glances at me. Presently she was squatting close by the box, examining the bananas with greedy eyes. She gave me a quick glance and then, as I seemed preoccupied with my fruit, she leant forward and her head and shoulders disappeared inside the crate. I hurled my weight against the back of the box so that it toppled over her, and then jumped up and sat heavily on top so that she could not bounce it off. Bob rushed into the compound and added his weight and then, with infinite caution, we edged the lid underneath the crate, turned the whole thing over and nailed the lid in place, while Minnie sat surveying me malevolently through a knot hole and plaintively crying "Ooo . . . Oooo . . . Oooo," as if shocked to the core by my perfidy. Wiping the sweat from my face and lighting a much-needed cigarette, I glanced at my watch. It had taken four and a quarter hours to catch Minnie; I reflected that it could not have taken much longer if she had been a wild chimpanzee leaping about in the forest. A little tired, we loaded her on to the Land-Rover and set out for Bafut again.

At Bafut, we had already constructed a large cage out of Dexion for Minnie. It was not, of course, anywhere near as big as the one she was used to, but big enough to prevent her feeling too confined to begin with. Later she would have to get used to quite a small crate for the voyage home, but after all her customary freedom I wanted to break her gradually to the idea of being closely confined. When we put her into her new cage she explored it thoroughly with grunts of approval, banging the wire with her hands and swinging on the perches to see how strong they were. Then we gave her a big box of mixed fruit and a large white plastic bowl full of milk, which she greeted with hoots of delight.

The Fon had been very interested to hear that we were getting Minnie, for he had never seen a large, live chimpanzee before. So that evening I sent him a note inviting him to come over for a drink and to view the ape. He arrived just after dark, wearing a green and purple robe, accompanied by six council members and his two favourite wives. After the greetings were over and we had exchanged small chat over the first drink of the evening, I took the pressure lamp and led the Fon and his retinue down the verandah to Minnie's cage which, at first sight, appeared to be empty. Only when I lifted the lamp higher we discovered Minnie was in bed. She had made a nice pile of dry banana leaves at one end of the cage and she had settled down in this, lying on her side, her cheek pillowed on one hand, with an old sack we had given her carefully draped over her body and tucked under her armpits.

"Wah!" said the Fon in astonishment, " 'e sleep like man."

"Yes, yes," chorused the council members, " 'e sleep like man."

Minnie, disturbed by the lamplight and the voices, opened one eye to see what the disturbance was about. Seeing the Fon and his party she decided that they might well repay closer investigation, so she threw back her sacking cover carefully and waddled over to the wire.

"Wah!" said the Fon, " 'e same same for man, dis beef."

Minnie looked the Fon up and down, plainly thought that he might be inveigled into playing with her, beat a loud tattoo on the wire with her big hands. The Fon and his party retreated hurriedly.

"No de fear," I said, "na funning dis."

The Fon approached cautiously, an expression of astonished delight on his face. Cautiously he leant forward and banged on the wire with the palm of his hand. Minnie, delighted, answered him with a positive fusillade of bangs, that made him jump back and then crow with laughter.

"Look 'e hand, look 'e hand," he gasped, " 'e get hand like man."

"Yes, yes, 'e get hand same same for man," said the councillors.

The Fon leant down and banged on the wire again and Minnie once more responded.

"She play musica with you," I said.

"Yes, yes, na chimpanzee musica dis," said the Fon, and went off into peals of laughter. Greatly excited by her success, Minnie ran round the cage two or three times, did a couple of backward somersaults on her perches and then came and sat in the front of the cage, seized her plastic milk bowl and placed it on her head, where it perched looking incongruously like a steel helmet. The roar of laughter that this manœuvre provoked from the Fon and his councillors and wives caused half the village dogs to start barking.

"'E get hat, 'e get hat," gasped the Fon, doubling up with mirth.

Realizing that it was going to be almost impossible to drag the Fon away from Minnie, I called for the table, chairs and drinks to be brought out and placed on the verandah near the chimp's cage. So for half an hour the Fon sat there alternately sipping his drink and spluttering with laughter, while Minnie showed off like a veteran circus performer. Eventually, feeling somewhat tired by her performance, Minnie came and sat near the wire by the Fon, watching him with great interest as he drank, still wearing her plastic bowl helmet. The Fon beamed down at her. Then he leant forward until his face was only six inches away from Minnie's and lifted his glass.

"Shin-shin!" said the Fon.

To my complete astonishment Minnie responded by protruding her long, mobile lips and giving a prolonged raspberry of the juiciest variety.

The Fon laughed so loud and so long at this witticism that at last we were all thrown into a state of hysterical mirth by merely watching him enjoy the jest. At length, taking a grip on himself, he wiped his eyes, leant forward and blew a raspberry at Minnie. But his was a feeble amateur effort compared to the one with which Minnie responded, which echoed up and down the verandah like a machine-gun. So, for the next five minutes —until the Fon had to give up because he was laughing so much and out of breath—he and Minnie kept up a rapid crossfire of raspberries. Minnie was definitely the winner, judged by quality and quantity; also she had better breath control, so that her efforts were much more prolonged and sonorous than the Fon's.

At length the Fon left us, and we watched him walking back across the great compound, occasionally blowing raspberries at his councillors, whereupon they all doubled up with laughter. Minnie, with the air of a society hostess after an exhausting dinner party, yawned loudly and then went over and lay down on her banana-leaf bed, covered herself carefully with the sack, put her cheek on her hand and went to sleep. Presently her snores reverberated along the verandah almost as loudly as her raspberries.

PART THREE

COASTWARDS AND ZOOWARDS

MAIL BY HAND

Sir,

I have the honour most respectfully beg to submit this letter
to you stating as follows:

(1) I regret extremely at your leaving me, though not for bad
but for good.

(2) At this juncture, I humbly and respectfully beg that you as
my kind master should leave a good record of recommenda-
tion about me which will enable your successor to know all
about me.

(3) Though I have worked with several Masters I have highly appreciated your ways then all.

Therefore should the Master leave some footprints behind on my behalf, I shall price that above all my dukedoms.

I have the honour to me, Sir,

Your obedient Servent,

Phillip Onaga (Cook).

CHAPTER SEVEN

A ZOO IN OUR LUGGAGE

IT was time for us to start making preparations to leave Bafut
and travel the three-hundred-odd miles down to the coast. But
there was a lot to be done before we could set out on the journey.
In many ways this is the most harassing and dangerous part
of a collecting trip. For one thing to load your animals on to
lorries and take them that distance, over roads that resemble
a tank-training ground more than anything else, is in itself a
major undertaking. But there are many other vital things to
arrange as well. Your food supply for the voyage must be
waiting for you at the port, and here again you cannot afford
to make any mistakes, for you cannot take two hundred and
fifty animals on board a ship for three weeks unless you have
an adequate supply of food. All your cages have to be carefully
inspected and any defects caused by six months' wear-and-tear
have to be made good, because you cannot risk having an escape
on board ship. So, cages have to be rewired, new fastenings
fixed on doors, new bottoms fitted on to cages that show signs
of deterioration, and a hundred and one other minor jobs.

So, taking all this into consideration, it is not surprising that
you have to start making preparations for departure sometimes
a month before you actually leave your base camp for the coast.
Everything, it seems, conspires against you. The local population, horrified at the imminent loss of such a wonderful source
of revenue, redouble their hunting efforts so as to make the

maximum profit before you leave, and this means that you are not only renovating old cages, but constructing new ones as fast as you can to cope with this sudden influx of creatures. The local telegraph operator undergoes what appears to be a mental breakdown, so that the vital telegrams you send and receive are incomprehensible to both you and the recipient. When you are waiting anxiously for news of your food supplies for the voyage it is not soothing to the nerves to receive a telegram which states, "MESSAGE REPLIED REGRET CANNOTOB VARY GREEN BALAS WELL HALF PIPE DO?" which, after considerable trouble and expense, you get translated as: MESSAGE RECEIVED REGRET CANNOT OBTAIN VERY GREEN BANANAS WILL HALF RIPE DO?

Needless to say, the animals soon become aware that something is in the wind and try to soothe your nerves in their own particular way: those that are sick get sicker, and look at you in such a frail and anaemic way you are quite sure they will never survive the journey down to the coast; all the rarest and most irreplaceable specimens try to escape, and if successful hang around taunting you with their presence and making you waste valuable time trying to catch them again; animals that had refused to live unless supplied with special food, whether avocado pear or sweet potato, suddenly decide that they do not like this particular food any more, so frantic telegrams have to be sent cancelling the vast quantities of the delicacies you had just ordered for the voyage. Altogether this part of a collecting trip is very harassing.

The fact that we were worried and jumpy, of course, made all of us do silly things that only added to the confusion. The case of the clawed toads is an example of what I mean. Anyone might be pardoned for thinking that clawed toads were frogs at first glance. They are smallish creatures with blunt, froglike heads and a smooth, slippery skin which is most untoadlike. Also they are almost completely aquatic, another untoad-like characteristic. To my mind they are rather dull creatures who spend ninety per cent of their time floating in the water in various abandoned attitudes, occasionally shooting to the surface to take a quick gulp of air. But, for some reason which I could never ascertain, Bob was inordinately proud of these wretched toads. We had two hundred and fifty of them and we kept them in a gigantic plastic

bath on the verandah. Whenever Bob was missing, one was almost sure to find him crouched over this great cauldron of wriggling toads, an expression of pride on his face. Then came the day of the great tragedy.

The wet season had just started and the brilliant sunshine of each day was being interrupted by heavy downpours of rain; they only lasted an hour or so, but during that hour the quantity of water that fell was quite prodigious. On this particular morning Bob had been crooning over his clawed toads and when it started to rain he thought that they would be grateful if he put their bowl out in it. So he carefully carried the toads' bowl down the verandah and placed it on the top step, brilliantly positioned so that it not only received the rain itself but all the water that ran off the roof. Then he went away to do something else and forgot all about it. The rain continued to rain as if determined to uphold the Cameroons' reputation for being one of the wettest places on earth, and gradually the bowl filled up. As the water level rose so the toads rose with it until they were peering over the plastic rim. Another ten minutes of rain and, whether they wanted to or not, they were swept out of the bowl by the overflow.

My attention was drawn to this instructive sight by Bob's

moan of anguish when he discovered the catastrophe, a long-drawn howl of emotion that brought us all running from wherever we were. On the top step stood the plastic bowl, now completely empty of toads. From it the water gushed down the steps carrying Bob's precious amphibians. The steps were black with toads, slithering, hopping and rolling over and over in the water. In this Niagara of amphibians Bob, with a wild look in his eye, was leaping to and fro like an excited heron, picking up toads as fast as he could. Picking up a clawed toad is quite a feat. It is almost as difficult as trying to pick up a drop of quicksilver; apart from the fact that their bodies are incredibly slippery, the toads are very strong for their size and kick and wriggle with surprising energy. In addition their hind legs are armed with small, sharp claws and when they kick out with these muscular hind legs they are quite capable of inflicting a painful scratch. Bob, alternately moaning and cursing in anguish, was not in the calm collected mood that is necessary for catching clawed toads, and so every time he had scooped up a handful of the creatures and was bounding up the steps to return them to their bath, they would squeeze from between his fingers and fall back on to the steps, to be immediately swept downwards again by the water. In the end it took five of us three-quarters of an hour to collect all the toads and put them back in their bowl, and just as we had finished and were soaked to the skin it stopped raining.

"If you must release two hundred and fifty specimens you might at least choose a fine day and an animal that is reasonably easy to pick up," I said to Bob bitterly.

"I can't think what made me do such a silly thing," said Bob, peering dismally into the bowl in which the toads, exhausted after their romp, hung suspended in the water, peering up at us in their normal pop-eyed, vacant way. "I do hope they're not damaged in any way."

"Oh, never mind about us. We can all get pneumonia galloping about in the rain, just as long as those repulsive little devils are all right. Would you like to take their temperatures?"

"You know," said Bob frowning, and ignoring my sarcasm, "I'm sure we've lost quite a lot . . . there doesn't seem to be anything like the number we had before."

"Well, I am not going to help you count them. I've been scratched enough by clawed toads to last me a lifetime. Why don't you go and change and leave them alone? If you start counting them you'll only have the whole damn lot out again."

"Yes," said Bob, sighing, "I suppose you're right."

Half an hour later I let Cholmondely St John, the chimp, out of his cage for his morning exercise, and stupidly took my eye off him for ten minutes. As soon as I heard Bob's yell, the cry of a mind driven past breaking point, I took a hasty look round and, not seeing Cholmondely St John, I knew at once that he was the cause of Bob's banshee wail. Hurrying out on to the verandah I found Bob wringing his hands in despair, while on the top step sat Cholmondely, looking so innocent that you could almost see his halo gleaming. Halfway down the steps, upside down, was the plastic bowl, and the steps below it and the compound beyond was freckled with hopping, hurrying toads.

We slithered and slipped in the red mud of the compound for an hour before the last toad was caught and put in the bowl. Then, breathing hard, Bob picked it up and in silence we made our way back to the verandah. As we reached the top step Bob's muddy shoes slipped under him and he fell, and the bowl rolled to the bottom, and for the third time the clawed toads set off joyfully into the wide world.

Cholmondely St John was responsible for another escape, but this was less strenuous and more interesting than the clawed toad incident. In the collection we had about fourteen of the very common local dormice, a creature that closely resembled the European dormouse, except that it was a pale ash grey, and had a slightly more bushy tail. This colony of dormice lived in a cage together in perfect amity and in the evenings gave us a lot of pleasure with their acrobatic displays. There was one in particular that we could distinguish from all the others for he had a very tiny white star on his flank, like a minute cattle brand. He was a much better athlete than the others and his daring leaps and somersaults had earned our breathless admiration. Because of his circus-like abilities we had christened him Bertram.

One morning, as usual, I had let Cholmondely St John out for his constitutional and he was behaving himself in an exemplary fashion. But a moment came when I thought Jacquie was watching him, and she thought I was. Cholmondely was always on the lookout for such opportunities. When we had discovered our mistake and had gone in search of him we found we were too late. Cholmondely had amused himself by opening the doors of the dormouse sleeping-compartments and then tipping the cage over so that the unfortunate rodents, all in a deep and peaceful sleep, cascaded out on to the floor. As we arrived on the scene they were all rushing frantically for cover while Cholmondely, uttering small "Oooo's" of delight, was galloping around trying to stamp on them. By the time the ape had been caught and chastized there was not a dormouse in sight, for they had all gone to continue their interrupted slumbers behind our rows of cages. So the entire collection had to be moved, cage by cage, so that we could recapture the dormice. The first one to break cover from behind a monkey cage was Bertram, who fled down the verandah hotly pursued by Bob. As he hurled himself at the flying rodent, I shouted a warning.

"Remember the tail . . . don't catch it by the tail. . . ." I yelled. But I was too late. Seeing Bertram wriggling his fat body behind another row of cages Bob grabbed him by his tail, which was the only part of his anatomy easily grabbed. The result was disastrous. All small rodents, and particularly these dormice, have very fine skin on the tail, and if you catch hold of it and the animal pulls away the skin breaks and peels off the bone like the finger of a glove. This is such a common thing among small rodents that I am inclined to think it may be a defence mechanism, like the dropping of the tail in lizards when caught by an enemy. Bob knew this as well as I did, but in the excitement of the chase he forgot it, and so Bertram continued on his way behind the cage and Bob was left holding a fluffy tail dangling limply between finger and thumb. Eventually we unearthed Bertram and examined him. He sat plumply in the palm of my hand, panting slightly; his tail was now pink and skinless, revoltingly reminiscent of an ox-tail before it enters a stew. As usual when this happens, the animal appeared to be completely unaffected by what is the equivalent in human terms, of having all the skin suddenly ripped off one leg, leaving nothing but the bare bone and muscle. I knew from experience that eventually, deprived of skin, the tail would wither and dry, and then break off like a twig, leaving the animal none the worse off. In the case of Bertram, of course, the loss would be a little more serious as he used his tail quite extensively as a balancing organ during his acrobatics, but he was so agile I did not think he would miss it much. But, from our point of view, Bertram was now useless, for he was a damaged specimen. The only solution was to amputate his tail and let him go. This I did, and then, very sorrowfully, we put him among the thick twining stems of the bougainvillaea that grew along the verandah rail. We hoped that he would set up house in the place and perhaps entertain future travellers with his acrobatic feats when he had grown used to having no tail.

He sat on a bougainvillaea stem, clutching it tightly with his little pink paws, and looking about him through a quivering windscreen of whiskers. Then, very rapidly, and apparently with his sense of balance completely unimpaired, he jumped down on to the verandah rail, from there to the floor, and then scurried across to the line of cages against the far wall. Thinking that perhaps he was a bit bewildered I picked him up and returned him to the bougainvillaea. But as soon as I released him he did exactly the same thing again. Five times I put him in the bougainvillaea and five times he jumped to the verandah floor and made a bee-line for the cages. After that, I tired of his stupidity and carried him right down to the other end of the verandah, put him once more in the creeper and left him thinking that this would finish the matter.

On top of the dormouse cage we kept a bundle of cotton waste which we used to change their beds when they became too unhygienic, and that evening, when I went to feed them, I decided that they could do with a clean bed. So, removing the extraordinary treasure trove that dormice like to keep in their bedrooms, I pulled out all the dirty cotton waste and prepared to replace it with clean. As I seized the bundle of waste on top of the cage, preparatory to ripping off a handful, I was suddenly and unexpectedly bitten in the thumb. It gave me a considerable shock, for not only was I not expecting it, but I also thought for a moment that it might be a snake. However, my mind was quickly set at rest for as soon as I touched the bundle of cotton waste an indignant face poked out of its depths and Bertram chittered and squeaked at me in extremely indignant terms. Considerably annoyed, I hauled him out of his cosy bed, carried him along the verandah and pushed him back into the bougainvillaea. He clung indignantly to a stem, teetering to and fro and chittering furiously. But within two hours he was back in the bundle of cotton waste.

Giving up the unequal struggle we left him there, but Bertram had not finished yet. Having beaten us into submission over the matter of accommodation, he started to work on our sympathies in another direction. In the evening, when the other dormice came out of their bedroom and discovered their food plate with squeaks of surprise and delight, Bertram would come out of his bed and crawl down the wire front of the cage. There he would hang, peering wistfully through the wire, while the other dormice nibbled their food and carried away choice bits of banana and avocado pear to hide in their beds, a curious habit that dormice have, presumably to guard against night starvation. He looked so pathetic, hanging on the wire, watching the others stagger about with their succulent titbits, that eventually we gave in, and a small plate of food was placed on top of the cage for him. At last his cunning served its purpose: it seemed silly, since we had to feed him, to let him live outside, so we caught him and put him back in the cage with the others, where he settled down again as if he had never left. It merely seemed to us that he looked a trifle more smug than before. But what other course could one adopt with an animal that refused to be released?

Gradually we got everything under control. All the cages that needed it were repaired, and each cage had a sacking curtain hung in front, which could be lowered when travelling. The poisonous snake-boxes had a double layer of fine gauze tacked over them, to prevent accidents, and their lids were screwed down. Our weird variety of equipment—ranging from mincers to generators, hypodermics to weighing machines—was packed away in crates and nailed up securely, and netting film tents were folded together with our giant tarpaulins. Now we had only to await the fleet of lorries that was to take us down to the coast. The night before they were due to arrive the Fon came over for a farewell drink.

"Wah!" he exclaimed sadly, sipping his drink, "I sorry too much you leave Bafut, my friend."

"We get sorry too," I replied honestly. "We done have happy time here for Bafut. And we get plenty fine beef."

"Why you no go stay here?" inquired the Fon. "I go give

you land for build one foine house, and den you go make dis your zoo here for Bafut. Den all dis European go come from Nigeria for see dis your beef."

"Thank you, my friend. Maybe some other time I go come

back for Bafut and build one house here. Na good idea dis."

"Foine, foine," said the Fon, holding out his glass.

Down in the road below the Rest House a group of the Fon's children were singing a plaintive Bafut song I had never heard before. Hastily I got out the recording machine, but just as I had it fixed up, the children stopped singing. The Fon watched my preparations with interest.

"You fit get Nigeria for dat machine?" he inquired.

"No, dis one for make record only, dis one no be radio."

"Ah!" said the Fon intelligently.

"If dis your children go come for up here and sing dat song I go show you how dis machine work," I said.

"Yes, yes, foine," said the Fon, and roared at one of his wives who was standing outside on the dark verandah. She scuttled down the stairs and presently reappeared herding a small flock of shy, giggling children before her. I got them assembled round the microphone and then, with my fingers on the switch, looked at the Fon.

"If they sing now I go make record," I said.

The Fon rose majestically to his feet and towered over the group of children.

"Sing," he commanded, waving his glass of whisky at them.

Overwhelmed with shyness the children made several false starts, but gradually their confidence increased and they started to carol lustily. The Fon beat time with his whisky glass, swaying to and fro to the tune, occasionally bellowing out a few words of the song with the children. Presently, when the song came to an end he beamed down at his progeny.

"Foine, foine, drink," he said, and as each child stood before him with cupped hands held up to their mouths he proceeded to pour a tot of almost neat whisky into their pink palms. While the Fon was doing this I wound back the tape and set the machine for playback. Then I handed the earphones to the Fon, showed him how to adjust them, and switched on.

The expressions that chased one another across the Fon's face were a treat to watch. First there was an expression of blank disbelief. He removed the headphones and looked at them suspiciously. Then he replaced them and listened with astonishment. Gradually as the song progressed a wide urchin grin of pure delight spread across his face.

"Wah! Wah! Wah!" he whispered in wonder, "na wonderful, dis." It was with the utmost reluctance that he relinquished the earphones so that his wives and councillors could listen as well. The room was full of exclamations of delight and the clicking of astonished fingers. The Fon insisted on singing three more songs, accompanied by his children, and then listening to the playback of each one, his delight undiminished by the repetition.

"Dis machine na wonderful," he said at last, sipping his drink and eyeing the recorder. "You fit buy dis kind of machine for Cameroons?"

"No, they no get um here. Sometime for Nigeria you go find um . . . maybe for Lagos," I replied.

"Wah! Na wonderful," he repeated dreamily.

"When I go for my country I go make dis your song for proper record, and then I go send for you so you fit put um for dis your gramophone," I said.

"Foine, foine, my friend," he said.

An hour later he left us, after embracing me fondly and assuring us that he would see us in the morning before the lorries left. We were just preparing to go to bed, for we had a strenuous day ahead of us, when I heard the soft shuffle of feet on the verandah outside, and then the clapping of hands. I went to the door and there on the verandah stood Foka, one of the Fon's elder sons, who bore a remarkable resemblance to his father.

"Hallo, Foka, welcome. Come in," I said.

He came into the room carrying a bundle under his arm, and smiled at me shyly.

"De Fon send dis for you, sah," he said, and handed the bundle to me. Somewhat mystified, I unravelled it. Inside was a carved bamboo walking stick, a small heavily embroidered skull cap, and a set of robes in yellow and black, with a beautifully embroidered collar.

"Dis na Fon's clothes," explained Foka. " 'E send um for you. De Fon 'e tell me say dat now you be second Fon for Bafut."

"Wah!" I exclaimed, genuinely touched. "Na fine ting dis your father done do for me."

Foka grinned delightedly at my obvious pleasure.

"Which side you father now. 'E done go for bed?" I asked.

"No, sah, 'e dere dere for dancing house."

I slipped the robes over my head, adjusted my sleeves, placed the ornate little skull cap on my head, grasped the walking stick in one hand and a bottle of whisky in the other, and turned to Foka.

"I look good?" I inquired.

"Fine, sah, na fine," he said, beaming.

"Good. Then take me to your father."

He led me across the great, empty compound and through the maze of huts towards the dancing house, where we could hear the thud of drums and the pipe of flutes. I entered the door and paused for a moment. The band in sheer astonishment stopped dead. There was a rustle of amazement from the assembled company, and I could see the Fon seated at the far end of the room, his glass arrested halfway to his mouth. I knew what I had to do, for on many occasions I had watched the councillors approaching the Fon to pay homage or ask a favour. In dead silence I made my way down the length of the dance hall, my robes swishing round my ankles. I stopped in front of the Fon's chair, half crouched before him and clapped my hands three times in greeting. There was a moment's silence and then pandemonium broke loose.

The wives and the council members screamed and hooted with delight, the Fon, his face split in a grin of pleasure, leapt from his chair and, seizing my elbows, pulled me to my feet and embraced me.

"My friend, my friend, welcome, welcome," he roared, shaking with gusts of laughter.

"You see," I said, spreading my arms so that the long sleeves of the robe hung down like flags, "You, see, I be Bafut man now."

"Na true, na true, my friend. Dis clothes na my own one. I give for you so you be Bafut man," he crowed.

We sat down and the Fon grinned at me.

"You like dis ma clothes?" he asked.

"Yes, na fine one. Dis na fine ting you do for me, my friend," I said.

"Good, good, now you be Fon same same for me," he laughed.

Then his eyes fastened pensively on the bottle of whisky I had brought.

"Good," he repeated, "now we go drink and have happy time." It was not until three thirty that morning that I crawled tiredly out of my robes and crept under my mosquito net.

"Did you have a good time?" inquired Jacquie sleepily from her bed.

"Yes," I yawned. "But it's a jolly exhausting process being Deputy Fon of Bafut."

The next morning the lorries arrived an hour and a half before the time they had been asked to put in an appearance. This extraordinary circumstance—surely unparalleled in Cameroon history—allowed us plenty of time to load up. Loading up a collection of animals is quite an art. First of all you have to put all your equipment into the lorry. Then the animal cages are placed towards the tailboard of the vehicle, where they will get the maximum amount of air. But cages cannot be pushed in haphazardly. They have to be wedged in such a way that there are air spaces between each cage, and you have to make sure that the cages are not facing each other, or during the journey a monkey will go and push its hand through the wire of a cage opposite and get itself bitten by a civet; or an owl (merely by being an owl and peering), if placed opposite a cage of small birds, will work them into such a state of hysteria that they will probably all be dead at the end of your journey. On top of all this you must pack your cages in such a way that all the stuff that is liable to need attention *en route* is right at the back and easily accessible. By nine o'clock, the last lorry had been loaded and driven into the shade under the trees, and we could wipe the sweat from our faces and have a brief rest on the verandah. Here the Fon joined us presently.

"My friend," he said, watching me pour out the last enormous whisky we were to enjoy together, "I sorry too much you go. We done have happy time for Bafut, eh?"

"Very happy time, my friend."

"Shin-shin," said the Fon.

"Chirri-ho," I replied.

He walked down the long flight of steps with us, and at the bottom shook hands. Then he put his hands on my shoulders and peered into my face.

"I hope you an' all dis your animal walka good, my friend," he said, "and arrive quick-quick for your country."

Jacquie and I clambered up into the hot, airless interior of the lorry's cab and the engine roared to life. The Fon raised his large hand in salute, the lorry jolted forward and, trailing a cloud of red dust, we shuddered off along the road, over the golden-green hills towards the distant coast.

The trip down to the coast occupied three days, and was as unpleasant and nerve-racking as any trip with a collection of animals always is. Every few hours the lorries had to stop so that the small bird cages could be unloaded, laid along the side of the road, and their occupants allowed to feed. Without this halt the small birds would all die very quickly, for they seemed to lack the sense to feed while the lorry was in motion. Then the delicate amphibians had to be taken out in their cloth bags and dipped in a local stream every hour or so, for as we got down into the forested lowlands the heat became intense, and unless this was done they soon dried up and died. Most of the road surfaces were pitted with potholes and ruts, and as the lorries dipped and swayed and shuddered over them we sat uncomfortably in the front seats, wondering miserably what precious creature had been maimed or perhaps killed by the last bump. At one point we were overtaken by a heavy rainfall, and the road immediately turned into a sea of glutinous red mud, that sprayed up from under the lorry wheels like bloodstained porridge; then one of the lorries—an enormous four-wheel-drive Bedford—got into a skid from which the driver could not extricate himself, and ended on her side in the ditch. After an hour's digging round her wheels and laying branches so that her tyres could get a grip, we managed to get her out; and fortunately none of the animals were any the worse for their experience.

But we were filled with a sense of relief as the vehicles roared down through the banana groves to the port. Here the animals and equipment were unloaded and then stacked on the little flat-topped railway waggons used for ferrying bananas to the side of the ship. These chugged and rattled their way through half a mile of mangrove swamp and then drew up on the wooden jetty where the ship was tied up. Once more the collection was unloaded and stacked in the slings, ready to be hoisted aboard. On the ship I made my way down to the forward hatch, where the animals were to be stacked, to supervise the unloading. As the first load of animals was touching down on the deck a sailor appeared, wiping his hands on a bundle of cotton waste. He peered over the rail at the line of railway trucks, piled high with cages and, then he looked at me and grinned.

"All this lot yours, sir?" he inquired.

"Yes," I said, "and all that lot down on the quay."

He went forward and peered into one of the crates.

"Blimey!" he said, "These all animals?"

"Yes, the whole lot."

"Blimey," he said again, in a bemused tone of voice, "You're the first chap I've ever met with a zoo in his luggage."

"Yes," I said happily, watching the next load of cages swing on board, "and it's my own zoo, too."

POSTCARD

Yes, bring the animals here. Don't know what the neighbours will say, but never mind. Mother very anxious to see chimps so hope you are bringing them as well. See you all soon. Much love from us all.

Margo.

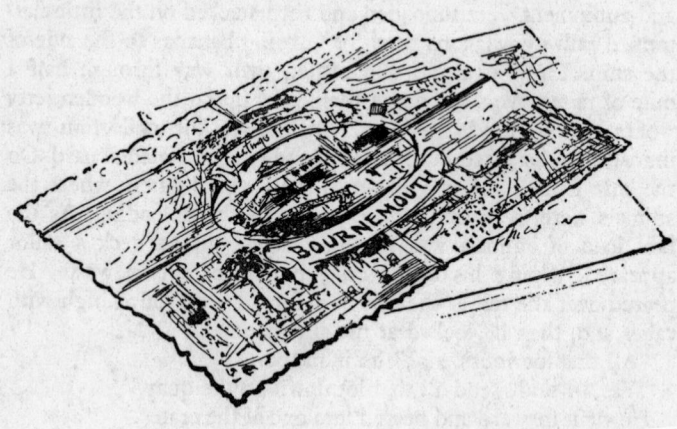

CHAPTER EIGHT

ZOO IN SUBURBIA

MOST people who lived in this suburban road in Bournemouth could look out on their back gardens with pride, for each one resembled its neighbour's. There were minor differences, of course: some preferred pansies to sweet peas, or hyacinths to lupins, but basically they were all the same. But anyone looking out at my sister's back garden would have been forced to admit that it was, to say the least, unconventional. In one corner stood a huge marquee, from inside which came a curious chorus of squeaks, whistles, grunts and growls. Alongside it stretched a line of Dexion cages from which glowered eagles, vultures, owls and hawks. Next to them was a large cage containing Minnie, the Chimp. On the remains of what had once been a lawn, fourteen monkeys rolled and played on long leashes, while in the garage frogs croaked, touracos called throatily, and squirrels gnawed loudly on hazel-nut shells. At all hours of the day the fascinated, horrified neighbours stood trembling behind their lace curtains and watched as my sister, my mother Sophie, Jacquie and I trotted to and fro through the shambles of the garden, carrying little pots of bread and milk, plates of chopped fruit or, what was worse, great hunks of gory meat or dead rats. We had, the neighbours felt, taken an unfair advantage of them. If it had been a matter of a crowing cockerel, or a barking dog, or our cat having kittens in their best flower-bed, they would have been able to cope with the situation. But the action of suddenly planting what amounted to a sizeable zoo in their midst was so unprecedented and unnerving that it took their breath away, and it was some time before they managed to rally their forces and start to complain.

In the meantime I had started on my search for a zoo in which to put my animals. The simplest thing to do, it occurred to me, was to go to the local council, inform them that I had the contents of a fine little zoo and wanted them to let me rent or purchase a suitable site for it. Since I already had the animals, it seemed to me in my innocence that they would be delighted to help. It would cost them nothing, and they would be getting what was, after all, another amenity for the town. But the Powers-that-Be had other ideas. Bournemouth is nothing if not conservative. There had never been a zoo in the town, so they did not see why there should be one now. This is what is known by local councils as progress. Firstly, they said that the animals would be dangerous; then they said they would smell; and then, searching their minds wildly for ideas, they said they had not got any land anyway.

I began to get a trifle irritable. I am never at my best when dealing with pompous illogicalities of the official mind. But I was beginning to grow worried in the face of such complete lack of co-operation. The animals were sitting in the back garden, eating their heads off and costing me a small fortune weekly in meat and fruit. The neighbours, now thoroughly indignant that we were not conforming to pattern, kept bombarding the local health authorities with complaints, so that on an average twice a week the poor inspector was forced to come up to the house, whether he wanted to or not. The fact that he could find absolutely nothing to substantiate the wild claims of the neighbours made no difference: if he received a complaint he had to come and investigate. We always gave the poor man a cup of tea, and he grew quite fond of some of the animals, even bringing his little daughter to see them. But I was chiefly worried by the fact that winter was nearly upon us, and the animals could not be expected to survive its rigours in an unheated marquee. Then Jacquie had a brilliant idea.

"Why not let's offer them to one of the big stores in town as a Christmas show?" she suggested.

So I rang every big store in town. All of them were charming but unhelpful; they simply had not the space for such a show, however desirable. Then I telephoned the last on my list, the huge emporium owned by J. J. Allen. They, to my delight, expressed great interest and asked me to go and discuss it with them. And "Durrell's Menagerie" came into being.

A large section of one of their basements was set aside, roomy cages were built with tastefully painted murals on the walls depicting a riot of tropical foliage, and the animals were moved out of the cold and damp which had already started, into the luxury of brilliant electric light and a constant temperature. The charge for admission just covered the food bills, and so the animals were warm, comfortable and well fed without being a drain on my resources. With this worry off my mind I could turn my attention once more to the problem of getting my zoo.

It would be wearisome to go into all the details of frustration during this period, or to make a catalogue of the number of mayors, town councillors, parks superintendents and sanitary officers I met and argued with. Suffice it to say that I felt my brain creaking at times with the effort of trying to persuade supposedly intelligent people that a zoo in any town should be considered an attraction rather than anything else. To judge by the way they reacted one would have thought I wanted to set off an atomic bomb on one of the piers.

In the meantime the animals, unaware that their fate hung in the balance, did their best to make life exciting for us. There was, for example, the day that Georgina the baboon decided that she wanted to see a little more of Bournemouth than the inside of J. J. Allen's basement. Fortunately it was a Sunday morning, so there was no one in the store: otherwise I dread to think what would have happened.

I was sipping a cup of tea, just before going down to the store and cleaning and feeding the animals, when the telephone rang. Without a care in the world I answered it.

"Is that Mr Durrell," inquired a deep, lugubrious voice.

"Yes, speaking."

"This is the Police 'ere, sir. One of them monkeys of yours 'as got out, and I thought I'd better let you know."

"Good God, which one is it?" I asked.

"I don't know, sir, really. It's a big brown one. Only it looks rather fierce, sir, so I thought I'd let you know."

"Yes, thanks very much. Where is it?"

"Well, it's in one of the windows at the moment. But I don't see as 'ow it'll stay there very long. Is it liable to bite, sir?"

"Well, it may do. Don't go near it. I'll be right down," I said, slamming down the receiver.

I grabbed a taxi and we roared down to the centre of the town, ignoring all speed limits. After all, I reflected, we were on police business of a sort.

As I paid off the taxi the first thing that greeted my eyes was the chaos in one of the big display windows of Allens. The window had been carefully set out to exhibit some articles of bedroom furniture. There was a large bed, made up, a tall bedside light and several eiderdowns tastefully spread over the floor. At least, that was how it had been when the window dresser had finished it. Now it looked as if a tornado had hit it. The light had been overturned and had burned a large hole in one of the eiderdowns; the bedclothes had been stripped off the bed and the pillow and sheets were covered with a tasteful pattern of paw marks. On the bed itself sat Georgina, bouncing up and down happily, and making ferocious faces at a crowd of scandalized church-goers who had gathered on the pavement outside the window. I went into the store and found two enormous constables lying in ambush behind a barricade of turkish towelling.

"Ah!" said one with relief, "there you are sir. We didn't like to try and catch it, see, because it didn't know us, and we thought it might make it worse, like."

"I don't think anything could make that animal worse," I said bitterly. "Actually she's harmless, but she makes a hell of a row and looks fierce . . . it's all bluff, really."

"Really?" said one of the constables, polite but unconvinced.

"I'll try and get her in the window there if I can, but if she breaks away I want you two to head her off. Don't, for the love of Allah, let her get into the china department."

"She came through the china department already," said one of the constables with gloomy satisfaction.

"Did she break anything?" I asked faintly.

"No, sir, luckily; she just galloped straight through. Me and Bill was chasing 'er, of course, so she didn't stop."

"Well, don't let's let her get back in there. We may not be so lucky next time."

By this time Jacquie and my sister Margo had arrived in another taxi, so our ranks had now swelled to five. We should, I thought, be able to cope with Georgina between us. I stationed the two constables, my sister and wife at suitable points guarding the entrance to the china department, and then went round and entered the window in which Georgina was still bouncing up and down on the ruined bed, making obscene faces at the crowd.

"Georgina," I said in a quiet but soothing voice, "come along then, come to Dad."

Georgina glanced over her shoulder in surprise. She studied my face as I moved towards her, and decided that my expression belied my honeyed accents. She gathered herself and leapt through the air, over the still smouldering eiderdown, and grabbed at the top of the great rampart of turkish towelling that formed the background of the window display. This, not having been constructed to take the weight of a large baboon hurtling through the air, immediately collapsed, and Georgina fell to the ground under a cascade of many-hued towelling. She struggled madly to free herself, and just succeeded in doing so as I flung myself forward to catch her. She gave a hysterical squawk and fled out of the window into the interior of the shop. I unravelled myself from the towelling and followed her. A piercing shriek from my sister told me of Georgina's whereabouts; my sister always tends to go off like a locomotive in moments of crisis. Georgina had slipped past her and was now perched on a counter, surveying us with glittering eyes, thoroughly enjoying the game. We approached her in a grim-faced body. At the end of the counter, suspended from the ceiling, hung a Christmas decoration made out of holly, tinsel and cardboard stars. It was shaped somewhat like a chandelier, and looked, as far as Georgina was concerned, ideal for swinging. She poised herself on the end of the counter and as we ran forward she leaped up and grabbed at the decoration in a manner vaguely reminiscent of the elder Fairbanks. The decoration promptly gave way, and Georgina fell to the ground, leapt to her feet and galloped off wearing a piece of tinsel over one ear.

For the next half-hour we thundered to and fro through the deserted store, always with Georgina one jump ahead of us, as it were. She knocked down a huge pile of account books in the stationery department, paused to see if a pile of lace doilies was edible, and made a large and decorative puddle at the foot of the main staircase. Then, just as the constables were beginning to breathe rather stertorously and I was beginning to despair of ever catching the wretched animal, Georgina made a miscalculation. Loping easily ahead of us she came upon what looked like the perfect hiding-place constructed of rolls of linoleum arranged on end. She fled between the rolls and was lost, for the rolls had been arranged in the form of a hollow square, a three-sided trap from which there was no escape. Quickly we closed in and blocked the entrance to the linoleum trap. I advanced towards her, grim-faced, and she sat there and screamed wildly, begging for mercy. As I made a lunge to grab her she ducked under my hand, and as I swung round to prevent her escape I bumped into one of the massive rolls of linoleum. Before I could stop it this toppled forward like a gigantic truncheon and hit one of the constables accurately on the top of his helmet. As the poor man staggered backwards, Georgina took one look at my face and decided that she was in need of police protection. She rushed to the still sway-ing constable and wrapped her arms tightly round his legs, looking over her shoulder at me and screaming. I jumped forward and grabbed her by her hairy legs and the scruff of her neck, and dragged her away from the constable's legs.

"Cor!" said the constable, in a voice of deep emotion, "I thought I'd 'ad me chips that time."

"Oh, she wouldn't have bitten you," I explained, raising my voice above Georgina's harsh screams. "She wanted you to protect her from me."

"Cor!" said the constable again. "Well, I'm glad *that's* over."

We put Georgina back in her cage, thanked the constables, cleared up the mess, cleaned and fed the animals and then went home to a well-earned rest. But for the rest of that day, every time the telephone rang I nearly jumped out of my skin.

Another animal that did his best to keep us on our toes was, of course, Cholmondely St John, the chimp. To begin with, after establishing himself in the house and getting my mother and sister well under control, he proceeded to catch a nasty chill that rapidly developed into bronchitis. Having recovered from this he was still very wheezy, and I therefore decreed that he should, for the first winter at any rate, wear clothes to keep him warm. As he lived in the house with us he already was wearing plastic pants and paper nappies, so he was used to the idea of clothes.

As soon as I had made this decision my mother, a delighted gleam in her eye, set to work, her knitting-needles clicking ferociously, and in record time had provided the ape with a variety of woolly pants and jerseys, in brilliant colours and the most complicated Fair-Isle patterns. So Cholmondely St John would loll on the window-sill of the drawing-room, nonchalantly eating an apple, clad in a different suit for each day of the week, completely ignoring the fascinated groups of local children that hung over our front gate and watched him absorbedly.

The attitude of people towards Cholmondely I found very interesting. Children, for example, did not expect him to be anything more than an animal with a curious resemblance to a human being, and with the ability to make them laugh. The adults who saw him, I'm afraid, were much less bright. On numerous occasions I was asked by apparently intelligent people whether he could talk. I always used to reply that chimps have, of course, a limited language of their own. But this is not what my questioners meant; they meant could he talk like a human being, could he discuss the political situation or the cold war, or some equally fascinating topic.

But the most extraordinary question I was ever asked about Cholmondely was asked by a middle-aged woman on the local golf-links. I used to take Cholmondely up there on fine days and let him scramble about in some pine trees, while I sat on the ground beneath, reading or writing. On this particular day Cholmondely had played for half an hour or so in the branches above me and then, growing bored, he had come down to sit on my lap and see if he could inveigle me into tickling him. Just at that moment this strange woman strode out of the gorse bushes and, on seeing Cholmondely and me, stopped short and looked at us. She displayed none of the surprise that most people evince at finding a chimpanzee in a Fair-Isle pullover occupying the golf-links. She came closer and watched Cholmondely closely as he sat on my lap. Then she turned to me and fixed me with a gimlet eye.

"Do they have souls?" she inquired.

"I don't know, madam," I replied. "I can't speak with any

certainty for myself on that subject, so you can hardly expect me to vouch for a chimpanzee."

"Um," she said, and walked off. Cholmondely had that sort of effect on people.

Having Cholmondely living in the house with us was, of course, a fascinating experience. His personality and intelligence made him one of the most interesting animals I have ever kept. One of the things about him that impressed me most was his memory, which I considered quite phenomenal.

I possessed at that time a Lambretta and side-car, and I decided that, providing Cholmondely sat well in the side-car and didn't try to jump out, I would be able to take him for excursions into the countryside. The first time I introduced him to it, I took him for a round trip of the golf-links, just to see how he would behave. He sat there with the utmost decorum, watching the passing scenery with a regal air. Apart from a tendency to lean out of the side-car and try to grab any cyclist we overtook, his behaviour was exemplary. Then I drove the Lambretta down to the local garage to have her filled up with petrol. Cholmondely was as fascinated with the garage as the garage man was with Cholmondely. The ape leaned out of the side-car and carefully watched the unscrewing of the petrol tank; and the introduction of the hose and splash and gurgle of the petrol made him "Ooo" softly to himself in astonishment.

A Lambretta can travel an incredible distance on a very small amount of petrol and, as I did not use it a great deal, about two weeks had passed before she needed filling up again. We had just come back from a local water-mill where we had been visiting Cholmondely's friend, the miller. This kind man, a great admirer of Cholmondely's, always had a brew of tea ready for us, and we would sit in a row above the weir, watching the moorhens paddling by, sipping our tea and meditating. On the way home from this tea party I noticed that the Lambretta was getting low on fuel, so we drove down to the garage.

As I was passing the time of day with the garage man, I noticed that he was gazing over my shoulder, a somewhat stupefied expression on his face. I turned round quickly to see what mischief the ape was up to. I found that Cholmondely had climbed out of the side-car on to the saddle, and was busy trying to unscrew the cap of the petrol tank. Now this was

surely quite a feat of memory. Firstly, he had only seen the filling-up process once, and that had been two weeks previously. Secondly, he had remembered, out of all the various gadgets on the Lambretta, which was the correct one to open in these circumstances. I was almost as impressed as the garage man.

But the time Cholmondely impressed me most, not only with his memory but with his powers of observation, was on the occasions when I had to take him up to London, once to appear on TV and later for a lecture. My sister drove me up to London, while Cholmondely sat on my lap and watched the passing scenery with interest. About halfway to our destination I suggested that we stopped for a drink. You had to be rather careful about pubs when you had Cholmondely with you, for it was not every landlord that appreciated a chimpanzee in his private bar. Eventually we found a pub that had a homely look about it, and stopped there. To our relief, and Cholmondely's delight, we found that the woman who ran the pub was a great animal lover, and she and Cholmondely took an immediate fancy to each other. He was allowed to play catch-as-catch-can among the tables in the bar, he was stuffed with orange juice and potato crisps, he was even allowed to get up on the bar itself and do a war dance, thumping his feet and shouting "Hoo . . . Hoo . . . Hoo." In fact he and the landlady got on so well that he was very reluctant to leave the place at all. If he had been an R.A.C. inspector he would have given that pub twelve stars.

Three months later I had to take Cholmondely up for the lecture; by that time I had forgotten all about the pub in which he had had such a good time, for we had, since then, been in many other licensed establishments which had given him a warm welcome. As we drove along Cholmondely, who was sitting on my lap as usual, started to bounce up and down excitedly. I thought at first he had seen a herd of cows or a horse, animals in which he had the deepest interest, but there was not a farm animal to be seen. Cholmondely went on bouncing, faster and faster, and presently started "Oo . . . ooing" to himself. I still could not see what was exciting him. Then his "Ooing" rose to a screaming crescendo, and he leaped about on my lap in an ecstasy of excitement, and we rounded a corner and there, a hundred yards ahead, was his favourite pub. Now this meant that he had recognized the countryside we were passing through, and had connected it with his memory of the good time he had had in the pub, a mental process which I had not come across in any other animal. Both my sister and I were so shaken by this that we were very glad to stop for a drink, and let Cholmondely renew his acquaintance with his friend the landlady, who was delighted to see him again.

In the meantime I was still continuing my struggle to find my zoo, but my chance of success seemed to recede farther and farther each day. The collection had to be moved from J. J. Allen's, of course, but here Paignton Zoo came to my rescue. With extreme kindness they allowed me to board my collection with them, on deposit, until such time as I could find a place of my own. But this, as I say, began to seem more and more unlikely. It was the old story. In the initial stages of a project, when you need people's help most, it is never forthcoming. The only solution, if at all possible, is to go ahead and accomplish it by yourself. Then, when you have made a success of it, all the people who would not help you launch it gather round, slap you on the back and offer their assistance.

"There must be an intelligent local council *somewhere*," said Jacquie one evening, as we pored over a map of the British Isles.

"I doubt it," I said gloomily, "and anyway I doubt whether I have the mental strength to cope with another round of mayors and town clerks. No, we'll just have to get a place and do it ourselves."

"But you'll have to get their sanction," Jacquie pointed out, "and then there's Town and Country Planning and all that."

I shuddered. "What we should really do is to go to some remote island in the West Indies, or somewhere," I said, "where they're sensible enough not to clutter their lives with all this incredible red tape."

Jacquie moved Cholmondely St John from the portion of the map on which he was squatting.

"What about the Channel Isles?" she asked suddenly.

"What about them?"

"Well, they're a very popular holiday resort, and they've got a wonderful climate."

"Yes, it would be an excellent place, but we don't know anyone there," I objected, "and you need someone on the spot to give you advice in this sort of thing."

"Yes," said Jacquie, reluctantly, "I suppose you're right."

So, reluctantly (for the idea of starting my zoo on an island had a very strong appeal for me) we forgot about the Channel Islands. It was not until a few weeks later that I happened to be in London and was discussing my zoo project with Rupert Hart-Davis that a gleam of daylight started to appear. I confessed to Rupert that my chances of having my own zoo now seemed so slight that I was on the verge of giving up the idea altogether. I said that we had thought of the Channel Islands, but that we had no contact there to help us. Rupert sat up, and with an air of a conjurer performing a minor miracle, said he had a perfectly good contact in the Channel Islands (if only he was asked) and a man moreover who had spent his whole life in the islands and would be only too willing to help us in any way. His name was Major Fraser, and that evening I telephoned him. He did not seem to find it at all unusual that a complete stranger should ring him up and ask his advice about starting a zoo, which made me warm to him from the start. He suggested that Jacquie and I should fly across to Jersey and he would show us round the island, and give us any information he could. And this accordingly we arranged to do.

So we flew to Jersey. As the plane came in to land the island seemed like a toy continent, a patchwork of tiny fields, set in a vivid blue sea. A pleasantly carunculated rocky coastline was broken here and there with smooth stretches of beach, along which the sea creamed in ribbons. As we stepped out on to the tarmac the air seemed warmer, and the sun a little more brilliant. I felt my spirits rising.

In the car park Hugh Fraser awaited us. He was a tall, slim man, wearing a narrow-brimmed trilby tilted so far forward that the brim almost rested on his aquiline nose. His blue eyes twinkled humorously as he shepherded us into his car and drove us away from the airport. We drove through St Helier, the capital of the island, which reminded me of a sizeable English market town; it was something of a surprise to find, at a cross-roads, a policeman in a white coat and white helmet, directing the traffic. It suddenly gave the place a faintly tropical atmosphere. We drove through the town and then out along narrow roads with steep banks, where the trees leaned over and entwined branches, turning it into a green tunnel. The landscape, with its red earth and rich green grass, reminded me very much of Devon, but the landscape was a miniature one, with tiny fields, narrow valleys stuffed with trees, and small farmhouses built of the beautiful Jersey granite, which contains a million autumn tints in its surface where the sun touches it. Then we turned off the road, drove down a long drive and suddenly, before us, was Hugh's home, Les Augres Manor.

The Manor was built like an E without the centre bar; the main building was in the upright of the E, while the two cross pieces were wings of the house, ending in two massive stone arches which allowed access to the courtyard. These beautiful arches were built in about 1660 and, like the rest of the building, were of the lovely local granite. Hugh showed us round his home with obvious pride, the old granite cider-press and cow-sheds, the huge walled garden, the small lake with its tattered fringe of bulrushes, the sunken water-meadows with the tiny streams trickling through them. At last we walked slowly back under the beautiful archways and into the courtyard, flooded with sunshine.

"You know, Hugh, you've got a wonderful place here," I said.

"Yes, it is lovely . . . I think one of the loveliest Manors on the island," said Hugh.

I turned to Jacquie. "Wouldn't it make a wonderful place for our zoo?" I remarked.

"Yes, it would," agreed Jacquie.

Hugh eyed me for a moment. "Are you serious?" he inquired.

"Well, I *was* joking, but it would make a wonderful site for a zoo. Why?" I asked.

"Well," said Hugh, thoughtfully, "I'm finding the upkeep too much for my resources, and I want to move to the mainland. Would you be interested in renting the place?"

"Would I?" I said. "Just give me the chance."

"Come inside, dear boy, and we'll discuss it," said Hugh, leading the way across the courtyard.

So, after a frustrating year of struggling with councils and other local authorities, I had gone to Jersey, and within an hour of landing at the airport I had found my zoo.

THE LAST WORD

MY zoo in Jersey has now been open to the public for nearly a year. We are probably the newest zoo in Europe and, I like to think, one of the nicest. We are small, of course (at the moment we have only about six hundred and fifty mammals, birds and reptiles), but we will continue to expand. Already we have on show a number of creatures which no other zoo possesses and we hope in the future when funds permit to concentrate on those species which are threatened with extinction.

Many of the animals on show are ones I collected myself. This is, as I said before, the best part of having one's own zoo; one can bring the animals back for it, watch their progress, watch them breed, go out and visit them at any hour of the day or night. This is the selfish pleasure of one's own zoo. But also I hope that, in a small way, I am interesting people in animal life and in its conservation. If I accomplish this I will consider that I have achieved something worthwhile. And if I can, later on, help even slightly towards preventing an animal from becoming extinct, I will be more than content.

ACKNOWLEDGMENTS

BRITAIN

All the members of the expedition are very grateful to the following manufacturers who supported them in a most generous way:

S. Allcock & Co. Ltd.	Fishing lines
Ashton Brothers & Co. Ltd.	Bedding
Black & Decker Ltd.	Drill
Bovril Ltd.	Food
Brand & Co. Ltd.	Food
British Bata Shoe Co.	Baseball boots
British Berkefeld Filters Ltd.	Filters
British Nylon Spinners Ltd.	Clothing
Cerebos Ltd.	Food
Coleman Quick Lite Co. Ltd.	Lighting and heating
Joseph Cookson Ltd.	Rope
Cussons Sons & Co.	Toilet goods
W. M. Delf (L'pool) Ltd.	Disinfectant
Electrical Equipment Co.	Generator
Ever-Ready Co. (GB) Ltd.	Batteries
Joseph Farrow & Co. Ltd.	Food
Granta Works	Folding canoe
Horlicks Ltd.	Food
Hugon & Co. Ltd.	Food
Jeyes-Ibco Sales Ltd.	Disinfectant
Percy Jones (Twinlock) Ltd.	Files
G. B. Kalee Ltd.	Ciné Equipment
Kimberly-Clark Ltd.	Tissues
Latex Upholstery Ltd.	Foam rubber
Linen Thread Company Ltd.	Special line
Lustraphone Ltd.	Microphone
Marmite Ltd.	Food
William Marples & Sons Ltd.	Tools
Minnesota Mining & Manu-facturing Co. Ltd.	Tapes
Don S. Momand Ltd.	Alka-Seltzer
The Nestlé Company Ltd.	Food
Olympia Ltd.	Typewriter
Oxo Ltd.	Food
Pifco Ltd.	Lighting
Polarisers (UK) Ltd.	Sunglasses
Prestige Group Ltd.	Cooking equipment
Rael-Brook Ltd.	Clothing
Reckitt & Colman Ltd.	Medical supplies
Revlon	Toilet goods
Ross Ensign Ltd.	Binoculars
Geo. Salter & Co. Ltd.	Scales

Adhesive Tapes Ltd.	Sellotape
Scott & Turner	Vitamin food
Selfset Ltd.	Traps
The Sheffield Twist Drill & Steel Co. Ltd.	Drills
Smiths Clocks and Watches Ltd.	Watches
Spear & Jackson Ltd.	Spades
Spong & Co. Ltd.	Mincers
Smith & Nephew Ltd.	Medical supplies
Stanley Works (G.B.) Ltd.	Tools
Tate & Lyle Ltd.	Food
Templeton Patents Ltd.	Dried foods
Joseph Tetley & Co. Ltd.	Tea
Tilley Lamp Co. Ltd.	Lamps and heaters
United Yeast Co. Ltd.	Yeast
Venesta Ltd.	Plymax board
Venner Accumulators Ltd.	Batteries for recorder
Vitamins Ltd.	Bemax
Windolite Ltd.	Windolite
Yeo Bros. Paull Ltd.	Tent
S. Young & Sons (Misterton) Ltd.	Animal equipment

Manufacturers whose products were of tremendous value and without which the expedition would have been seriously hampered were:

Allen & Hanburys	Entavet
Barnards Ltd.	Wire netting
B.D.H.	Medical supplies
British Nylon Spinners Ltd., Pontypool	Tarpaulins, etc.
Dexion Ltd.	Dexion
Glaxo Labs Ltd.	Animal food
Greengate & Irwell Rubber Co. Ltd.	Nylon tarpaulins
Joseph Gundry & Co. Ltd.	Special nets
Halex Ltd.	Plastic goods
Kenneth G. Hayes Ltd.	Finch nest baskets
Hounsfield Ltd.	Camp beds
Imperial Chemical (Pharmaceuticals) Ltd.	Medical supplies
The Oppenheimer Casing Co. (UK) Ltd.	Polythene bags
Parke-Davis & Co. Ltd.	Medical supplies
William Smith (Poplar) Ltd.	Tarpaulins, tent, etc.
Thomas's Ltd.	Cages and special equipment
J. H. Thompson (Cutlery) Ltd.	Cutlery

Transatlantic Plastics Ltd.   Polythene bags
Varley Dry Accumulators Ltd.   for ciné camera
Wire-Bands Ltd.   Banding machine.

London: Mr Miles, of Grindlay's Bank Shipping Department, without whose efforts no members of the expedition would ever have arrived in the Cameroons.

CAMEROONS

Victoria: Mr Eric Saward, Acting Manager, U.A.C., and his wife, Sheila, who generously welcomed us to the Cameroons.

Mr MacCarney, Manager U.A.C., who went out of his way to help us.

Mr Walker, of Elders and Fyffes Ltd., who saw that all food supplies for the animals were safely put upon the ship.

Mr Dudding, Assistant Commissioner, for all his help in arranging all our permits to catch animals.

Mr Austin, of the Agricultural Co-operative, who most kindly sent a large truck all the way up from the coast to Bafut to ensure that both we and our animals caught the ship on time.

Kumba: Dr William Crewe, who so lavishly entertained both us and our animal cargo on our way down to the coast.

Mr Gordon, Manager U.A.C., who supplied us with a 4-wheel drive Bedford truck to take our animals down to the coast.

Mamfe: Mr John Henderson, Manager U.A.C., for whom our gratitude knows no bounds.

Mr John Topham, who invited both us and our animals to invade his house at the dead of night and did everything he could to assist us. He also provided a truck to take the animals down to the coast.

Mr John Thrupp, District Officer of the Mamfe Division, who bore our complaints and protests with fortitude.

Mr Martin Davis, Forestry Officer, who helped us in every way and brought us Tavy, our second black-footed mongoose.

Bamenda: Dr Paul Gebauer, of the Cameroons Baptist Mission, who, as on previous expeditions, suffered much at our hands yet always welcomed us.

Mr Brandt, Manager U.A.C., and his wife Rona, who did everything they could to make our stay in Bamenda enjoyable.

Mr Shadock, A.D.O., who helped us in many ways to smooth our departure.

Mr Macfarlane, Veterinary Officer of the Cameroons, who gave us invaluable assistance with our animal charges.

Mr Stan Marriot, of the Agricultural Department, who recharged our camera batteries and repaired our Land-Rover on countless occasions. Mr Dennison, Manager U.A.C., who helped us in any way he could.

Tiko: Mr Bowerman, of C.D.C., who made all arrangements for us to stay in the Rest House prior to our sailing.

Our thanks also to the Captain, officers and men of the M.V. *Nicoya,* and in particular to Mr Terrance Huxtable, the Chief Steward, who bore with us and our animals with great fortitude and understanding.

Last of all we would like to thank our good friend, the Fon of Bafut, for giving us "a happy time".

ENCOUNTERS
WITH
ANIMALS

INTRODUCTION

DURING the past nine years, between leading expeditions to various parts of the world, catching a multitude of curious creatures, getting married, having malaria and writing several books, I made a number of broadcasts on different animal subjects for the B.B.C. As a result of these I had many letters from people asking if they could have copies of the scripts. The simplest way of dealing with this problem was to amass all the various talks in the form of a book, and this I have now done.

That the original talks were at all popular is entirely due to the producers I have had, and in particular Miss Eileen Molony, to whom this book is dedicated. I shall always remember her tact and patience during rehearsals. In a bilious green studio with the microphone leering at you from the table like a Martian monster, I am never completely at ease. So it was Eileen's unenviable task to counteract the faults in delivery that these nerves produced. I remember with pleasure her voice coming over the intercom. with such remarks as: "Very good, Gerald, but at the rate you're reading it will be a five-minute talk, not a fifteen-minute one." Or, "Try to get a little enthusiasm into your voice there, will you? It sounds as if you hated the animal . . . and try not to sigh when you say your opening sentence . . . you nearly blew the microphone away, and you've no idea how lugubrious it sounded." Poor Eileen suffered much attempting to teach me the elements of broadcasting, and any success I have achieved in this direction has been entirely due to her guidance. In view of this, it seems rather uncharitable of me to burden her with the dedication of this book, but I know of no other way of thanking her publicly for her help. And anyway, I don't expect her to read it.

PART ONE

BACKGROUND

FOR

ANIMALS

I AM constantly being surprised by the number of people, in different parts of the world, who seem to be quite oblivious to the animal life around them. To them the tropical forests or the savannah or the mountains in which they live, are apparently devoid of life. All they see is a sterile landscape. This was brought home most forcibly to me when I was in Argentina. In Buenos Aires I met a man, an Englishman who had spent his whole life in Argentina, and when he learnt that my wife and I intended to go out into the pampa to look for animals he stared at us in genuine astonishment.

"But, my dear chap, you won't find anything *there*," he exclaimed.

"Why not?" I inquired, rather puzzled, for he seemed an intelligent person.

"But the pampa is just a lot of grass," he explained, waving his arms wildly in an attempt to show the extent of the grass, "nothing, my dear fellow, absolutely nothing but grass punctuated by cows."

Now, as a rough description of the pampa this is not so very wide of the mark except that life on this vast plain does not consist entirely of cows and gauchos. Standing in the pampa you can turn slowly round and on all sides of you, stretching away to the horizon, the grass lies flat as a billiard-table, broken here and there by the clumps of giant thistles, six or seven feet high, like some extraordinary surrealist candelabra. Under the hot blue sky it does seem to be a dead landscape, but under the shimmering cloak of grass, and the small forests of dry, brittle thistle-stalks the amount of life is extraordinary. During the hot part of the day, riding on horseback across the thick carpet of grass, or pushing through a giant thistle-forest so that the brittle stems cracked and rattled like fireworks, there was little to be seen except the birds. Every forty or fifty yards there would be burrowing owls, perched straight as guardsmen on a tussock of grass near their holes, regarding you with astonished frosty-cold eyes, and, when you got too close, doing a little bobbing dance of anxiety before taking off and wheeling over the grass on silent wings.

Inevitably your progress would be observed and reported on by the watchdogs of the pampa, the black-and-white spur-winged plovers, who would run furtively to and fro, ducking their heads and watching you carefully, eventually taking off and swooping round and round you on piebald wings, screaming "Tero-tero-tero . . . tero . . . tero," the alarm cry that warned everything for miles around of your presence. Once this strident warning had been given, other plovers in the distance would take it up, until it seemed as though the whole pampa rang with their cries. Every living thing was now alert and suspicious. Ahead, from the skeleton of a dead tree, what appeared to be two dead branches would suddenly take wing and soar up into the hot blue sky: chimango hawks with handsome rust-and-white plumage and long slender legs. What you had thought was merely an extra-large tussock of sun-dried grass would suddenly hoist itself up on to long stout legs and speed away across the grass in great loping strides, neck stretched out, dodging and twisting between the thistles, and you realized that your grass tussock had been a rhea, crouching low in the hope that you would pass it by. So, while the plovers were a nuisance in advertising your advance, they helped to panic the other inhabitants of the pampa into showing themselves.

Occasionally you would come across a "laguana", a small shallow lake fringed with reeds and a few stunted trees. Here there were fat green frogs, but frogs which, if molested, jumped *at* you with open mouth, uttering fearsome gurking noises. In pursuit of the frogs were slender snakes marked in grey, black and vermilion red, like old school ties, slithering through the grass. In the rushes you would be almost sure to find the nest of a screamer, a bird like a great grey turkey: the youngster crouching in the slight depression in the sun-baked ground, yellow as a buttercup, but keeping absolutely still even when your horse's legs straddled it, while its parents paced frantically about, giving plaintive trumpeting cries of anxiety, intermixed with softer instructions to their chick.

This was the pampa during the day. In the evening, as you rode homeward, the sun was setting in a blaze of coloured clouds, and on the laguanas various ducks were flighting in, arrowing the smooth water with ripples as they landed. Small flocks of spoonbills drifted down like pink clouds to feed in the shallows among snowdrifts of black-necked swans.

As you rode among the thistles and it grew darker you might meet armadillos, hunched and intent, trotting like strange mechanical toys on their nightly scavenging; or perhaps a skunk who would stand, gleaming vividly black and white in the twilight, holding his tail stiffly erect while he stamped his front feet in petulant warning.

This, then, was what I saw of the pampa in the first few days. My friend had lived in Argentina all his life and had never realized that this small world of birds and animals existed. To him the pampa was "nothing but grass punctuated by cows". I felt sorry for him.

THE BLACK BUSH

AFRICA is an unfortunate continent in many ways. In Victorian times it acquired the reputation of being the Dark Continent, and even today, when it contains modern cities, railways, macadam roads, cocktail bars and other necessary adjuncts of civilization, it is still looked upon in the same way. Reputations, whether true or false, die hard, and for some reason a bad reputation dies hardest of all.

Perhaps the most maligned area of the whole continent is the West Coast, so vividly described as the White Man's Grave. It has been depicted in so many stories—quite inaccurately —as a vast, unbroken stretch of impenetrable jungle. If you ever manage to penetrate the twining creepers, the thorns and undergrowth (and it is quite surprising how frequently the impenetrable jungle is penetrated in stories), you find that every bush shakes and quivers with a mass of wild life waiting its chance to leap out at you: leopards with glowing eyes, snakes hissing petulantly, crocodiles in the streams straining every nerve to look more like a log of wood than a log of wood does. If you should escape these dangers there are always the savage native tribes to give the unfortunate traveller the *coup de grâce*. The natives are of two kinds, cannibal and non-cannibal: if they are cannibal, they are always armed with spears; if non-cannibal, they are armed with arrows whose tips drip deadly poison of a kind generally unknown to science.

Now, no one minds giving an author a bit of poetic licence, provided it is recognizable as such. But unfortunately the West Coast of Africa has been libelled to such an extent that anyone who tries to contradict the accepted ideas is branded as a liar who has never been there. It seems to me a great pity that an area of the world where you find nature at its most bizarre, flamboyant and beautiful should be so abused, though I realize that I am a voice crying rather plaintively in the wilderness.

My work has enabled me, one way and another, to see quite a lot of tropical forest, for when you collect live wild animals for a living you have to go out into the so-called impenetrable jungle and look for them. They do not, unfortunately, come to you. It has been brought home to me that in the average tropical forest there is an extraordinary *lack* of wild life: you can walk all day and see nothing more exciting than an odd bird or butterfly. The animals are there, of course, and in rich profusion, but they very wisely avoid you, and in order to see or capture them you have to know exactly where to look. I remember once, after a six months' collecting trip in the forests of the Cameroons, that I showed my collection of about one hundred and fifty different mammals, birds and reptiles to a gentleman who had spent some twenty-five years in that area, and he was astonished that such a variety should have been living, as it were, on his doorstep, in the forest he had considered uninteresting and almost devoid of life.

In the pidgin-English dialect spoken in West Africa, the forest is called the Bush. There are two kinds of Bush: the area that surrounds a village or a town and which is fairly well trodden by hunters and in some places encroached on by farmland. Here the animals are wary and difficult to see. The other type is called the Black Bush, areas miles away from the nearest village, visited by an odd hunter only now and then; and it is here, if you are patient and quiet, that you will see the wild life.

To catch animals, it is no use just scattering your traps wildly about the forest, for, although at first the movements of the animals seem haphazard, you very soon realize that the majority of them have rooted habits, following the same paths year in and year out, appearing in certain districts at certain times when the food supply is abundant, disappearing again when the food fails, always visiting the same places for water. Some of them even have special lavatories which may be some distance away from the place where they spend most of their lives. You may set a trap in the forest and catch nothing in it, then shift that trap three yards to the left or right on to a roadway habitually used by some creature; and thus make your capture at once. Therefore, before you can start on your trapping, you must patiently and carefully investigate the area around you, watching to see which routes are used through the tree-tops or on the forest floor; where supplies of wild fruit are ripening; and which holes are used as bedrooms during the daytime by the nocturnal animals. When I was in West Africa I spent many hours in the Black Bush, watching the forest creatures, studying their habits, so that I would find it more easy to catch and keep them.

I watched one such area over a period of about three weeks. In the Cameroon forests you occasionally find a place where the soil is too shallow to support the roots of the giant trees, and here their place has been taken by the lower growth of shrubs and bushes and long grass which manages to exist on the thin layer of earth covering a grey carapace of rock beneath. I soon found that the edge of one of these natural grassfields, which was about three miles from my camp, was an ideal place to see animal life, for here there were three distinct zones of vegetation: first, the grass itself, five acres in extent, bleached almost white by the sun; then surrounding it a narrow strip of shrubs and bushes thickly entwined with parasitic creepers and hung with the vivid flowers of the wild convolvulus; and finally, behind this zone of low growth spread the forest proper, the giant tree-trunks a hundred and fifty feet high like massive columns supporting the endless roof of green leaves. By choosing your vantage-point carefully you could get a glimpse of a small section of each of these types of vegetation.

I would leave the camp very early in the morning; even at that hour the sun was fierce. Leaving the camp clearing, I then plunged into the coolness of the forest, into a dim green light that filtered through the multitude of leaves above. Picking my way through the gigantic tree-trunks, I moved across the forest floor, so thickly covered with layer upon layer of dead leaves that it was as soft and springy as a Persian carpet. The only sounds were the incessant zithering of the millions of cicadas, beautiful green-and-silver insects that clung to the bark of the trees, making the air vibrate with their cries, and when you approached too closely zooming away through the forest like miniature aeroplanes, their transparent wings glittering as they flew. Then there would be an occasional plaintive "whowee" of some small bird which I never managed to identify, but which always accompanied me through the forest, asking questions in its soft liquid tones.

In places there would be a great gap in the roof of leaves above, where some massive branch had perhaps been undermined by insects and damp until it had eventually broken loose and crashed hundreds of feet to the forest floor below, leaving this rent in the forest canopy through which the sunlight sent its golden shafts. In these patches of brilliant light you would find butterflies congregating: large ones with long, narrow, orange-red wings that shone against the darkness of the forest like dozens of candle flames; delicate little white ones like snow-flakes would rise in clouds about my feet, then drift slowly back on to the dark leaf-mould, pirouetting as they went. Eventually I reached the banks of a tiny stream which whispered its way through the water-worn boulders, each wearing a cap of green moss and tiny plants. This stream flowed through the forest, through the rim of short growth and out into the grassfield. Just before it reached the edge of the forest, however, the ground sloped and the water flowed over a series of miniature waterfalls, each decorated with clumps of wild begonias whose flowers were a brilliant waxy yellow. Here, at the edge of the forest, the heavy rains had gradually washed the soil from under the massive roots of one of the giant trees which had crashed down and now lay half in the forest and half in the grassfield, a great hollow, gently rotting shell, thickly overgrown with convolvulus, moss, and with battalions of tiny toadstools marching over its peeling bark. This was my hideout, for in one part of the trunk the bark had given way and the hollow interior lay revealed, like a canoe, in which I could sit well hidden by the low growth. When I had made sure that the trunk had no other occupant I would conceal myself and settle down to wait.

For the first hour or so there would be nothing—only the cries of cicadas, an occasional trill from a tree-frog on the banks of the stream, and sometimes a passing butterfly. Within a short time the forest would have forgotten and absorbed you, and within the hour, if you kept still, you would be accepted just as another, if rather ungainly, part of the scenery.

Generally, the first arrivals were the giant plantain-eaters who came to feed on the wild figs which grew round the edge of the grassfield. These huge birds, with long, dangling magpie-like tails, would give notice of their arrival when they were half a mile or so away in the forest, by a series of loud, ringing and joyful cries . . . caroo, coo, coo, coo. They would appear, flying swiftly from the forest with a curious dipping flight and land in the fig trees, shouting delightedly to each other, flipping their long tails so that their golden-green plumage gleamed iridescently. They would run along the branches in a totally unbirdlike way and leap from one branch to another with great kangaroo jumps, plucking off the wild figs and gulping them down. The next arrivals to the feast would be a troop of Mona monkeys, with their russet-red fur, grey legs and the two strange, vivid white patches like giant thumbprints on each side of the base of the tail. To hear the monkeys approaching sounded like a sudden wind roaring and rustling through the forest, but if you listened carefully you would hear in the background a peculiar sort of whoop-whoop noise followed by loud and rather drunken honkings, like a fleet of ancient taxicabs caught in a traffic jam. This was the sound of the hornbills, birds who always followed the monkey troops around, feeding not only on the fruit that the monkeys discovered but also on the lizards, tree-frogs and insects that the movements of the monkeys through the tree-tops disturbed.

On reaching the edge of the forest, the leader of the monkeys would climb to a vantage-point and, uttering suspicious grunts, survey the grassfield in front of him with the greatest care. Behind him the troop, numbering perhaps fifty individuals, would be silent except for the wheezy cry now and again from some tiny baby. Presently, when he was satisfied that the clearing contained nothing, the old male would stalk along a branch slowly and gravely, his tail curled up over his back like a question mark, and then give a prodigious leap that sent him crashing into the fig-tree leaves. Here he paused again and once more examined the grassfield; then he plucked the first fruit and uttered a series of loud imperative calls: oink, oink, oink. Immediately, the still forest behind him was alive with movement, branches swishing and roaring like giant waves on a beach as the monkeys leapt out of cover and landed in the fig-trees, grunting and squeaking to each other as they plummeted through the air. Many of the female monkeys carried tiny babies which clung under their bellies, and as their mothers jumped you could hear the infant squeaking shrilly, though whether from fear or excitement it was difficult to judge.

The monkeys settled down on the branches to feed on the ripe figs, and presently with loud swishings and honks of delight the hornbills discovered their whereabouts and came crashing among the branches in the wild disorderly way in which hornbills always land. Their great round eyes, thickly fringed with heavy eyelashes, stared roguishly and slightly idiotically at the monkeys, while with their enormous and apparently cumbersome beaks they delicately and with great precision plucked the fruit and tossed it carelessly into the air, so that it fell back into their gaping mouths and disappeared. The hornbills were by no means such wasteful feeders as the monkeys, for they would invariably eat each fruit they plucked, whereas the monkeys would take only one bite from a fruit before dropping it to the ground below and moving along the branch to the next delicacy.

The arrival of such rowdy feeding companions was evidently distasteful to the giant plantain-eaters, for they moved off as soon as the monkeys and hornbills arrived. After half an hour or so the ground beneath the fig-trees was littered with half-eaten fruit, and the monkeys then made their way back into the forest, calling oink-oink to each other in a self-satisfied kind of way. The hornbills paused to have just one more fig and then flew excitedly after the monkeys, and as the sound of their wings faded away the next customers for the fig-tree arrived on the scene. They were so small and appeared so suddenly and silently out of the long grass that unless you had field-glasses and kept a careful watch they would come and go without giving a sign of their presence. They were the little striped mice whose homes were amongst the tussocks of grass, the tree-roots and the boulders along the edge of the forest. Each about the size of a house mouse, with a long and delicately tapering tail, they were clad in sleek, fawny-grey fur which was boldly marked with creamy white stripes from nose to rump. They would drift out from among the grass stalks, moving in little fits and starts, with many long pauses when they sat on their haunches, their tiny pink claws clenched into fists, their noses and whiskers quivering as they tested the wind for enemies. When they froze thus into immobility against the grass stalks, their striped coats, which when they were moving seemed so bright and decorative, acted like an invisible cloak and made them almost disappear.

Having assured themselves that the hornbills had really left (for a hornbill is occasionally partial to a mouse), they set about the serious task of eating the fruit that the monkeys had so lavishly scattered on the ground. Unlike a lot of the other forest mice and rats, these little creatures were of a quarrelsome disposition and would argue over the food, sitting up on their hind legs and abusing each other in thin, reedy squeaks of annoyance. Sometimes two of them would come upon the same fruit and both lay hold of it, one at either end, digging their little pink paws into the leaf mould and tugging frantically in an effort to break the other's grip. If the fig were exceptionally ripe, it generally gave way in the middle so that both mice fell over backwards, each clutching his share of the trophy. They then sat quite peacefully within six inches of one another, each eating his portion. At times, if some sudden noise alarmed them, they all leapt vertically into the air six inches or even more as though suddenly plucked upwards by strings, and on landing they sat quivering and alert until they were sure the danger had passed, when they once more started bickering and fighting over the food.

Once I saw a tragedy enacted among these striped mice as they squabbled amongst the monkeys' left-overs. Suddenly a genet appeared out of the forest. This is perhaps one of the most lithe and beautiful animals to be seen in the forest, with its long sinuously weasel-shaped body and cat-like face, handsome golden fur heavily blotched with a pattern of black spots and long tail banded in black and white. It is not an animal you generally see in the early morning, for its favourite hunting time is in the evenings or at night. I presume this particular one must have had a fruitless night's hunting, and so when morning arrived he was still searching for something to fill his

stomach. When he appeared at the edge of the grassfield and saw the striped mice, he flattened close to the ground and then launched himself as smoothly as a skimming stone across the intervening space, and was in amongst the rodents before they knew what was happening. As usual, they all leapt perpendicularly into the air and then fled, looking like portly little business men in their striped suits, rushing through the grass stems; but the genet had been too quick and he walked off into the forest, carrying in his mouth two limp little bodies which had so recently been abusing each other as to the sole ownership of a fig and had consequently left it too late to retreat.

Towards midday the whole country fell quiet under the hot rays of the sun, and even the incessant cries of the cicadas seemed to take on a sleepy note. This was siesta time, and very few creatures were to be seen. In the grassfield only the skinks, who loved the sun, emerged to bask on the rocks or to stalk the grasshoppers and locusts. These brilliant lizards, shining and polished as though freshly painted, had skins like mosaic work, made up of hundreds of tiny scales coloured cherry-red, cream and black. They would run swiftly through the grass stalks, their bodies glinting in the sun, so that they looked like some weird firework. Apart from these reptiles, there was practically nothing to be seen until the sun dipped and the day became a trifle cooler, so it was during this period of inactivity that I used to eat the food I had brought with me and smoke a much-needed cigarette.

Once during my lunch break I witnessed an extraordinary comedy that was performed almost, I felt, for my special benefit. On the tree-trunk where I was sitting, not six feet away, out of a tangle of thick undergrowth, up over the bark of the trunk, there glided slowly and laboriously and very regally a giant land-snail, the size of an apple. I watched it as I ate, fascinated by the way the snail's body glided over the bark, apparently without any muscular effort whatever, and the way its horns with the round, rather surprised eyes on top, twisted this way and that as it picked its route through the miniature landscape of toadstools and moss. Suddenly I realized that as the snail was making its slow and rather vague progress along the trunk it was leaving behind it the usual glistening trail, and this trail was being followed by one of the most ferocious and bloodthirsty animals, for its size, to be found in the West African forest.

The twining convolvulus was thrust aside, and out on to the log strutted a tiny creature only as long as a cigarette, clad in jet-black fur and with a long slender nose that it kept glued to the snail's track, like a miniature black hound. It was one of the forest's shrews, whose courage is incredible and whose appetite is prodigious and insatiable. If anything lives to eat, this forest shrew does. They will even in a moment of peckishness think nothing of eating one another. Chittering to himself, the shrew trotted rapidly after the snail and very soon overtook it. Uttering a high-pitched squeak, it flung itself on that portion of the snail which protruded from the rear of the shell and sank its teeth into it. The snail, finding itself so suddenly and unceremoniously attacked from the rear, did the only possible thing and drew its body rapidly back inside its shell. This movement was performed so swiftly and the muscular contraction of the snail was so strong, that as the tail disappeared inside the shell the shrew's face was banged against it and his grip was broken. The shell, having now nothing to balance it, fell on its side, and the shrew, screaming with frustration, rushed forward and plunged his head into the interior, in an effort to retrieve the retreating mollusc. However, the snail was prepared for this attack and as soon as the shrew's head was pushed into the opening of the shell it was greeted by a sudden fountain of greenish-white froth that bubbled out and enveloped nose and head. The shrew leapt back with surprise, knocking against the shell as it did so. The snail teetered for a moment and then rolled sideways and dropped into the undergrowth beneath the log. The shrew meanwhile was sitting on its hind legs, almost incoherent with rage, sneezing violently and trying to wipe the froth from its face with its paws. The whole thing was so ludicrous that I started to laugh, and the shrew, casting a hasty and frightened glance in my direction, leapt down into the undergrowth and hurried away. It was not often during the forest's siesta-time that I could enjoy such a scene as this.

At mid-afternoon, when the heat had lessened, the life of the forest would start again. There were new visitors to the fig-trees, in particular the squirrels. There was one pair who obviously believed in combining business with pleasure, for they ran and leapt among the fig-tree branches, playing hide-and-seek and leap-frog, courting each other in this way, and occasionally breaking off their wild and exuberant activities to sit very quietly and solemnly, their tails draped over their backs, eating figs. As the shadows grew longer, you might, if you were lucky, see a duiker coming down to drink at the stream. These small antelopes, clad in shining russet coats, with their long, pencil-slim legs, would pick their way slowly and suspiciously through the forest trees, pausing frequently while their large liquid eyes searched the path ahead, and their ears twitched backwards and forwards, picking up the sounds of the forest. As they drifted their way without a sound through the lush plants bordering the stream, they would generally disturb some of the curious aquatic mice who were feeding there. These little grey rodents have long, rather stupid-looking faces, big semi-transparent ears shaped like a mule's, and long hind legs on which they would at times hop like miniature kangaroos. At this hour of the evening it was their habit to wade through the shallow water, combing the water-weed with their slender front paws and picking out tiny water-insects, baby crabs and water-snails. At this time rats of another type would also come out, and these were probably the most fussy, pompous and endearing of the rodents. They were clad all over in greenish fur, with the exception of their noses and their behinds which were, rather incongruously, a bright foxy red, and made them look rather as though they were wearing red running shorts and masks. Their favourite hunting-ground was in the soft leaf-mould between the towering buttress roots of the great trees. Here they would waddle about, squeaking to each other, turning over leaves and bits of rock and twigs for the insects which were concealed underneath. Occasionally they would stop and hold conversations, sitting on their hind legs, facing each other, their whiskers trembling as they chittered and squeaked very rapidly and in a complaining sort of tone as though commiserating with one another on the lack of food in that particular part of the forest. There were times when, sniffing about in certain patches, they became terribly excited, squeaking loudly and digging, like terriers, down into the soft leaf-mould. Eventually they would triumphantly unearth a big chocolate-coloured beetle, almost as large as themselves. These insects were horny and very strong, and it took the rats a good deal of effort to subdue them. They would turn them on to their backs and then rapidly nip off the spiky, kicking legs. Once they had immobilized their prey, a couple of quick bites and the beetle was dead. Then the little rat would sit up on its hind legs, clasping the body of the beetle in both hands and proceed to eat it, as though it were a stick of rock, with loud scrunchings and occasional muffled squeaks of delight.

By now, although still light in the grassfield, it was gloomy and difficult to see in the forest itself. You might, if you were fortunate, catch a glimpse of some of the nocturnal animals venturing out on their hunting: perhaps a brush-tailed porcupine would trot past, portly and serious, his spines rustling through the leaves as he hurried on his way. Now the fig-trees would once again become the focal-point, as these nocturnal animals appeared. The galagos, or bush-babies, would materialize magically, like fairies, and sit among the branches, peering about them with their great saucer-shaped eyes, and their little incredibly human-looking hands held up in horror, like a flock of pixies who had just discovered that the world was a sinful place. They would feed on the figs and sometimes take prodigious leaps through the branches in pursuit of a passing moth, while overhead, across a sky already flushed with sunset colours, pairs of grey parrots flew into the forest to roost, whistling and cooing to each other, shrilly, so that the forest echoed. Far away in the distance a chorus of hoots suddenly rose, screams and wild bursts of maniacal laughter, the hair-raising noise of a troop of chimpanzees going to bed. The galagos would now have disappeared as quickly and as silently as they had come, and through the darkening sky the fruit bats would appear in great tattered clouds, flapping down, giving their ringing cries, diving into the trees to fight and flutter round the remains of the fruit, so that the sound of their wings was like a hundred wet umbrellas being shaken amongst the trees. There would be one more shrill and hysterical outburst from the chimpanzees, and then the forest was completely dark, but still alive and vibrating with a million little rustles, squeaks, patters and grunts, as the night creatures took over.

I rose to my feet, cramped and stiff, and stumbled off through the forest, the glow of my torch seeming pathetically frail and tiny among the great silent tree-trunks. This, then, was the tropical forest that I had read about as savage, dangerous and unpleasant. To me it seemed a beautiful and incredible world made up of a million tiny lives, plants and animals, each different and yet dependent on the other, like the many parts of a gigantic jigsaw puzzle. It seemed to me such a pity that people should still cling to their old ideas of the unpleasantness of the jungle when here was a world of magical beauty waiting to be explored, observed and understood.

LILY-TROTTER LAKE

BRITISH GUIANA, lying in the northern part of South America, is probably one of the most beautiful places in the world, with its thick tropical forest, its rolling savannah land, its jagged mountain ranges and giant foaming waterfalls. To me, however, one of the most lovely parts of Guiana is the creek lands. This is a strip of coastal territory that runs from Georgetown to the Venezuelan border; here a thousand forest rivers and streams have made their way down towards the sea, and on reaching the flat land have spread out into a million creeks and tiny waterways that glimmer and glitter like a flood of quicksilver. The lushness and variety of the vegetation is extraordinary, and its beauty has turned the place into an incredible fairyland. In 1950 I was in British Guiana collecting wild animals for zoos in England, and during my six months there I visited the savannah lands to the north, the tropical forest and, of course, the creek lands, in pursuit of the strange creatures living there.

I had chosen a tiny Amerindian village near a place called Santa Rosa as my headquarters in the creek lands, and to reach it required a two-day journey. First, by launch down the Essequibo River and then through the wider creeks until we reached the place where the launch could go no farther, for the water was too shallow and too choked with vegetation. Here we took to dug-out canoes, paddled by the quiet and charming Indians who were our hosts, and leaving the broad main creek we plunged into a maze of tiny waterways on one of the most beautiful journeys I can remember.

Some of the creeks along which we travelled were only

about ten feet wide, and the surface of the water was completely hidden under a thick layer of great creamy water-lilies, their petals delicately tinted pink, and a small fern-like water-plant that raised, just above the surface of the water, on a slender stem, a tiny magenta flower. The banks of the creek were thickly covered with undergrowth and great trees, gnarled and bent, leant over the waters to form a tunnel; their branches were festooned with long streamers of greenish-grey Spanish moss and clumps of bright pink-and-yellow orchids. With the water so thickly covered with vegetation, you had the impression when sitting in the bows of the canoe that you were travelling smoothly and silently over a flower-studded green lawn that undulated gently in the wake of your craft. Great black woodpeckers, with scarlet crests and whitish beaks, cackled loudly as they flipped from tree to tree, hammering away at the rotten bark, and from the reeds and plants along the edges of the creek there would be a sudden explosion of colour as we disturbed a marsh bird which flew vertically into the air, with its hunting-pink breast flashing like a sudden light in the sky.

The village, I discovered, was situated on an area of high ground which was virtually an island, for it was completely surrounded by a chess-board of creeks. The little native hut that was to be my headquarters was some distance away from the village and placed in the most lovely surroundings. On the edge of a tiny valley an acre or so in extent, it was perched amongst some great trees which stood round it like a group of very old men, with long grey beards of Spanish moss. During the winter rains the surrounding creeks had overflowed so that the valley was now drowned under some six feet of water out of which stuck a number of large trees, their reflections shimmering in the sherry-coloured water. The rim of the valley had grown a fringe of reeds and great patches of lilies. Sitting in the doorway of the hut, one had a perfect view of this miniature lake and its surroundings, and it was sitting here quietly in the early morning or evening that I discovered what a wealth of animal life inhabited this tiny patch of water and its surrounding frame of undergrowth.

In the evening, for example, a crab-eating raccoon would come down to drink. They are strange-looking animals, about the size of a small dog, with bushy tails ringed in black and white, large, flat, pink paws, the grey of their body-fur relieved only by a mask of black across the eyes, which gives the creature a rather ludicrous appearance. These animals walk in a curious humpbacked manner with their feet turned out, shuffling along in this awkward fashion like someone afflicted with chilblains. The raccoon came down to the water's edge and, having stared at his reflection dismally for a minute or so, drank a little and then with a pessimistic air shuffled slowly round the outer rim of the valley in search of food. In patches of shallow water he would wade in a little way and, squatting on his haunches, feel about in the dark water with the long fingers of his front paws, patting and touching and running them through the mud, and he would suddenly extract something with a look of pleased surprise and carry it to the bank to be eaten. The trophy was always carried delicately between his front paws and dealt with when he arrived on dry land. If it was a frog, he would hold it down and with one quick snap decapitate it. If, however, as was often the case, it was one of the large freshwater crabs, he would hurry shorewards as quickly as possible, and on reaching land flick the crab away from him. The crab would recover its poise and menace him with open pincers, and the raccoon would then deal with it in a very novel and practical way. A crab is very easily discomfited, and if you keep tapping at it and it finds that every grab it makes at you with its pincers misses the mark, it will eventually fold itself up and sulk, refusing to participate any more in such a one-sided contest. So the raccoon simply followed the crab around, tapping him on his carapace with his long fingers and whipping them out of the way every time the pincers came within grabbing distance. After five minutes or so of this the frustrated crab would fold up and just squat. The raccoon, who till then had resembled a dear old lady playing with a Pekinese, would straighten up and become businesslike, and, leaning forward, with one quick snap would cut the unfortunate crab almost in two.

Along one side of the valley some previous Indian owner of the hut had planted a few mango and guava trees, and while I was there the fruit ripened and attracted a great number of creatures. The tree-porcupines were generally the first on the scene. They lumbered out of the undergrowth, looking like portly and slightly inebriated old men, their great bulbous noses whiffling to and fro, while their tiny and rather sad little eyes, that always seemed full of unshed tears, peered about them hopefully. They climbed up into the mango-trees very skilfully, winding their long, prehensile tails round the branches to prevent themselves from falling, their black-and-white spines rattling among the leaves. They then made their way along to a comfortable spot on a branch, anchored themselves firmly with a couple of twists of the tail, then sat up on their hind legs, and plucked off a fruit. Holding it in their front paws, they turned it round and round while their large buck teeth got to work on the flesh. When they had finished a mango they sometimes began playing a rather odd game with the big seed. Sitting there they looked round in a vague and rather helpless manner while juggling the seed from paw to paw as though not quite certain what to do with it, and occasionally pretending to drop it and recovering it at the last moment. After about five minutes of this they tossed the seed down to the ground below and shuffled about the tree in search of more fruit.

Sometimes when one porcupine met another face to face on a branch, they both anchored themselves with their tails, sat up on their hind legs and indulged in the most ridiculous boxing-match, ducking, and slapping with their front paws, feinting and lunging, giving left hooks, uppercuts and body blows, but never once making contact. Throughout this performance (which lasted perhaps for a quarter of an hour) their expression never changed from one of bewildered and benign interest. Then, as though prompted by an invisible signal, they went down on all fours and scrambled away to different parts of the tree. I could never discover the purpose of these boxing bouts nor identify the winner, but they afforded me an immense amount of amusement.

Another fascinating creature that used to come to the fruit trees was the douroucouli. These curious little monkeys, with long tails, delicate, almost squirrel-like bodies and enormous owl-like eyes are the only nocturnal species of monkey in the world. They arrived in small troops of seven or eight and, though they made no noise as they jumped into the fruit trees, you could soon tell they were there by the long and complicated conversation they held while they fed. They had the biggest range of noises I have ever heard from a monkey, or for that matter from any animal of similar size. First they could produce a loud purring bark, a very powerful vibrating cry which they used as a warning; when they delivered it their throats would swell up to the size of a small apple with the effort. Then, to converse with one another, they would use shrill squeaks, grunts, a mewing noise not unlike a cat's and a series of liquid, bubbling sounds quite different from anything else I have ever heard. Sometimes one of them in an excess of affection would drape his arm over a companion's shoulder and they would sit side by side, arms round each other, bubbling away, peering earnestly into each other's faces. They were the only monkeys I know that would on the slightest provocation give one another the most passionate human kisses, mouth to mouth, arms round each other, tails entwined.

Naturally these animals made only sporadic appearances; there were, however, two creatures which were in constant evidence in the waters of the drowned valley. One was a young cayman, the South American alligator, about four feet long. He was a very handsome reptile with black-and-white skin as knobbly and convoluted as a walnut, a dragon's fringe on his tail, and large eyes of golden-green flecked with amber. He was the only cayman to live in this little stretch of water. I could never understand why no others had joined him, for the creeks and waterways, only a hundred feet or so away, were alive with them. None the less this little cayman lived in solitary state in the pool outside my hut and spent the day swimming round and round with a rather proprietory air. The other creature always to be seen was a jacana, probably one of the strangest birds in South America. In size and appearance it is not unlike the English moorhen, but its neat body is perched on long slender legs which end in a bunch of enormously elongated toes. It is with the aid of these long toes and the even distribution of weight they give that the jacana manages to walk across water, using the water-lily leaves and other water-plants as its pathways. It has thus earned its name of lily-trotter.

The jacana disliked the cayman, while the cayman had formed the impression that Nature had placed the jacana in his pool to add a little variety to his diet. He was, however, a young and inexperienced reptile, and at first his attempts to stalk and capture the bird were ridiculously obvious. The jacana would come mincing out of the undergrowth, where it used to spend much of its time, and walk out across the water, stepping delicately from one lily leaf to the next, its long toes spreading out like spiders and the leaves dipping gently under its weight. The cayman, on spotting it, immediately submerged until only his eyes showed above water. No ripple disturbed the surface, yet his head seemed to glide along until he got nearer and nearer to the bird. The jacana, always pecking busily among the water-plants in search of worms and snails and tiny fish, rarely noticed the cayman's approach and would probably have fallen an easy victim if it had not been for one thing. As soon as the cayman was within ten or twelve feet he would become so excited that instead of submerging and taking the bird from underneath he would suddenly start to wag his tail vigorously and shoot along the surface of the water like a speedboat, making such large splashes that not even the most dim-witted bird could have been taken unawares; and the jacana would fly up into the air with a shrill cry of alarm, wildly flapping its buttercup-yellow wings.

For a long time it did not occur to me to wonder why the bird should spend a greater part of the day in the reed-bed at one end of the lake. But on investigating this patch of reed I soon discovered the reason, for there on the boggy ground I found a mat neatly made of weed on which lay four round creamy eggs heavily blotched with chocolate and silver. The bird must have been sitting for some time, for only a couple of days later I found the nest empty and a few hours after that saw the jacana leading out her brood for its first walk into the world.

She emerged from the reed-bed, trotted out on to the lily leaves, then paused and looked back. Out of the reeds her four babies appeared, with the look of outsize bumble-bees, in their golden-and-black fluff, while their long slender legs and toes seemed as fragile as spider-webs. They walked in single file behind their mother, always a lily leaf behind, and they waited patiently for their mother to test everything before moving forward. They could all cluster on one of the great plate-like leaves, and they were so tiny and light that it scarcely dipped beneath their weight. Once the cayman had seen them, of course, he redoubled his efforts, but the jacana was a very careful mother. She kept her brood near the edge of the lake, and if the cayman showed any signs of approaching, the babies immediately dived off the lily leaves and vanished into the water, to reappear mysteriously on dry land a moment later.

The cayman tried every method he knew, drifting as close as possible without giving a sign, concealing himself by plunging under a mat of water-weeds and then surfacing so that the weeds almost covered eyes and nose. There he lay patiently, sometimes even moving very close inshore, presumably in the hope of catching the jacanas before they ventured out too far. For a week he tried each of these methods in turn, and only once did he come anywhere near success. On this particular day he had spent the hot noon hours lying, fully visible, in the very centre of the lake, revolving slowly round and round so that he could keep an eye on what was happening on the shore. In the late afternoon he drifted over to the fringe of lilies and weeds and managed to catch a small frog that had been sunning itself in the centre of a lily. Fortified by this, he swam over to a floating raft of green weeds, studded with tiny flowers, and dived right under it. It was only after half an hour of fruitless search in other parts of the little lake that I realized he must be concealed under the weeds. I trained my field-glasses on them, and although the entire patch was no larger than a door, it took me at least ten minutes to spot him. He was almost exactly in the centre and as he had risen to the surface a frond of weed had become draped between his eyes; on the top of this was a small cluster of pink flowers. He looked somewhat roguish with this weed on his head, as though he were wearing a vivid Easter bonnet, but it served to conceal him remarkably well. Another half an hour passed before the jacanas appeared and the drama began.

The mother, as usual, emerged suddenly from the reed-bed, and stepping daintily on to the lily leaves paused and called her brood, who pattered out after her like a row of quaint clockwork toys and then stood patiently clustered on a lily leaf, awaiting instructions. Slowly the mother led them out into the lake, feeding as they went. She would poise herself on one leaf and bending over, catch another in her beak, which she would pull and twist until it was sufficiently out of the water to expose the underside. A host of tiny worms and leeches, snails and small crustaceans, generally clung to it. The babies clustered round and pecked vigorously, picking off all this small fry until the underside of the leaf was clean, whereupon they all moved off to another.

Quite early in the proceedings I realized that the female was leading her brood straight towards the patch of weeds beneath which the cayman was hiding, and I remembered then that this particular area was one of her favourite hunting-grounds. I had watched her standing on the lily pads, pulling out the delicate, fern-like weed in large tangled pieces and draping it across a convenient lily flower so that her babies could work over it for the mass of microscopic life it contained. I felt sure that, having successfully managed to evade the cayman so far, she would notice him on this occasion, but although she paused frequently to look about her, she continued to lead her brood towards the reptile's hiding-place.

I was now in a predicament. I was determined that the cayman was not going to eat either the female jacana or her brood if I could help it, but I was not quite sure what to do. The bird was quite used to human noises and took no notice of them whatever, so there was no point in clapping my hands. Nor was there any way of getting close to her, for this scene was being enacted on the other side of the lake, and it would have taken me ten minutes to work my way round, by which time it would be too late, for already she was within twenty feet of the cayman. It was useless to shout, too far to throw stones, so I could only sit there with my eyes glued to my field-glasses, swearing that if the cayman so much as touched a feather of my jacana family I would hunt him out and slaughter him. And then I suddenly remembered the shotgun.

It was, of course, too far for me to shoot at the cayman: the shot would have spread out so much by the time it reached the other side of the lake that only a few pellets would hit him, whereas I might easily kill the birds I was trying to protect. It occurred to me, however, that as far as I knew the jacana had never heard a gun, and a shot fired into the air might therefore frighten her into taking her brood to safety. I dashed into the hut and found the gun, and then spent an agonizing minute or two trying to remember where I had put the cartridges. At last I had it loaded and hurried out to my vantage-point again. Holding the gun under my arm, its barrels pointing into the soft earth at my feet, I held the field-glasses up in my other hand and peered across the lake to see if I was in time.

The jacana had just reached the edge of the lilies nearest the weed patch. Her babies were clustered on a leaf just behind and to one side of her. As I looked she bent forward, grabbed a large trailing section of weed and pulled it on to the lily leaves, and at that moment the caymen, only about four feet away, rose suddenly from his nest of flowers and weeds and, still wearing his ridiculous bonnet, charged forward. At the same moment I let off both barrels of the shotgun, and the roar echoed round the lake.

Whether it was my action that saved the jacana or her own quick-wittedness I do not know, but she rose from the leaf with extraordinary speed just as the cayman's jaws closed and cut the leaf in half. She swooped over his head, he leapt half out of the water in an effort to grab her (I could hear the clop of his jaws) and she flew off unhurt but screaming wildly.

The attack had been so sudden that she had apparently given no orders to her brood, who had meanwhile been crouching on the lily leaf. Now, hearing her call, they were galvanized into action, and as they dived overboard the cayman swept towards them. By the time he reached the spot, they were under water, so he dived too and gradually the ripples died away and the surface of the water became calm. I watched anxiously while the female jacana, calling in agitation, flew round and round the lake. Presently she disappeared into the reed-bed and I saw her no more that day. Nor did I see the cayman for that matter. I had a horrible feeling that he had succeeded in catching all those tiny bundles of fluff as they swam desperately under water, and I spent the evening planning revenge.

The next morning I went round to the reed-bed, and there to my delight I found the jacana, and with her three rather subdued-looking babies. I searched for the fourth one, but as he was nowhere to be seen it was obvious that the cayman had been at any rate partially successful. To my consternation the jacana, instead of being frightened off by her experience of the previous day, proceeded once more to lead her brood out to the water-lilies, and for the rest of the day I watched her with my heart in my mouth. Though there was no sign of the cayman, I spent several nerve-wracking hours, and by evening I decided I could stand it no longer. I went to the village and borrowed a tiny canoe which two Indians kindly carried down to the little lake for me. As soon as it was dark I armed myself with a powerful torch and a long stick with a slip-knot of rope on the end, and set off on my search for the cayman. Though the lake was so small, an hour had passed before I spotted him, lying on the surface near some lilies. As the torch-beam caught him, his great eyes gleamed like rubies. With infinite caution I edged closer and closer until I could gently lower the noose and pull it carefully over his head, while he lay there quietly, blinded or mesmerized by the light. Then I jerked the noose tight and hauled his thrashing and wriggling body on board, his jaws snapping and his throat swelling as he gave vent to loud harsh barks of rage. I tied him up in a sack and the next day took him five miles deep into the creeks and let him go. He never managed to find his way back, and for the rest of my stay in the little hut by the drowned valley I could sit and enjoy the sight of my lily-trotter family pottering happily over the lake in search of food, without suffering any anxiety every time a breeze ruffled the surface of the rich tawny water.

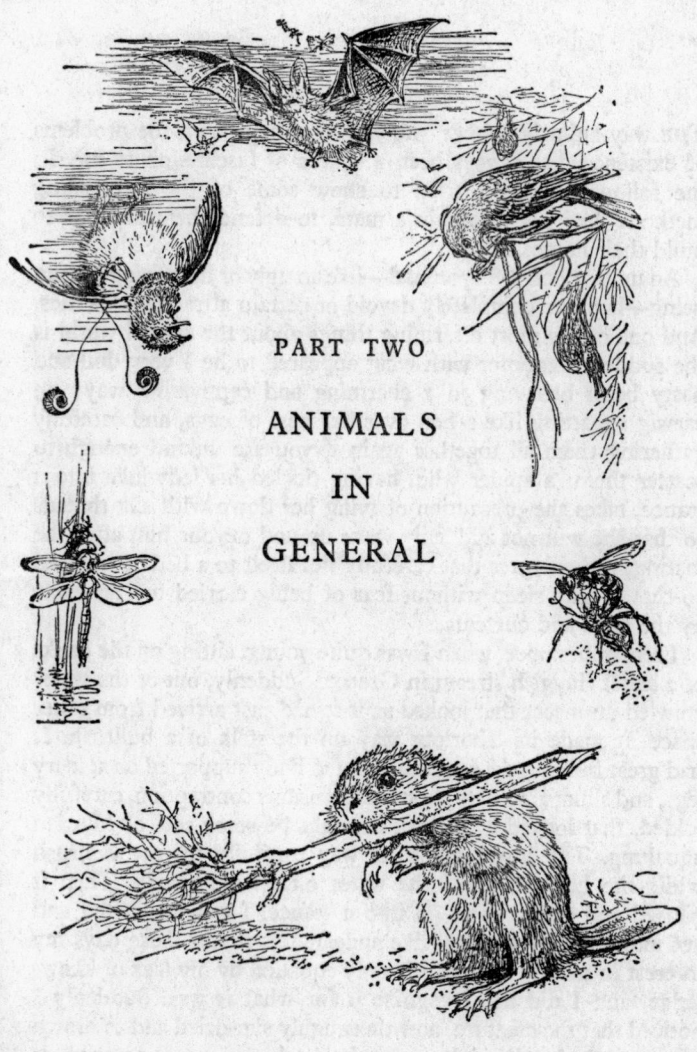

PART TWO

ANIMALS

IN

GENERAL

THE way animals behave, the way they cope with the problems of existence, has always been a source of fascination to me. In the following talks I tried to show some of the astonishing methods they use to obtain a mate, to defend themselves or to build their homes.

An ugly or horrifying animal—like an ugly or horrifying human being—is never completely devoid of certain attractive qualities. And one of the most disarming things about the animal world is the sudden encounter with what appeared to be a very dull and nasty beast behaving in a charming and captivating way: an earwig squatting like a hen over her nest of eggs, and carefully gathering them all together again if you are unkind enough to scatter them; a spider who, having tickled his lady-love into a trance, takes the precaution of tying her down with silk threads so that she will not suddenly wake up and devour him after the mating; the sea-otter that carefully ties itself to a bed of seaweed so that it may sleep without fear of being carried too far away by the tides and currents.

I remember once, when I was quite young, sitting on the banks of a small sluggish stream in Greece. Suddenly, out of the water crawled an insect that looked as if it had just arrived from outer space. It made its laborious way up the stalk of a bullrush. It had great bulbous eyes, a carunculated body supported on spidery legs, and slung across its chest was a curious contraption, carefully folded, that looked as though it might be some sort of Martian aqualung. The insect made its way carefully up the bullrush while the hot sun dried the water off its ugly body. Then it paused and appeared to go into a trance. I was fascinated and yet interested by its repulsive appearance, for in those days my interest in natural history was only equalled by my lack of knowledge, and I did not recognize it for what it was. Suddenly I noticed that the creature, now thoroughly sun-dried and as brown as a nut, had split right down its back and, as I watched, it seemed as though the animal inside was struggling to get out. As the minutes passed, the struggles grew stronger and the split grew larger, and presently the creature inside hauled itself free of its ugly skin and crawled feebly on to the rush stalk, and I saw it was a dragonfly. Its wings were still wet and crumpled from this strange birth, and its body soft, but, as I watched, the sun did its work and the wings dried stiff and straight, as fragile as snowflakes and as intricate as a cathedral window. The body also stiffened, and changed to a brilliant sky-blue. The dragonfly whirred its wings a couple of times, making them shimmer in the sun, and then flew unsteadily away, leaving behind, still clinging to the stem, the unpleasant shell of its former self.

I had never seen such a transformation before, and as I gazed with amazement at the unattractive husk which had housed the beautiful shining insect, I made a vow that never again would I judge an animal by its appearance.

ANIMAL COURTSHIPS

MOST animals take their courtship very seriously, and through the ages some of them have evolved fascinating ways of attracting the female of their choice. They have grown a bewildering mass of feathers, horns, spikes and dewlaps, and have developed an astonishing variety of colours, patterns and scents, all for the purpose of obtaining a mate. Not content with this, they will sometimes bring the female a gift, or construct a flower show for her, or intrigue her with an acrobatic display, or a dance, or a song. When the animals are courting they put their heart and soul into it, and are even, if necessary, ready to die.

The Elizabethan lovers of the animal world are, of course, the birds: they dress themselves magnificently, they dance and posture and they are prepared at a moment's notice to sing a madrigal or fight a duel to the death.

The most famous are the birds of paradise, for not only do they possess some of the most gorgeous courting dresses in the world but they show them off so well.

Take, for example, the king bird of paradise. I was once lucky enough to see one of these birds displaying in a Brazilian zoo. Here, in a huge outdoor aviary full of tropical plants and trees, three king birds of paradise were living—two females and a male. The male is about the size of a blackbird, with a velvety orange head contrasting vividly with a snow-white breast and a brilliant scarlet back, the feathers having such a sheen on them that they seem polished. The beak is yellow and the legs are a beautiful cobalt blue. The feathers along the side of its body—since it was the breeding season—were long, and the middle pair of tail feathers were produced in long slender stalks about ten inches in length. The feather was tightly coiled like a watch spring, so that at the end of each of these wire-like feathers shone a disc of emerald green. In the sunlight he gleamed and glittered with every movement, and the slender tail-wire trembled and the green disc shook and scintillated in the sun. He was sitting on a long bare branch, and the two females were squatting in a bush close by, watching him. Suddenly he puffed himself out a little and gave a curious cry midway between a whine and a yap. He was silent for a minute as if watching the effect of this sound on the females; but they continued to sit there, observing him unemotionally. He bobbed once or twice on the branch, to fix their attention perhaps, then raised his wings above his back and flapped them wildly, just as if he were about to take off on a triumphant flight. He spread them out wide and ducked forward, so that his head was hidden by the feathers. Then he raised them again, flapped vigorously once more, and wheeled round so that the two females should be dazzled by his beautiful snow-white breast. He gave a lovely liquid warbling cry, while the long side-plumes on his body suddenly burst out, like a beautiful fountain of ash-grey, buff and emerald-green that quivered delicately in time to his song. He raised his short tail and pressed it closely to his back, so that the two long tail-wires curved over his head and on each side of his yellow beak hung the two emerald-green discs. He swayed his body gently to and fro; the discs swung like pendulums and gave the odd impression that he was juggling with them. He lifted and lowered his head, singing with all his might, while the green discs gyrated to and fro.

The females seemed completely oblivious. They sat there regarding him with the mild interest of a couple of housewives at an expensive mannequin parade, who, though they admired the gowns, realized they have no hope of purchasing them. Then the male, as if in a last desperate effort to work his audience into some show of enthusiasm, suddenly swung right round on the perch and showed his beautiful scarlet back to them, lowered himself to a crouch and opened wide his beak, revealing the interior of his mouth which was a rich apple-green in colour and as glossy as though it had just been painted. He stood like this, singing with open mouth, and then gradually, as his song died away, his gorgeous plumes ceased to twitch and tremble and fell against his body. He stood upright on the branch for a moment and regarded the females. They stared back at him with the expectant air of people who, having watched a conjurer performing one good trick, are waiting for the next. The male gave a few slight chirrups and then burst into song again and suddenly let himself drop, so that he hung beneath the branch. Still singing, he spread his wings wide and then walked to and fro upside down. This acrobatic display seemed to intrigue one of the females for the first time, for she cocked her head on one side in a gesture of enquiry. I could not for the life of me see how they could remain so unimpressed, for I was dazzled and captivated by the male's song and colouring. Having walked backwards and forwards for a minute or so, he closed his wings tightly and let his body dangle straight down, swaying softly from side to side, singing passionately all the while. He looked like some weird crimson fruit attached to the bough by the blue stalks of his legs, stirring gently in a breeze.

At this point, one of the females grew bored and flew off to another part of the aviary. The remaining one, however, with head cocked to one side, was peering closely at the male. With a quick flap of his wings he regained his upright position on the perch, looking a trifle smug I thought, as well he might. Now I waited excitedly to see what would happen next. The male was standing stock-still, letting his feathers shimmer in the sunlight, and the female was becoming decidedly excited. I felt sure that she had succumbed to his fantastic courtship which was as sudden and as beautiful as a burst of highly coloured fireworks. Sure enough, the female took wing. Now, I thought, she was going up to congratulate him on his performance and they would start married life together at once, but to my astonishment she merely flew on to the branch where the male sat, picked up a small beetle, which was wandering aimlessly across the bark, and with a satisfied chuck flew off to the other end of the aviary with it. The male puffed himself out and started to preen in a resigned sort of fashion, and I decided that the females must be especially hard-hearted, or especially inartistic, to have been able to resist such an exhibition. I felt very sorry for the male that his magnificent courtship should go unrewarded. However my sympathy was wasted, for with a squeak of triumph he had discovered another beetle which he was happily banging on the branch. He obviously did not mind in the least being turned down.

Not all birds are such good dancers as the birds of paradise, nor are they so well dressed, but they have compensated for this by the charming originality of their approach to the opposite sex. Take, for example, the bower-birds. They have, in my opinion, one of the most delightful courtship methods in the world. The satin bower-bird, for instance, is not particularly impressive to look at: about the size of a thrush, he is clad in dark blue feathers that have a metallic glint when the light catches on them. He looks, quite frankly, as if he is wearing an old and shiny suit of blue serge, and you would think that his chances of inducing the female to overlook the poverty of his wardrobe were non-existent. But he contrives it by an extremely cunning device: he builds a bower.

Once again it was in a zoo that I was lucky enough to see a satin bower-bird building his temple of love. He had chosen two large tussocks of grass in the middle of his aviary and had carefully cleared a large circular patch all round and a channel between them. Then he had carried twigs, pieces of string and straw, and woven them into the grass, so that the finished building was like a tunnel. It was at this stage that I first noticed what he was doing, and by then, having built his little week-end cottage, he was in the process of decorating it. Two empty snail-shells were the first items, and they were followed by the silver paper from a packet of cigarettes, a piece of wool that he had picked up, six coloured pebbles and a bit of string with a blob of sealing wax on it. Feeling that he might like some more decoration, I brought him some strands of coloured wool, a few multi-coloured sea-shells and some bus-tickets.

He was delighted; he came down to the wire to take them carefully from my fingers, and then hopped back to his bower to arrange them. He would stand staring at the decorations for a minute and then hop forward and move a bus-ticket or a strand of wool into what he considered a more artistic position.

When the bower was finished it really looked very charming and decorative, and he stood in front of it preening himself and stretched out one wing at a time as if indicating his handiwork with pride. Then he dodged to and fro through his little tunnel, rearranged a couple of sea-shells, and started posturing again with one wing outspread. He had really worked hard on his bower, and I felt sorry for him, for the whole effort was in vain: his mate had apparently died some time previously and he now shared the aviary with a few squawking common finches that took no interest whatsoever in his architectural abilities or in his display of household treasures.

In the wild state, the satin bower-bird is one of the few birds that uses a tool, for he will sometimes paint the twigs used in the construction of his bower with highly coloured berries and moist charcoal, using a piece of some fibrous material as a brush. Unfortunately, by the time I had remembered this and had made plans to provide my bower-bird with a pot of blue paint and a piece of old rope—the bower-birds are particularly fond of blue—he had lost interest in his bower and not even the presentation of a complete set of cigarette cards, depicting soldiers' uniforms through the ages, could arouse his enthusiasm again.

Another species of bower-bird builds an even more impressive structure, four to six feet high, by piling sticks round two trees and then roofing it over with creepers. The inside is carefully laid with moss, and the outside, for this bower-bird is plainly a man of the world with expensive tastes, is decorated with orchids. In front of the bower he constructs a little bed of green moss on which he places all the brightly coloured flowers and berries he can find; being a fastidious bird, he renews these every day, taking the withered decorations and piling them carefully out of sight behind the bower.

Among the mammals, of course, you do not come across quite such displays as among the birds. On the whole, mammals seem to have a more down-to-earth, even modern attitude, towards their love problems.

I was able to watch the courtship of two tigers when I worked at Whipsnade Zoo. The female was a timid, servile creature, cringing at the slightest snarl from her mate until the day she came into season. Then she changed suddenly into slinking, dangerous creature, fully aware of her attraction but biding her time. By the end of the morning the male was following her round, belly-crawling and abject, while on his nose were several deep, bloody grooves caused by slashing backhands from his mate. Every time he forgot himself and approached too closely he got one of these backhand swipes across the nose. If he seemed at all offended by this treatment and lay down under a bush, the female would approach him, purring loudly, and rub herself against him until he got up and followed her again, moving closer and closer until he received another blow on the nose for his pains.

Eventually the female led him down into a little dell where the grass was long, and there she lay down and purred to herself, with her green eyes half-closed. The tip of her tail, like a big black-and-white bumble-bee, twitched to and fro in the grass, and the poor besotted male chased it from side to side, like a kitten, slapping it gently with his great paws. At last the female tired of her vamping; she crouched lower in the grass and gave a curious purring cry. The male, rumbling in his throat, moved towards her. She cried again, and raised her head, while the male gently bit along the line of her arched neck, a gentle nibble with his great teeth. Then the female cried again, a self-satisfied purr, and the two great striped bodies seemed to melt together in the green grass.

Not all mammals are so decorative and highly coloured as the tiger, but they generally compensate by being brawny. They therefore have to rely on cave-man tactics for obtaining their mates. Take, for example, the hippopotamus. To see one of these great chubby beasts lying in the water, staring at you with a sort of benign innocence out of bulbous eyes, sighing occasionally in a smug and lethargic manner, would scarcely lead you to believe that they could be roused to bursts of terrible savagery when it came to choosing a mate. If you have ever seen a hippo yawning, displaying on each side of its mouth four great curved razor-sharp tusks (hidden among which, two more point outwards like a couple of ivory spikes) you will realize what damage they could do.

When I was collecting animals in West Africa we once camped on the banks of a river in which lived a hippo herd of moderate size. They seemed a placid and happy group, and every time we

went up or down the stream by canoe they would follow us a short distance, swimming nearer and nearer, wiggling their ears and occasionally snorting up clouds of spray, as they watched us with interest. As far as I could make out, the herd consisted of four females, a large elderly male and a young male. One of the females had a medium-sized baby with her which, though already large and fat, was still occasionally carried on her back. They seemed, as I say, a very happy family group. But one night, just as it was growing dark, they launched into a series of roars and brays which sounded like a choir of demented donkeys. These were interspersed with moments of silence broken only by a snort or a splash, but as it grew darker the noise became worse, until, eventually realizing I would be unlikely to get any sleep, I decided to go down and see what was happening. Taking a canoe, I paddled down to the curve of the river a couple of hundred yards away, where the brown water had carved a deep pool out of the bank and thrown up a great half-moon of glittering white sand. I knew the hippos liked to spend the day here, and it was from this direction that all the noise was coming. I knew something was wrong, for usually by this time each evening they had hauled their fat bodies out of the water and trekked along the bank to raid some unfortunate native's plantation, but here they were in the pool, long past the beginning of their feeding-time. I landed on the sandbank and walked along to a spot which gave me a good view. There was no reason for me to worry about noise: the terrible roars and bellows and splashes coming from the pool were quite sufficient to cover the scrunch of my footsteps.

At first I could see nothing but an occasional flash of white where the hippos' bodies thrashed in the water and churned it into foam, but presently the moon rose, and in its brilliant light I could see the females and the baby gathered at one end of the pool in a tight bunch, their heads gleaming above the surface of the water, their ears flicking to and fro. Now and again they would open their mouths and bray, rather in the manner of a Greek chorus. They were watching with interest both the old male and the young who were in the shallows at the centre of the pool. The water reached up only to their tummies, and their great barrel-shaped bodies and the rolls of fat under their chins gleamed as though they had been oiled. They were facing each other with lowered heads, snorting like a couple of steam-engines.

Suddenly the young male lifted his great head, opened his mouth so that his teeth flashed in the moonlight, gave a prolonged and blood-curdling bray, and, just as he was finishing, the old male rushed at him with open mouth and with incredible speed for such a bulky animal. The young male, equally quick, twisted to one side. The old male splashed in a welter of foam like some misshapen battleship, and was now going so fast that he could not stop. As he passed, the young male, with a terrible sideways chop of his huge jaws, bit him in the shoulder. The old male swerved round and charged again, and just as he reached his opponent the moon went behind a cloud. When it came out again, they were standing as I had first seen them, facing each other with lowered heads, snorting.

I sat on that sandbank for two hours, watching these great roly-poly creatures churning up the water and sand as they duelled in the shallows. As far as I could see, the old male was getting the worst of it, and I felt sorry for him. Like some once-great pugilist who had now grown flabby and stiff, he seemed to be fighting a battle which he knew was already lost. The young male, lighter and more agile, seemed to dodge him every time, and his teeth always managed to find their mark in the shoulder or neck of the old male. In the background the females watched with semaphoring ears, occasionally breaking into a loud lugubrious chorus which may have been sorrow for the plight of the old male, or delight at the success of the young one, but was probably merely the excitement of watching the fight. Eventually, since the fight did not seem as if it would end for several more hours, I paddled home to the village and went to bed.

I awoke just as the horizon was paling into dawn, and the hippos were quiet. Apparently the fight was over. I hoped that the old male had won, but I very much doubted it. The answer was given to me later that morning by one of my hunters; the corpse of the old male, he said, was about two miles downstream, lying where the current of the river had carried it into the curving arms of a sandbank. I went down to examine it and was horrified at the havoc the young male's teeth had wrought on the massive body. The shoulders, the neck, the great dewlaps that hung under the chin, the flanks and the belly: all were ripped and tattered, and the shallows around the carcase were still tinged with blood. The entire village had accompanied me, for such an enormous windfall of meat was a red-letter day for them. They stood silent and interested while I examined the old male's carcase, and when I had finished and walked away they poured over it like ants, screaming and pushing with excitement, vigorously wielding their knives and machetes. It seemed to me, watching the huge hippo's carcase disintegrate under the pile of hungry humans, that it was a heavy price to pay for love.

A notably romantic member of the human race is described as hot-blooded; yet in the animal world it is among the cold-blooded creatures that you find some of the best courtship displays. The average crocodile looks as though he would prove a pretty cold-blooded lover as he lies on the bank, watching with his perpetual, sardonic grin and unwinking eyes the passing pageant of river life. Yet when the time and the place and the lady are right, he will fling himself into battle for her hand; and the two males, snapping and thrashing, will roll over and over in the water. At last the winner, flushed with victory, proceeds to do a strange dance on the surface of the water, whirling round and round with his head and tail thrust into the air, bellowing like a foghorn in what is apparently the reptilian equivalent of an old-fashioned waltz.

It is among the terrapins or water-tortoises that we find an example of the "treat 'em rough and they'll love you" school of thought. In one of these little reptiles the claws on the front flippers are greatly elongated. Swimming along, the male sees a suitable female and starts to head her off. He then beats her over the head with his long fingernails, an action so quickly performed that his claws are a mere blur. This does not seem to make the female suffer in any way; it may even give her pleasure. But at any rate, even a female terrapin cannot succumb at the very first sign of interest on the part of the male. She must play hard to get, even if only for a short time, and she therefore breaks away and continues swimming in the stream. The male now roused to a frenzy, swims after her, heads her off again, backs her up to the bank and proceeds to give her another beating. And this may happen several times before the female agrees to take up housekeeping with him. Whatever one may say against this reptile, he is certainly no hypocrite; he starts as he means to go on. And the female does not appear to mind these somewhat hectic advances. In fact, she seems to find them a pleasant and rather original form of approach. But there is no accounting for tastes—even among human beings.

However, for bewildering variety and ingenuity in the management of their love affairs, I think one must give pride of place to the insects.

Take the praying mantis—mind you, one look at their faces and nothing would surprise you about their private lives. The small head, the large bulbous eyes dominating a tiny, pointed face that ends in a little quivering moustache; and the eyes themselves, a pale watery straw colour with black cat-like pupils that give them a wild and maniacal look. Under the chest a pair of powerful, savagely barbed arms are bent in a permanent and hypocritical attitude of prayer, being ready at a moment's notice to leap out and crush the victim in an embrace as though he had been caught in a pair of serrated scissors. Another unpleasant habit of the mantis is the way it looks at things, for it can turn its head to and fro in the most human manner and, if puzzled, will cock its little chinless face on one side, staring at you with wild eyes. Or, if you walk behind it, it will peer at you over its shoulder with an unpleasant air of expectancy. Only a male mantis, I feel, could see anything remotely attractive in the female, and you would think he would be sensible enough not to trust a bride with a face like that. But no, I have seen one, his heart overflowing with love, clasp a female passionately, and while they were actually consummating their marriage his spouse leaned tenderly over her shoulder and proceeded to eat him, browsing with the air of a gourmet over his corpse still clasped to her back, while her whiskers quivered and twitched as each delicate, glistening morsel was savoured to the full.

Female spiders, of course, have this same rather anti-social habit of eating their husbands; and the male's approach to the web of the female is thus fraught with danger. If she happens to be hungry, he will hardly have a chance to get the first words of his proposal out, as it were, before he finds himself a neatly trussed bundle being sucked of his vital juices by the lady. In one such species of the spider, the male has worked out a method to make certain he can get close enough to the female to tickle and massage her into a receptive frame of mind, without being eaten. He brings her a little gift—may be a bluebottle or something of the sort—neatly wrapped up in silk. While she is busily devouring this, he creeps up behind her and strokes her into a sort of trance with his legs. Sometimes, when the nuptials are over, he manages to get away, but in most cases he is eaten at the end of the honeymoon, for it appears that the only true way to a female spider's heart is through her stomach.

In another species of spider the male has evolved an even more brilliant device for subduing his tigerish wife. Having approached her, he then starts to massage her gently with his legs until, as is usual with female spiders, she enters a sort of hypnotic state. Then the male, as swiftly as he can, proceeds to bind her to the ground with a length of silken cord, so that, when she awakes from her trance in the marriage bed, she finds herself unable to turn her husband into a wedding breakfast until she has set about the tedious business of untying herself. This generally saves the husband's life.

But if you want a really exotic romance you need not go to the tropical jungle to find it: just go into your own back-garden and creep up on the common snail. Here you have a situation as complex as the plot of any modern novel, for snails are hermaphrodite, and so each one can enjoy the pleasure of both the male and female side of courtship and mating. But apart from this dual sex, the snail possesses something even more extraordinary, a small sack-like container in its body in which is manufactured a tiny leaf-shaped splinter of carbonate of lime, known as the love-dart. Thus when one snail—who, as I say, is both male and female—crawls alongside another snail, also male and female, the two of them indulge in the most curious courtship action. They proceed to stab each other with their love-darts, which penetrate deeply and are quite quickly dissolved in the body. It seems that this curious duel is not as painful as it appears; in fact, the dart sinking into its side seems to give the snail a pleasant feeling, perhaps an exotic tickling sensation. But, whatever it is, it puts both snails into an enthusiastic frame of mind for the stern business of mating. I am no gardener, but if I were I would probably have a soft spot for any snails in my garden, even if they did eat my plants. Any creature who has dispensed with Cupid, who carries his own quiverful of arrows around with him is, in my opinion, worth any number of dull and sexless cabbages. It is an honour to have him in the garden.

ANIMAL ARCHITECTS

SOME time ago I received a small parcel from a friend of mine in India. Inside the box I found a note which read: "I bet you don't know what this is." Greatly intrigued, I lifted off the top layer of wrapping paper, and underneath I found what appeared to be two large leaves which had been rather inexpertly sewn together.

My friend would have lost his bet. As soon as I saw the large and rather amateur stitches, I knew what it was: the nest of a tailor-bird, a thing I had always wanted to see. The two leaves were about six inches long, shaped rather like laurel leaves, and only the edges had been sewn together, so that it formed a sort of pointed bag. Inside the bag was a neat nest of grass and moss, and inside that were two small eggs. The tailor-bird is quite small, about the size of a tit, but with a rather long beak. This is its needle. Having found the two leaves it likes, hanging close together, it then proceeds to sew them together, using fine cotton as thread. The curious thing about it is not so much that the tailor-bird stitches the leaves together as that nobody seems to know where he finds the cotton material with which to do the sewing. Some experts insist that he weaves it himself, others that he has some source of supply that has never been discovered. As I say, the stitches were rather large and inartistic, but then how many people could make a success of sewing up two leaves, using only a beak as a needle?

Architecture in the animal world differs a great deal. Some animals, of course, have only the haziest idea of constructing a suitable dwelling, while others produce most complicated and delightful homes. It is strange that even among closely related animals there should be such a wide variety of taste in the style, situation and size of the home and the choice of materials used in its construction.

In the bird world, of course, one finds homes of every shape and size. They range from the tailor-bird's cradle of leaves to the emperor penguin, who, with nothing but snow for his building, has dispensed with the idea of a nest altogether. The egg is simply carried on the top of the large flat foot, and the skin and feathers of the stomach form a sort of pouch to cover it. Then you have the edible swift who makes a fragile, cup-shaped nest of saliva and bits of twigs and sticks it to the wall

of a cave. Among the weaver-birds of Africa, too, the variety of nests is bewildering. One species lives in a community which builds a nest half the size of a haystack, rather like a block of flats, in which each bird has its own nesting-hole. In these gigantic nests you sometimes get an odd variety of creatures living as well as the rightful occupants. Snakes are very fond of them; so are bush-babies and squirrels. One of these nests, if taken to pieces, might display an extraordinary assortment of inmates. No wonder that trees have been known to collapse under the weight of these colossal nests. The common weaver-bird of West Africa builds a neat round nest, like a small basket woven from palm fibres. They also live in communities and hang their nests on every available branch of a tree, until it seems festooned with some extraordinary form of fruit. In the most human way the brilliant and shrill-voiced owners go about the business of courting, hatching the eggs, feeding their young, and bickering with their neighbours, so that the whole thing rather resembles an odd sort of council estate.

To construct their nests, the weaver-birds have become adept not only at weaving but at tying knots, for the nest is strapped very firmly to the branch and requires considerable force to remove it. I once watched a weaver-bird starting its nest, a fascinating performance. He had decided that the nest should hang from the end of a delicate twig half-way up a tree, and he arrived on the spot carrying a long strand of palm fibre in his beak. He alighted on the branch, which at once swung to and fro so that he had to flap his wings to keep his balance. When he was fairly steady he juggled with the palm fibre until he got to the centre of it. Then he tried to drape it over the branch, so that the two ends hung one side and the loop hung the other. The branch still swayed about, and twice he dropped the fibre and had to fly down to retrieve it, but at last he got it slung over the branch to his satisfaction. He then placed one foot on it to keep it in position and leaning forward precariously he pulled the two dangling ends from one side of the branch through the loop on the other and tugged it tight. After this he flew off for some more fibre and repeated the performance. He went on in this way for the whole day, until by evening he had twenty or thirty pieces of fibre lashed to the branch, the ends dangling down like a beard.

Unfortunately I missed the following stages in the construction of this nest, and I next saw it empty, for the bird had presumably reared its young and moved off. The nest was flask-shaped—a small round entrance, guarded by a small porch of plaited fibre. I tried to pull the nest off the branch, but it was impossible, and in the end I had to break the whole branch off. Then I tried to tear the nest in half so that I could examine the inside. But so intricately interlaced and knotted were the palm fibres that it took me a long time and all my strength before I could do so. It was really an incredible construction, when you consider the bird had only its beak and its feet for tools.

When I went to Argentina four years ago I noticed that nearly every tree-stump or rail-post in the pampa was decorated with a strange earthenware construction about the size and shape of a football. At first, I believed they were termite nests, for they were very similar to a common feature of the landscape in West Africa. It was not until I saw, perched on top of one of them, a small tubby bird about the size of a robin with a rusty-red back and grey shirt-front that I realized they were the nests of the oven-bird.

As soon as I found an unoccupied nest, I carefully cut it in half and was amazed at the skill with which it had been built. Wet mud had been mixed with tiny fragments of dried grass, roots and hair to act as reinforcement. The sides of the nest were approximately an inch and a half thick. The outside had been left rough—unrendered, as it were—but the inside had been smoothed to a glass-like finish. The entrance to the nest was a small arched hole, rather like a church door, which led into a narrow passage-way that curved round the outer edge of the nest and eventually led into the circular nesting-chamber lined with a pad of soft roots and feathers. The whole thing rather resembled a snail shell.

Although I searched a large area, I was never lucky enough to find a nest that had been newly started, for it was fairly well into the breeding season. But I did find one half-completed. Oven-birds are very common in Argentina, and in the way they move and cock their heads on one side and regard you with their shining dark eyes, they reminded me very much of the English robin. The pair building this nest took no notice of me whatever, provided I remained at a distance of about twelve feet, though occasionally they would fly over to take a closer look at me, and after inspecting me with their heads on one side, they would flap their wings as though shrugging and return to their building work. The nest, as I say, was half-finished: the base was firmly cemented on to a fence-post and the outer walls and inner wall of the passage-way were already some four or five inches high. All that remained now was for the whole thing to be covered with the domed roof.

The nearest place for wet mud was about half a mile away at the edge of a shallow lagoon. They would hop round the edge of the water in a fussy, rather pompous manner, testing the mud every few feet. It had to be of exactly the right consistency. Having found a suitable patch, they would hop about excitedly, picking up tiny rootlets and bits of grass until their beaks were full and they looked as though they had suddenly sprouted large walrus moustaches. They would carry these beakfuls of reinforcement down to the mud patch, and then by skilful juggling, without dropping the material, pick up a large amount of mud as well. By a curious movement of the beak they matted the two materials together until their walrus moustaches looked distinctively bedraggled and mudstained. Then, with a muffled squeak of triumph, they flew off to the nest. Here the bundle was placed in the right position and pecked and trampled on and pushed until it had firmly adhered to the original wall. Then they entered the nest and smoothed off the new patch, using their beaks, their breasts and even the sides of their wings to get the required shining finish.

When only a small patch on the very top of the roof needed to be finished, I took some bright scarlet threads of wool down to the edge of the lagoon and scattered them around the place where the oven-birds gathered their material. On my next trip down there, to my delight, they had picked them up, and the result, a small russet bird apparently wearing a bright scarlet moustache, was quite startling. They incorporated the wool into the last piece of building on the nest, and it was, I feel sure, the only Argentinian oven-bird's nest on the pampa flying what appeared to be a small red flag at half-mast.

If the oven-bird is a master-builder, whose nest is so solid that it takes several blows of a hammer to demolish it, members of the pigeon family go to the opposite extreme. They have absolutely no idea of proper nest-making. Four or five twigs laid across a branch: that is the average pigeon's idea of a highly complicated structure. On this frail platform the eggs, generally two, are laid. Every time the tree sways in the wind this silly nest trembles and shakes and the eggs almost fall out. How any pigeon ever reaches maturity is a mystery to me.

I knew that pigeons were stupid and inefficient builders, but I never thought that their nests might prove an irritating menace to a naturalist. When I was in Argentina I learned differently. On the banks of a river outside Buenos Aires I found a small wood. The trees, only about thirty feet high, were occupied by what might almost be called a pigeon colony. Every tree had about thirty or forty nests in it. Walking underneath the branches you could see the fat bellies of the young, or the gleam of the eggs, through the carelessly arranged twigs. The nests looked so insecure that I felt like walking on tip-toe for fear that my footsteps would destroy the delicate balance.

In the centre of the wood I found a tree full of pigeons' nests but for some odd reason devoid of pigeons. At the very top of the tree I noticed a great bundle of twigs and leaves which was obviously a nest of some sort and equally obviously not a pigeon's nest. I wondered if it was the occupant of this rather untidy bundle of stuff that had made the pigeons desert all the nests in the tree. I decided to climb and see if the owner was at home. Unfortunately, it was only when I had started to climb that I realized my mistake, for nearly every pigeon's nest in the tree contained eggs, and as I made my way slowly up the branches my movements created a sort of waterfall of pigeon eggs which bounced and broke against me, smearing my coat and trousers with yolk and bits of shell. I would not have minded this so much, but every single egg was well and truly addled, and by the time I had reached the top of the tree, hot and sweating, I smelt like a cross between a tannery and a sewage farm. To add insult to injury, I found that the occupant of the nest I had climbed up to was out, so I had gained nothing by my climb except a thick coating of egg and a scent that would have made a skunk envious. Laboriously I climbed down the tree again, looking forward to the moment when I would reach ground and could light a cigarette, to take the strong smell of rotten egg out of my nostrils. The ground under the tree was littered with broken eggs tastefully interspersed with the bodies of a few baby pigeons in a decomposed condition. I made my way out into the open as quickly as possible. With a sigh of relief, I sat down and reached into my pocket for my cigarettes. I drew them out dripping with egg-yolk. At some point during my climb, by some curious chance, an egg had fallen into my pocket and broken. My cigarettes were ruined. I had to walk two miles home without a smoke, breathing in a strong aroma of egg and looking as though I had rather unsuccessfully taken part in an omelette-making competition. I have never really liked pigeons since then.

Mammals, on the whole, are not such good builders as the birds, though, of course, a few of them are experts. The badger, for example, builds the most complicated burrow, which is sometimes added to by successive generations until the whole thing resembles an intricate underground system with passages, culs-de-sac, bedrooms, nurseries and feeding-quarters. The beaver, too, is another master-builder, constructing his lodge half in and half out of the water: thick walls of mud and logs with an underground entrance, so that he can get in and out even when the surface of the lake is iced over. Beavers also build canals, so that when they have to fell a tree some distance inland for food or repair work on their dam, they can float it down the canal to the main body of water. Their dams are, of course, masterpieces—massive constructions of mud and logs, welded together, stretching sometimes many hundreds of yards. The slightest breach in these is frantically repaired by the beavers, for fear that the water would drain away and leave their lodge, with its door no longer covered by water, an easy prey to any passing enemy. What with their home, their canals and their dams, one has the impression that the beaver must be a remarkably intelligent and astute animal. Unfortunately, however, this is not the case. It appears that the desire to build a dam is an urge which no self-respecting beaver can repress even when there is no need for the construction, and when kept in a large cement pool they will solemnly and methodically run a dam across it to keep the water in.

But, of course, the real master-architects of the animal world are, without a doubt, the insects. You need only look at the beautiful mathematical precision with which a common or garden honeycomb is built. Insects seem capable of building the most astonishing homes from a vast array of materials—wood, paper, wax, mud, silk and sand—and they differ just as widely in their design. In Greece, when I was a boy, I used to spend hours searching mossy banks for the nests of the trapdoor-spiders. These are one of the most beautiful and astonishing pieces of animal architecture in the world. The spider itself, with its legs spread out, would just about cover a two-shilling piece and looks as though it has been made out of highly polished chocolate. It has a squat fat body and rather short legs, and does not look at all the sort of creature you would associate with delicate construction work. Yet these rather clumsy-looking spiders sink a shaft into the earth of a bank about six inches deep and about the diameter of a shilling. This is carefully lined, so that when finished it is like a tube of silk. Then comes the most important part, the trapdoor. This is circular and with a neatly bevelled edge, so that it fits securely into the mouth of the tunnel. It is then fixed with a silken hinge, and the outside of it camouflaged with sprigs of moss or lichen; it is almost indistinguishable from the surrounding earth when closed. If the owner is not at home and you flip back the door, you will see on its silken underside a series of neat little black pinpricks. These are the handles, so to speak, in which the spider latches her claws to hold the door firmly shut against intruders. The only person, I think, who would not be amazed at the beauty of a trapdoor-spider's nest is the male trapdoor-spider himself, for once he has lifted the trapdoor and entered the silken shaft, it is for him both a tunnel of love and death. Once having gone down into the dark interior and mated with the female, he is promptly killed and eaten by her.

One of my first experiences with animal architects was when I was about ten years old. At that time I was extremely interested in freshwater biology and used to spend most of my spare time dredging about in ponds and streams, catching the minute fauna that lived there and keeping them in large jam-jars in my bedroom. Among other things, I had one jam-jar full of caddis larvae. These curious caterpillar-like creatures encase themselves in a sort of silken cocoon with one end open, and then decorate the outside of the cocoon with whatever materials they think will produce the best camouflage. The caddis I had were rather dull, for I had caught them in a very stagnant pool. They had merely decorated the outside of their cocoons with little bits of dead water-plant.

I had been told, however, that if you remove a caddis larva from its cocoon and place it in a jar of clean water, it would spin itself a new cocoon and decorate the outside with whatever materials you care to supply. I was a bit sceptical about this, but decided to experiment. I took four of my caddis larvae and very carefully removed them, wriggling indignantly, from their cocoons. Then I placed them in a jar of clean water and lined the bottom of the jar with a handful of tiny bleached seashells. To my astonishment and delight the creatures did exactly what my friend said they would do, and by the time the larvae had finished the new cocoons were like a filigree of seashells.

I was so enthusiastic about this that I gave the poor creatures a rather hectic time of it. Every now and then I would force them to manufacture new cocoons decorated with more and more improbable substances. The climax came with my discovery that by moving the larvae to a new jar with a new substance at the bottom when they were half-way through building operations, you could get them to build a parti-coloured cocoon. Some of the results I got were very odd. There was one, for example, who had half his cocoon magnificently arrayed in seashells and the other half in bits of charcoal. My greatest triumph, however, lay in forcing three of them to decorate their cocoons with fragments of blue glass, red brick and white seashells. Moreover, the materials were put on in stripes—rather uneven stripes, I grant you, but stripes nevertheless.

Since then I have had a lot of animals of which I have been proud, but I never remember feeling quite the same sort of satisfaction as I did when I used to show off my red, white and blue caddis larvae to my friends. I think the poor creatures were really rather relieved when they could hatch out and fly away and forget about the problems of cocoon-building.

ANIMAL WARFARE

I REMEMBER once lying on a sun-drenched hillside in Greece
—a hillside covered with twisted olive-trees and myrtle bushes
—and watching a protracted and bloody war being waged within inches of my feet. I was extremely lucky to be, as it were,
war correspondent for this battle. It was the only one of its
kind I have ever seen and I would not have missed it for the
world.

The two armies involved were ants. The attacking force was
a shining, fierce red, while the defending army was as black as
coal. I might quite easily have missed this if one day I had not
noticed what struck me as an extremely peculiar ants' nest. It
contained two species of ants, one red and one black, living
together on the most amicable terms. Never having seen two
species of ants living in the same nest before, I took the trouble
to check up on them, and discovered that the red ones, who
were the true owners of the nest, were known by the resounding title of the blood-red slave-makers, and the black ones were
in fact their slaves who had been captured and placed in their
service while they were still eggs. After reading about the habits
of the slave-makers, I kept a cautious eye on the nest in the
hope of seeing them indulge in one of their slave raids. Several
months passed and I began to think that either these slave-
makers were too lazy or else they had enough slaves to keep
them happy.

The slave-makers' fortress lay near the roots of an olive-
tree, and some thirty feet farther down the hillside was a nest
of black ants. Passing this nest one morning, I noticed several
of the slave-makers wandering about within a yard or so of it,
and I stopped to watch. There were perhaps thirty or forty of
them, spread over quite a large area. They did not appear to
be foraging for food, as they were not moving with their normal
brisk inquisitiveness. They kept wandering round in vague
circles, occasionally climbing a grass blade and standing pensively
on its tip, waving their antennae. Periodically, two of them would
meet and stand there in what appeared to be animated conversation, their antennae twitching together. It was not until
I had watched them for some time that I realized what they
were doing. Their wanderings were not as aimless as they

appeared, for they were quartering the ground very thoroughly like a pack of hunting-dogs, investigating every bit of the terrain over which their army would have to travel. The black ants seemed distinctly ill at ease. Occasionally one of them would meet one of the slave-makers and would turn tail and run back to the nest to join one of the many groups of his relatives who were gathered in little knots, apparently holding a council of war. This careful investigation of the ground by the scouts of the slave-makers' army continued for two days, and I had begun to think that they had decided the black ants' city was too difficult to attack. Then I arrived one morning to find that the war had started.

The scouts, accompanied by four or five small platoons, had now moved in closer to the black ants, and already several skirmishes were taking place within two or three feet of the nest. Black ants were hurling themselves on the red ones with almost hysterical fervour, while the red ones were advancing slowly but inexorably, now and then catching a black ant and with a swift, savage bite piercing it through the head or the thorax with their huge jaws.

Half-way up the hillside the main body of the slave-makers' army was marching down. In about an hour they had got within four or five feet of the black ants' city, and here, with a beautiful military precision which was quite amazing to watch, they split into three columns. While one column marched directly on the nest the other two spread out and proceeded to execute a flanking or pincer movement. It was fascinating to watch. I felt I was suspended in some miraculous way above the field of battle of some old military campaign—the battle of Waterloo or some similar historic battle. I could see at a glance the disposition of the attackers and the defenders; I could see the columns of reinforcements hurrying up through the jungle of grass; see the two outflanking columns of slave-makers moving nearer and nearer to the nest, while the black ants, unaware of their presence, were concentrating on fighting off the central column. It was quite obvious to me that unless the black ants very soon realized that they were being encircled, they had lost all hope of survival. I was torn between a desire to help the black ants in some way and a longing to leave things as they were and see how matters developed. I did pick up one of the black ants and place him near the encircling red-ant column, but he was set upon and killed rapidly, and I felt quite guilty.

Eventually, however, the black ants suddenly became aware of the fact that they were being neatly surrounded. Immediately they seemed to panic; numbers of them ran to and fro aimlessly, some of them in their fright running straight into the red invaders and being instantly killed. Others, however, seemed to keep their heads, and they rushed down into the depths of the fortress and started on the work of evacuating the eggs, which they brought up and stacked on the side of nest farthest away from the invaders. Other members of the community then seized the eggs and started to rush them away to safety. But they had left it too late.

The encircling columns of slave-makers, so orderly and neat, now suddenly burst their ranks and spread over the whole area, like a scuttling red tide. Everywhere there were knots of struggling ants. Black ones, clasping eggs in their jaws, were pursued by the slave-makers, cornered and then forced to give up the eggs. If they showed fight, they were immediately killed; the more cowardly, however, saved their lives by dropping the eggs they were carrying as soon as a slave-maker hove in sight. The whole area on and around the nest was littered with dead and dying ants of both species, while between the corpses the black ants ran futilely hither and thither, and the slave-makers gathered the eggs and started on the journey back to their fortress on the hill. At that point, very reluctantly, I had to leave the scene of battle, for it was getting too dark to see properly.

Early next morning I arrived at the scene again, to find the war was over. The black ants' city was deserted, except for the dead and injured ants littered all over it. Neither the black nor the red army were anywhere to be seen. I hurried up to the red ants' nest and was just in time to see the last of the army arrive there, carrying their spoils of war, the eggs carefully in their jaws. At the entrance to the nest their black slaves greeted them excitedly, touching the eggs with their antennae and scuttling eagerly around their masters, obviously full of enthusiasm for the successful raid on their own relations that the slave-makers had achieved. There was something unpleasantly human about the whole thing.

It is perhaps unfair to describe animals as indulging in warfare, because for the most part they are far too sensible to engage in warfare as we know it. The exceptions are, of course, the ants, and the slave-makers in particular. But for most other creatures warfare consists of either defending themselves against an enemy, or attacking something for food.

After watching the slave-makers wage war I had the greatest admiration for their military strategy, but it did not make me like them very much. In fact, I was delighted to find that there existed what might be described as an underground movement bent on their destruction; the ant-lions. An adult ant-lion is very like a dragonfly, and looks fairly innocent. But in its childhood, as it were, it is a voracious monster that has evolved an extremely cunning way of trapping its prey, most of which consists of ants.

The larva is round-bodied, with a large head armed with great pincer-like jaws. Picking a spot where the soil is loose and sandy, it buries itself in the earth and makes a circular depression like the cone of a volcano. At the bottom of this, concealed by sand, the larva waits for its prey. Sooner or later an ant comes hurrying along in that preoccupied way so typical of ants, and blunders over the edge of the ant-lion's cone. It immediately realizes its mistake and tries to climb out again, but it finds this difficult, for the sand is soft and gives way under its weight. As it struggles futilely at the rim of this volcano it dislodges grains of sand which trickle down inside the cone and awake the deadly occupant that lurks there. Immediately the ant-lion springs into action. Using its great head and jaws like a steam-shovel, it shoots a rapid spray of sand grains at the ant, still struggling desperately to climb over the lip of the volcano. The earth sliding away from under its claws, knocked off its balance by this stream of sand and unable to regain it, the ant rolls down to the bottom of the cone where the sand parts like a curtain and it is enfolded lovingly in the great curved jaws of the ant-lion. Slowly, kicking and struggling, it disappears, as though it were being sucked down by quicksand, and within a few seconds the cone is empty, while below the innocent-looking sand the ant-lion is sucking the vital juices out of its victim.

Another creature that uses this sort of machine-gunning to

bring down its prey is the archer-fish. This is a rather handsome creature found in the streams of Asia. It has evolved a most ingenious method of obtaining its prey, which consists of flies, butterflies, moths and other insects. Swimming slowly along under the surface it waits until it sees an insect alight on a twig or leaf overhanging the water. Then the fish slows down and approaches cautiously. When it is within range it stops, takes aim, and then suddenly and startlingly spits a stream of tiny water droplets at its prey. These travel with deadly accuracy, and the startled insect is knocked off its perch and into the water below, and the next minute the fish swims up beneath it, there is a swirl of water and a gulp, and the insect has vanished for ever.

I once worked in a pet-shop in London, and one day with a consignment of other creatures we received an archer-fish. I was delighted with it, and with the permission of the manager I wrote out a notice describing the fish's curious habits, arranged the aquarium carefully, put the fish inside and placed it in the window as the main display. It proved very popular, except that people wanted to see the archer-fish actually taking his prey, and this was not easy to manage. Eventually I had a brainwave. A few doors down from us was a fish shop, and I saw no reason why we should not benefit from some of their surplus bluebottles. So I suspended a bit of very smelly meat over the archer-fish's aquarium and left the door of the shop open. I did this without the knowledge of the manager. I wanted it to be a surprise for him.

It was certainly a surprise.

By the time he arrived, there must have been several thousand bluebottles in the shop. The archer-fish was having the time of his life, watched by myself inside the shop and fifty or sixty people on the pavement outside. The manager arrived neck and neck with a very unzoological policeman, who wanted to know the meaning of the obstruction outside. To my surprise the manager, instead of being delighted with my ingenious window display, tended to side with the policeman. The climax came when the manager, leaning over the aquarium to unfasten the bit of meat that hung above it, was hit accurately in the face by a stream of water which the fish had just released in the hope of hitting a particularly succulent bluebottle. The manager never referred to the incident again, but the next day the archer-fish disappeared, and it was the last time I was allowed to dress the window.

Of course, one of the favourite tricks in animal warfare is for some harmless creature to persuade a potential enemy that it is really a hideous, ferocious beast, best left alone. One of the most amusing examples of this I have seen was given to me by a sun bittern when I was collecting live animals in British Guiana. This slender bird, with a delicate, pointed beak and slow stately movements, had been hand-reared by an Indian and was therefore perfectly tame. I used to let it wander freely round my camp during the day and lock it in a cage only at night. Sun bitterns are clad in lovely feathering that has all the tints of an autumn woodland, and sometimes when this bird stood unmoving against a background of dry leaves she seemed to disappear completely. As I say, she was a frail, dainty little bird who, one would have thought, had no defence of any sort against an enemy. But this was not the case.

Three large and belligerent hunting-dogs followed their master into camp one afternoon, and before long one of them spotted the sun bittern, standing lost in meditation on the edge of the clearing. He approached her, his ears pricked, growling softly. The other two quickly joined him, and the three of them bore down on the bird with a swaggering air. The bird let them get within about four feet of her before deigning to notice them. Then she turned her head, gave them a withering stare and turned round to face them. The dogs paused, not quite sure what to do about a bird that did not run squawking at their approach. They moved closer. Suddenly the bittern ducked her head and spread her wings, so that the dogs were presented with a fan of feathers. In the centre of each wing was a beautiful marking, not noticeable when the wings were closed, which looked exactly like the two eyes of an enormous owl glaring at you. The whole transformation was done so slickly, from a slim meek little bird to something that resembled an infuriated eagle owl at bay, that the dogs were taken completely by surprise. They stopped their advance, took one look at the shivering wings and then turned tail and fled. The sun bittern shuffled her wings back into place, preened a few of her breast feathers that had become disarranged and fell to meditating again. It was obvious that dogs did not trouble her in the slightest.

Some of the most ingenious methods of defence in the animal

world are displayed by insects. They are masters of the art of disguise, of setting traps, and other methods of defence and attack. But, certainly, one of the most extraordinary is the bombardier beetle.

I was once the proud owner of a genuine wild black rat which I had caught when he was a half-grown youngster. He was an extremely handsome beast with his shining ebony fur and gleaming black eyes. He divided his time equally between cleaning himself and eating. His great passion was for insects of any shape or size: butterflies, praying mantis, stick-insects, cockroaches, they all went the same way as soon as they were put into his cage. Not even the largest praying mantis stood a chance against him, though they would occasionally manage to dig their hooked arms into his nose and draw a bead of blood before he scrunched them up. But one day I found an insect which got the better of him. It was a large, blackish beetle which had been sitting reflecting under a stone that I had inquisitively turned over; and, thinking it would make a nice titbit for my rat, I put it in a matchbox in my pocket. When I arrived home I pulled the rat out of his sleeping-box, opened the matchbox and shook the large succulent beetle on to the floor of his cage. Now the rat had two methods of dealing with insects, which varied according to their kind. If they were as fast-moving and as belligerent as a mantis, he would rush in and bite as quickly as possible in order to destroy it, but with anything harmless and slow, like a beetle, he would pick it up in his paws and sit scrunching it up as though it were a piece of toast.

Seeing this great fat delicacy wandering rather aimlessly around on the floor of his cage, he trotted forward, rapidly seized it with his little pink paws and then sat back on his haunches with the air of a gourmet about to sample the first truffle of the season. His whiskers twitched in anticipation as he lifted the beetle to his mouth, and then a curious thing happened. He uttered the most prodigious sniff, dropped the beetle and leaped backwards as though he had been stung, and sat rubbing his paws hastily over his nose and face. At first I thought he had merely been taken with a sneezing fit just as he was about to eat the beetle. Having wiped his face, he again approached it, slightly more cautiously this time, picked it up and lifted it to his mouth. Then he uttered a strangled snort, dropped it as though it were red-hot and sat wiping his face indignantly. The second experience had obviously been enough for him, for he refused to go near the beetle after that; in fact he seemed positively scared of it. Every time it ambled round to the corner of the cage where he was sitting, he would back away hurriedly. I put the beetle back in the matchbox and took it inside to identify it and it was only then that I discovered that I had offered my unfortunate rat a bombardier beetle. Apparently the beetle, when attacked, squirts out a liquid which, on reaching the air, explodes with a tiny crack and forms a sort of pungent and unpleasant gas, sufficiently horrible to make any creature who has experienced it leave the bombardier beetle severely alone in future.

I felt rather sorry for my black rat. It was, I felt, an unfortunate experience to pick up what amounted to a particularly delicious dinner, only to have it suddenly turn into a gas attack in your paws. It gave him a complex about beetles, too, because for days afterwards he would dash into his sleeping-box at the sight of one, even a fat and harmless dung-beetle. However, he was a young rat, and I suppose he had to learn at some time or another that one cannot judge by appearances in this life.

ANIMAL INVENTORS

I ONCE travelled back from Africa on a ship with an Irish captain who did not like animals. This was unfortunate, because most of my luggage consisted of about two hundred-odd cages of assorted wild life, which were stacked on the forward well deck. The captain (more out of devilment than anything else, I think) never missed a chance of trying to provoke me into an argument by disparaging animals in general and my animals in particular. But fortunately I managed to avoid getting myself involved. To begin with, one should never argue with the captain of a ship, and to argue with a captain who was also an Irishman was simply asking for trouble. However, when the voyage was drawing to an end, I felt the captain needed a lesson and I was determined to teach him one if I could.

One evening when we were nearing the English Channel, the wind and rain had driven us all into the smoking-room, where we sat and listened to someone on the radio giving a talk on radar, which in those days was still sufficiently new to be of interest to the general public. The captain listened to the talk with a gleam in his eye, and when it had finished he turned to me.

"So much for your animals," he said, "they couldn't produce anything like that, in spite of the fact that, according to you, they're supposed to be so clever."

By this simple statement the captain had played right into my hands, and I prepared to make him suffer.

"What will you bet," I enquired, "that I can't describe at least two great scientific inventions and prove to you that the principle was being used in the animal world long before man ever thought of it?"

"Make it four inventions instead of two and I'll bet you a bottle of whisky," said the captain, obviously feeling he was on to a good thing. I agreed to this.

"Well," said the captain smugly, "off you go."

"You'll have to give me a minute to think," I protested.

"Ha," said the captain triumphantly, "you're stuck already."

"Oh, no," I explained, "it's just that there are so many examples I'm not sure which to choose."

The captain gave me a dirty look.

"Why not try radar, then?" he enquired sarcastically.

"Well, I could," I said, "but I really felt it was too easy. However, since you choose it, I suppose I'd better."

It was fortunate for me that the captain was no naturalist; otherwise he would never have suggested radar. It was a gift, from my point of view, because I simply described the humble bat.

Many people must have been visited by a bat in their drawing-room or bedroom at one time or another, and if they have not been too scared of it, they will have been fascinated by its swift, skilful flight and the rapid twists and turns with which it avoids all obstacles, including objects like shoes and towels that are sometimes hurled at it. Now, despite the old saying, bats are not blind. They have perfectly good eyes, but these are so tiny that they are not easily detected in the thick fur. Their eyes, however, are certainly not good enough for them to perform some of the extraordinary flying stunts in which they indulge. It was an

Italian naturalist called Spallanzani, in the eighteenth century, who first started to investigate the flight of bats, and by the unnecessarily cruel method of blinding several bats he found that they could still fly about unhampered, avoiding obstacles as though they were uninjured. But how they managed to do this he could not guess.

It was not until fairly recently that this problem was solved, at least partially. The discovery of radar, the sending out of sound-waves and judging the obstacles ahead by the returning echo, made some investigators wonder if this was not the system employed by bats. A series of experiments was conducted, and some fascinating things were discovered. First of all, some bats were blindfolded with tiny pieces of wax over their eyes, and as usual they had no difficulty in flying to and fro without hitting anything. Then it was found that if they were blindfolded and their ears were covered they were no longer able to avoid collisions, and in fact did not seem at all keen on flying in the first place. If only one ear was covered they could fly with only moderate success, and would frequently hit objects. This showed that bats could get information about the obstacles ahead by means of sound-waves reflected from them. Then the investigators covered the noses and mouths of their bats, but left the ears uncovered, and again the bats were unable to fly without collision. This proved that the nose, ears and mouth all played some part in the bat's radar system. Eventually, by the use of extremely delicate instruments, the facts were discovered. As the bat flies along, it emits a continuous succession of supersonic squeaks, far too high for the human ear to pick up. They give out, in fact, about thirty squeaks a second. The echoes from these squeaks, bouncing off the obstacles ahead, return to the bat's ears and, in some species, to the curious fleshy ridges round the creature's nose, and the bat can thus tell what lies ahead, and how far away it is. It is, in fact, in every detail the principle of radar. But one thing rather puzzled the investigators: when you are transmitting sound-waves on radar, you must shut off your receiver when you are actually sending out the sound, so that you receive only the echo. Otherwise the receiver would pick up both the sound transmitted and the echo back, and the result would be a confused jumble. This might be possible on electrical apparatus, but they could not imagine how the bats managed to do it. It was then discovered that there was a tiny muscle in the bat's ear that did the job. Just at the moment the bat squeaks, this muscle contracts and puts the ear out of action. The squeak over, the muscle relaxes and the ear is ready to receive the echo.

But the amazing thing about this is not that bats have this private radar system—for after a while very little surprises one in Nature—but that they should have had it so long before man did. Fossil bats have been found in early Eocene rocks, and they differed very little from their modern relatives. It is possible, therefore, that bats have been employing radar for something like fifty million years. Man has possessed the secret for about twenty.

It was quite obvious that my first example had made the captain think. He did not seem quite so sure of winning the bet. I said that my next choice would be electricity, and this apparently cheered him up a bit. He laughed in a disbelieving way, and said I would have a job to persuade him that animals had electric lights. I pointed out that I had said nothing about electric lights, but merely electricity, and there were several creatures that employed it. There is, for example, the electric-ray or torpedo-fish, a curious creature that looks rather like a frying-pan run over by a steam-roller. These fish are excessively well camouflaged: not only does their colouring imitate the sandy bottom but they have also the annoying habit of half-burying themselves in the sand, which renders them really invisible. I remember once seeing the effect of this fish's electric organs, which are large and situated on its back. I was in Greece at the time, and was watching a young peasant boy fishing in the shallow waters of a sandy bay. He was wading up to his knees in the clear waters, holding in his hand a three-pronged spear such as the fishermen used for night-fishing. As he made his way round the bay, he was having quite a successful time: he had speared several large fish and a young octopus which had been concealed in a small group of rocks. As he came opposite where I was sitting a curious and rather startling thing happened. One minute he was walking slowly forward, peering down intently into the water, his trident at the ready; the next minute he had straightened up as stiffly as a guardsman and projected himself out of the water like a rocket, uttering a yell that could have been heard half a mile away. He fell back into the water with a splash and immediately uttered another and louder scream and leapt up again. This time he fell back into the water and seemed unable to regain his feet, for he struggled out on to the sand, half-crawling, half-dragging himself. When I got down to where he lay, I found him white and shaking, panting as though he had just run half a mile. How much of this was due to shock and how much to the actual effect of the electricity I could not tell, but at any rate I never again went bathing in that particular bay.

Probably the most famous electricity-producing creature is the electric-eel which, strangely enough, is not an eel at all but a species of fish that looks like an eel. These long, black creatures live in the streams and rivers of South America, and can grow to eight feet in length and the thickness of a man's thigh. No doubt a lot of stories about them are grossly exaggerated, but it is possible for a big one to shock a horse fording a river strongly enough to knock down the animal.

When I was collecting animals in British Guiana I very much wanted to catch some electric-eels to bring back to this country. At one place where we were camped the river was full of them, but they lived in deep caves hollowed out in the rocky shores. Most of these caves communicated with air by means of round pot-holes that had been worn by the flood waters, and in the cave beneath each pot-hole lived an electric-eel. If you made your way to a pot-hole and stamped heavily with your shoes it would annoy the eel into replying with a strange purring grunt, as though a large pig were entombed beneath your feet.

Try as I would I did not manage to catch one of these eels. Then one day my partner and I, accompanied by two Indians, went for a trip to a village a few miles away, where the inhabitants were great fishermen. We found several animals and birds in the village which we purchased from them, including a tame tree-porcupine. Then, to my delight, someone appeared with an electric-eel in a rather insecure fish-basket. Having bargained for and bought these creatures, including the eel, we piled them into the canoe and set out for home. The porcupine sat in the bow, apparently very interested in the scenery, and in front of him lay the eel in its basket. We were half-way home when the eel escaped.

We were first made aware of this by the porcupine. He was, I think, under the impression that the eel was a snake, for he galloped down from the bows and endeavoured to climb on to my head. Struggling to evade the porcupine's prickly embrace, I suddenly saw the eel wriggling determinedly towards me, and indulged in a feat which I would not have believed possible. I leapt into the air from a sitting position, clasping the porcupine to my bosom, and landed again when the eel had passed, without upsetting the canoe. I had a very vivid mental picture of what had happened to the young peasant who had trodden on the torpedo-fish, and I had no intention of indulging in a similar experience with an electric-eel. Luckily none of us received a shock from the eel, for while we were trying to juggle it back into its basket it wriggled over the side of the canoe and fell into the river. I cannot say any of us were really sorry to see it go.

I remember once feeding an electric-eel that lived in a large tank in a zoo, and it was quite fascinating to watch his method of dealing with his prey. He was about five feet long and could cope adequately with a fish of about eight or ten inches in length. These had to be fed to him alive, and as their death was instantaneous, I had no qualms about this. The eel seemed to know when it was feeding-time and he would be patrolling his tank with the monotonous regularity of a sentry outside Buckingham Palace. As soon as a fish was dropped into his tank he would freeze instantly and apparently watch it as it swam closer and closer. When it was within range, which was about a foot or so, he would suddenly appear to quiver all over as if a dynamo had started within his long dark length. The fish would be, as it were, frozen in its tracks; it was dead before you realized that anything was happening, and then very slowly it would tilt over and start floating belly uppermost. The eel would move a little closer, open his mouth and suck violently, and, as though he were an elongated vacuum-cleaner, the fish would disappear into him.

Having dispensed quite succesfully, I thought, with electricity, I now turned my attention to another field: medicine. Anaesthetics, I said, would be my next example, and the captain looked if anything even more sceptical than before.

The hunting-wasp is the Harley Street specialist of the insect world, and he performs an operation which would give a skilled surgeon pause. There are many different species of hunting-wasp, but most of them have similar habits. For the reception of her young the female has to build a nursery out of clay. This is neatly divided into long cells about the circumference of a cigarette and about half its length. In these the wasp intends to lay her eggs. However, she has another duty to perform before she can seal them up, for her eggs will hatch into grubs, and they will then require food until such time as they are ready to undergo the last stage of their metamorphosis into the perfect wasp. The hunting-wasp could stock her nursery with dead food, but by the time the eggs had hatched this food would have gone bad, so she is forced to evolve another method. Her favourite prey is the spider. Flying like some fierce hawk, she descends upon her unsuspecting victim and proceeds to sting it deeply and skilfully. The effect of this sting is extraordinary, for the spider is completely paralysed. The hunting-wasp then seizes it and carries it off to her nursery where it is carefully tucked away in one of the cells and an egg laid on it. If the spiders are small, there may be anything up to seven or eight in a cell. Having satisfied herself that the food-supply is adequate for her youngsters, the wasp then seals up the cells and flies off. Inside this grisly nursery the spiders lie in an unmoving row, in some cases for as much as seven weeks. To all intents and purposes the spiders are dead, even when you handle them, and not even under a magnifying glass can you detect the faintest sign of life. Thus they wait, so to speak, in cold storage until the eggs hatch out and the tiny grubs of the hunting-wasp start browsing on their paralysed bodies.

I think even the captain was a little shaken by the idea of being completely paralysed while something consumed you bit by bit, so I hastily switched to something a shade more pleasant. It was, in fact, the most delightful little creature, and a most ingenious one—the water-spider. Only recently in his history has man been able to live under water for any length of time, and one of his first steps in this direction was the diving-bell. Thousands of years before this the water-spider had evolved his own method of penetrating this new world beneath the surface of the water. To begin with, he can quite happily swim below the surface of the water, wearing his equivalent of the aqualung in the shape of an air bubble which he traps beneath his stomach and between his legs, so that he may breathe under water. This alone is extraordinary, but the water-spider goes even further: he builds his home beneath the surface of the

water, a web shaped like an inverted cup, firmly anchored to the water-weeds. He then proceeds to make several journeys to the surface, bringing with him air bubbles which he pushes into this dome-shaped web until it is full of them, and in this he can live and breathe as easily as if he were on land. In the breeding-season he picks out the house of a likely looking female and builds himself a cottage next door, and then, presumably being of a romantic turn of mind, he builds a sort of secret passage linking his house with that of his lady-love. Then he breaks down her wall, so that the air bubbles in each house intermix, and here in this strange underwater dwelling he courts the female, mates with her, and lives with her until the eggs are laid and hatched, and until their children, each carrying their little globule of air from their parent's home, swim out to start life on their own.

Even the captain seemed amused and intrigued by my story of the water-spider, and he was bound to admit, albeit reluctantly, that I had won my bet.

I suppose it must have been about a year later I was talking to a lady who had travelled on the same ship with the same captain.

"Wasn't he a delightful man?" she asked me. I agreed politely.

"He must have enjoyed having you on board," she went on, "because he was so keen on animals, you know. One night he kept us all spellbound for *at least* an hour, telling us about all these scientific discoveries—you know, things like radar—and how animals had been employing them for years and years before man discovered them. Really it was fascinating. I told him he ought to write it up into a talk and broadcast it on the B.B.C."

VANISHING ANIMALS

SOME time ago I was watching what must be the strangest group of refugees in this country, strange because they did not come here for the usual reasons, driven by either religious or political persecution from their own country. They came here quite by chance, and in doing so they were saved from extermination. They are the last of their kind, for in their country of origin their relatives were long ago hunted down, killed and eaten. They were, in fact, a herd of Père David deer.

Their existence was first discovered by a French missionary, one Father David, during the course of his work in China in the early eighteen hundreds. In those days China was as little known, zoologically speaking, as the great forests of Africa, and so Father David, who was a keen naturalist, spent his spare time collecting specimens of the flora and fauna to send back to the museum in Paris. In 1865 his work took him to Peking, and while he was there he heard a rumour that there was a strange herd of deer kept in the Imperial Hunting Park, just south of the city. This park had been for centuries a sort of combined hunting- and pleasure-ground for the Emperors of China, a great tract of land completely surrounded by a high wall forty-five miles long. It was strictly guarded by Tartar soldiers, and no one was allowed to enter or approach it. The French missionary was intrigued by the stories he heard about these peculiar deer, and he was determined that, guards or no guards, he was going to look inside the walled park and try to see the animals for himself. One day he got his opportunity and was soon lying up on top of the wall, looking down into the forbidden park and watching the various game animals feeding among the trees below him. Among them was a large herd of deer, and Father David realized that he was looking at an animal he had never seen before, and one which was, very probably, new to science.

Father David soon found out that the deer were strictly protected, and for anyone caught harming or killing them the sentence was death. He knew that any official request he might put forward for a specimen would be politely refused by the Chinese authorities, so he had to use other, less legal methods to get what he wanted. He discovered that the Tartar guards occasionally improved their rather sparse rations by the addition of a little venison; they were well aware what the penalty for their poaching would be if they were caught, and so, in spite of the missionary's pleadings, they refused to sell him the skins and antlers of the deer they killed, or indeed anything that might be evidence of their crime. However, Father David did not give up hope, and after a considerable time he was successful.

He met some guards who were either braver or perhaps poorer than the rest, and they obtained for him two deer skins, which he triumphantly shipped on to Paris. As he had expected, the deer turned out to be an entirely new species, and so it was named, in honour of its discoverer, the Père David deer—Father's David's deer.

Naturally, when zoos in Europe heard about this new kind of deer they wanted specimens for exhibition, and after protracted negotiations the Chinese authorities rather reluctantly allowed a few of the animals to be sent to the Continent. Although no one realized it at the time, it was this action that was to save the animals. In 1895, thirty years after the Père David deer first became known to the world, there were great floods around Peking; the Hun-Ho river overflowed its banks and caused havoc in the countryside, destroying the crops and bringing the population to near starvation. The waters also undermined the great wall round the Imperial Hunting Park. Parts of it collapsed, and through these gaps the herd of Père David deer escaped into the surrounding countryside, where they were quickly killed and eaten by the hungry peasants. So the deer perished in China, and the only ones left were the handful of live specimens in the various zoos in Europe.

Shortly before this disaster overtook the deer in China, a small herd of them had arrived in England. The present Duke of Bedford's father had, on his estate at Woburn in Bedfordshire, a wonderful collection of rare animals, and he had been most anxious to try to establish a herd of this new Chinese deer there. He bought as many specimens as he could from the Continental zoos, eighteen in all, and released them in his park. To the deer this must have seemed like home from home, for they settled down wonderfully, and soon started to breed. Today, the herd that started with eighteen now numbers over a hundred and fifty animals, the only herd of Père David deer in the world.

When I was working at Whipsnade Zoo four newly born Père David deer were sent over from Woburn for us to hand-rear. They were delightful little things, with long gangling limbs over which they had no control and strange slanted eyes that gave them a distinctly Oriental appearance. To begin with of course, they did not know what a feeding-bottle was for,

239

and we had to hold them firmly between our knees and force them to drink. But they very soon got the hang of it, and within a few days we had to open the stable door with extreme caution if we did not want to be knocked flying by an avalanche of deer, pushing and shoving in an effort to get at the bottle first.

They had to be fed once during the night, at midnight, and again at dawn, and so we worked out a system of night duties, one week on, one week off, between four keepers. I must say that I rather enjoyed the night duties. To pick one's way through the moonlit park towards the stable where the baby deer were kept, you had to pass several of the cages and paddocks, and the occupants were always on the move. The bears, looking twice as big in the half-light, would be snorting to each other as they shambled heavily through the riot of brambles in their cage, and they could be persuaded to leave their quest for snails and other delicacies if one had a bribe of sugar-lumps. They would come and squat upright in the moonlight, like a row of shaggy, heavy-breathing Buddhas, their great paws resting on their knees. They would throw back their heads and catch the flying lumps of sugar and eat them with much scrunching and smacking of lips. Then, seeing that you had no more in your pockets, they would sigh in a long-suffering manner and shamble off into the brambles again.

At one point the path led past the wolf wood, two acres or so of pines, dark and mysterious, with the moonlight silvering the trunks and laying dark shadows along the ground through which the wolf pack danced on swift, silent feet, like a strange black tide, swirling and twisting among the trunks. As a rule they made no sound, but occasionally you would hear them panting gently or the sudden snap of jaws and a snarl when one wolf barged against another.

Then you would reach the stable and light the lantern. The baby deer would hear you and start moving restlessly in their straw beds, bleating tremulously. As you opened the door they rushed forward, wobbling on their unsteady legs, sucking frantically at your fingers, the edge of your coat, and butting you suddenly in the legs with their heads, so that you were almost knocked down. Then came the exquisite moment when the teat was pushed into their mouths and they sucked frantically at the warm milk, their eyes staring, bubbles gathering like a moustache at the corners of their mouths. There is always a certain pleasure to be gained from bottle-feeding a baby animal, if only from its wholehearted enthusiasm and concentration on the job. But in the case of these deer there was something else as well. In the flickering light of the lantern, while the deer sucked and slobbered over the bottles, occasionally ducking their heads and butting at an imaginary udder with their heads, I was very conscious of the fact that they were the last of their kind.

At Whipsnade I had to look after another group of animals which belonged to a species now extinct in the wild state, and they were some of the most charming and comic animals I have ever had anything to do with. They were a small herd of white-tailed gnus.

The white-tailed gnu is a weird creature to look at: if you can imagine an animal with the body and legs of a finely built pony, a squat blunt face with very wide-spaced nostrils, a heavy mane of white hair on its thick neck, and a long white sweeping plume of a tail. The buffalo horns curve outward and upwards over the eyes, and the animal peers at you from under them with a perpetually indignant and suspicious expression. If the gnu behaved normally, this appearance would not be so noticeable, but the animal does not behave normally. Anything but, in fact. Its actions can only be described, very inadequately, as a cross between bebop and ballet, with a bit of yogi thrown in.

In the mornings, when I went to feed them, it always took me twice as long as it should have done because the gnus would start performing for me, and the sight was so ludicrous that I would lose all sense of time. They would prance and twist and buck, gallop, rear and pirouette, and while they did so they would throw their slim legs out at extraordinary and completely un-anatomical angles, and swish and curve their long tails as a circus ringmaster uses his whip. In the middle of the wild dance they would suddenly stop dead and glare at me, uttering loud, indignant belching snorts at my laughter. I watched them dancing their swift, wild dance across the paddock and they reminded me, in their antics and attitudes, of some strange heraldic creature from an ancient coat-of-arms, miraculously brought to life, prancing and posturing on a field of green turf.

It is difficult to imagine how anyone had the heart to kill these agile and amusing antelopes. However, the fact remains that the early settlers in South Africa found in the white-tailed gnu a valuable source of food, and so the great herds of high-spirited creatures were slaughtered unmercifully. The antelope contributed to its own downfall in an unusual way. They are incorrigibly curious creatures, and so when they saw the ox-drawn waggons of the early settlers moving across the veldt they simply had to go and investigate. They would dance and gallop round the waggons in circles, snorting and kicking their heels, and then suddenly stopping to stare. Naturally, with these habits of running away and then stopping to stare before they were out of range, they were used by enterprising "sportsmen" for rifle practice. So they were killed, and their numbers decreased so rapidly that it is amazing that they did not become extinct. Today there are under a thousand of these charming animals left alive, and these are split up into small herds on various estates in South Africa. If they were to become extinct, South Africa would have lost one of the most amusing and talented of her native fauna, an antelope whose actions could enliven any landscape, however dull.

Unfortunately, the Père David deer and the white-tailed gnu are not the only creatures in the world that are nearly extinct. The list of creatures that have vanished altogether, and others that have almost vanished, is a long and melancholy one. As man has spread across the earth he has wrought the most terrible havoc among the wild life by shooting, trapping, cutting and burning the forest, and by the callous and stupid introduction of enemies where there were no enemies before.

Take the dodo, for example, the great ponderous waddling pigeon, the size of a goose, that inhabited the island of Mauritius. Secure in its island home, this bird had lost the power of flight since there were no enemies to fly from, and, since there were no enemies, it nested on the ground in complete safety. But, as well as losing the power of flight, it seems to have the lost the power of recognizing an enemy when it saw one, for it was apparently an extremely tame and confiding creature. Then man discovered the dodo's paradise in about 1507, and with him came his evil familiars: dogs, cats, pigs, rats and goats. The dodo surveyed these new arrivals with an air of innocent interest. Then the slaughter began. The goats ate the undergrowth which provided the dodo with cover; dogs and cats hunted and harried the old birds; while pigs grunted their way round the island, eating the eggs and young, and the rats followed behind to finish the feast. By 1681 the fat, ungainly and harmless pigeon was extinct—as dead as the dodo.

All over the world the wild fauna has been whittled down steadily and remorselessly, and many lovely and interesting animals have been so reduced in numbers that, without protection and help, they can never re-establish themselves. If they cannot find sanctuary where they can live and breed undisturbed, their numbers will dwindle until they join the dodo, the quagga, and the great auk on the long list of extinct creatures.

Of course, in the last decade or so much has been done for the protection of wild life: sanctuaries and reserves have been started, and the reintroduction of a species into areas where it had become extinct is taking place. In Canada, for instance, beavers are now reintroduced into certain areas by means of aeroplane. The animal is put in a special box attached to a parachute, and when the plane flies over the area it drops the cage and its beaver passenger out. The cage floats down on the end of the parachute, and when it hits the ground it opens automatically and the beaver then makes its way to the nearest stream or lake.

But although much is being done, there is still a very great deal to do. Unfortunately, the majority of useful work in animal preservation has been done mainly for animals which are of some economic importance to man, and there are many obscure species of no economic importance which, although they are protected on paper, as it were, are in actual fact being allowed to die out because nobody, except a few interested zoologists, considers them important enough to spend money on.

As mankind increases year by year, and as he spreads farther over the globe burning and destroying, it is some small comfort to know that there are certain private individuals and some institutions who consider that the work of trying to save and give sanctuary to these harried animals is of some importance. It is important work for many reasons, but perhaps the best of them is this: man, for all his genius, cannot create a species, nor can he recreate one he has destroyed. There would be a dreadful outcry if anyone suggested obliterating, say, the Tower of London, and quite rightly so; yet a unique and wonderful species of animal which has taken hundreds of thousands of years to develop to the stage we see today, can be snuffed out like a candle without more than a handful of people raising a finger or a voice in protest. So, until we consider animal life to be worthy of the consideration and reverence we bestow upon old books and pictures and historic monuments, there will always be the animal refugee living a precarious life on the edge of extermination, dependent for existence on the charity of a few human beings.

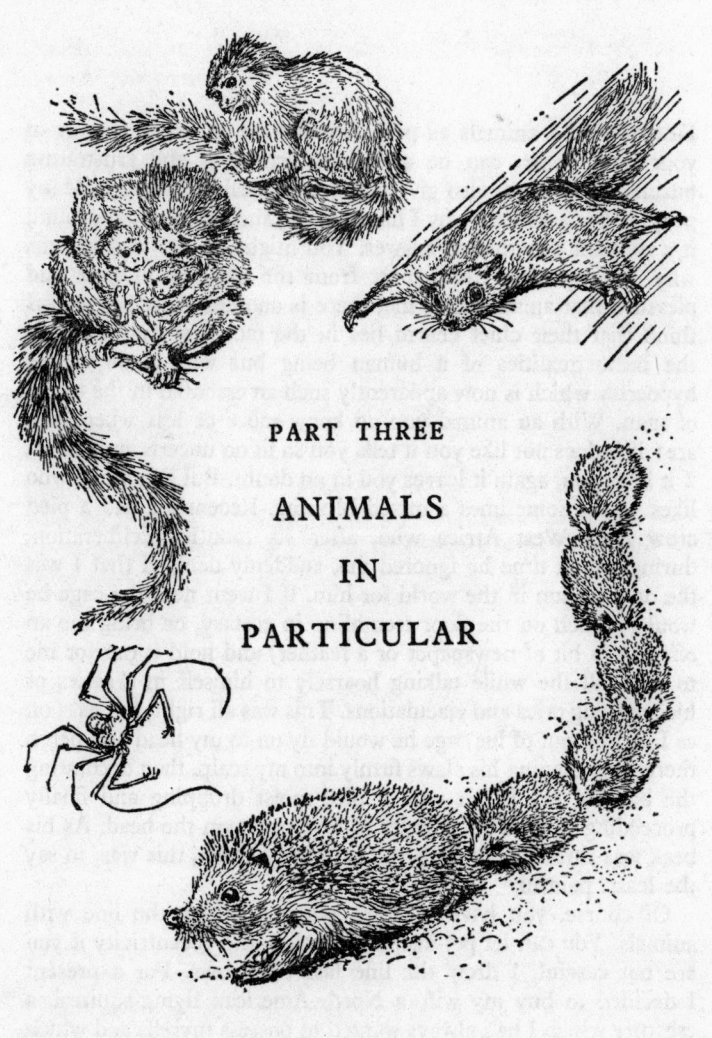

PART THREE

ANIMALS

IN

PARTICULAR

KEEPING wild animals as pets, whether on an expedition or in your own home, can be a tedious, irritating and frustrating business, but it can also give you a great deal of pleasure. Many people have asked me why I like animals, and I have always found it a difficult question to answer. You might just as well ask me why I like eating. But, apart from the obvious interest and pleasure that animals give me, there is another aspect as well. I think that their chief charm lies in the fact that they have all the basic qualities of a human being but with none of the hypocrisy which is now apparently such an essential in the world of man. With an animal you do know more or less where you are: if it does not like you it tells you so in no uncertain manner; if it likes you, again it leaves you in no doubt. But an animal who likes you is sometimes a mixed blessing. Recently I had a pied crow from West Africa who, after six months' deliberation, during which time he ignored me, suddenly decided that I was the only person in the world for him. If I went near the cage he would crouch on the floor trembling in ecstasy, or bring me an offering (a bit of newspaper or a feather) and hold it out for me to take, all the while talking hoarsely to himself in a series of hiccoughing cries and ejaculations. This was all right, but as soon as I let him out of his cage he would fly on to my head and perch there, first digging his claws firmly into my scalp, then decorating the back of my jacket with a nice moist dropping and finally proceeding to give me a series of love pecks on the head. As his beak was three inches long and extremely sharp, this was, to say the least, painful.

Of course, you have to know where to draw the line with animals. You can let pet-keeping develop into eccentricity if you are not careful. I drew the line last Christmas. For a present I decided to buy my wife a North American flying-squirrel, a creature which I had always wanted to possess myself, and which I was sure she would like. The animal duly arrived, and we were both captivated by it. As it seemed extremely nervous, we thought it would be a good idea to keep it in our bedroom for a week or two, so that we could talk to it at night when it came out, and let it grow used to us. This plan would have worked quite well but for one thing. The squirrel cunningly gnawed its way out of the cage and took up residence behind the wardrobe. At first this did not seem too bad. We could sit in bed at night and watch it doing acrobatics on the wardrobe, scuttling up and and down the dressing-table, carrying off the nuts and apple we had left there for it. Then came New Year's Eve when we had been invited to a party for which I had to don my dinner-jacket. All was well until I opened a drawer in my dressing-table, when I discovered the answer to the question that had puzzled us for some time: where did the flying-squirrel store all the nuts, apple, bread and other bits of food? My brand-new cummerbund, which I had never even worn, looked like a piece of delicate Madeira lacework. The bits that had been chewed out of it had been very economically saved and used to build little nests, one on the front of each of my dress shirts. In these nests had been collected seventy-two hazel nuts, five walnuts, fourteen pieces of bread, six mealworms, fifty-two bits of apple and twenty grapes. The grapes and the apple had, of course, disintegrated somewhat with the passage of time and had left most interesting Picasso designs in juice across the front of my shirts.

I had to go to the party in a suit. The squirrel is now in Paignton Zoo.

The other day my wife said that she thought a baby otter would make a delightful pet, but I changed the subject hurriedly.

ANIMAL PARENTS

I HAVE the greatest respect for animal parents. When I was young I tried my hand at rearing a number of different creatures, and since then, on my animal-collecting trips for zoos to various parts of the world, I have had to mother quite a number of baby animals, and I have always found it a most nerve-racking task.

The first real attempt I made at being a foster-mother was to four baby hedgehogs. The female hedgehog is a very good mother. She constructs an underground nursery for the reception of her young; a circular chamber about a foot below ground-level, lined with a thick layer of dry leaves. Here she gives birth to her babies, which are blind and helpless. They are covered with a thick coating of spikes, but these are white and soft, as though made of rubber. They gradually harden and turn brown when the babies are a few weeks old. When they are old enough to leave the nursery the mother leads them out and shows them how to hunt for food; they walk in line, rather like a school crocodile, the tail of one held in the mouth of the baby behind. The baby at the head of the column holds tight to mother's tail with grim determination, and they wend their way through the twilit hedgerows like a strange prickly centipede.

To a mother hedgehog the rearing of her babies seems to present no problems. But when I was suddenly presented with four blind, white, rubbery-spiked babies to rear, I was not so sure. We were living in Greece at the time, and the nest, which was about the size of a football and made of oak leaves, had been dug up by a peasant working in his fields. The first job was to feed the babies, for the ordinary baby's feeding-bottle only took a teat far too large for their tiny mouths. Luckily, the young daughter of a friend of mine had a doll's feeding-bottle, and after much bribery I got her to part with it. After a time the hedgehogs took to this and thrived on a diet of diluted cow's milk.

I kept them at first in a shallow cardboard box where I had put the nest. But in record time the original nest was so unhygienic that I found myself having to change the leaves ten or twelve times a day. I began to wonder if the mother hedgehog spent her day rushing to and fro with piles of fresh leaves to keep her nest clean, and, if she did, how on earth she found time to satisfy the appetites of her babies. Mine were always ready for food at any hour of the day or night. You had only to touch the box and a chorus of shrill screams arose from four little pointed faces poking out of the leaves, each head decorated with a crew-cut of white spikes; and the little black noses would whiffle desperately from side to side in an effort to locate the bottle.

Most baby animals know when they have had enough, but in my experience this does not apply to baby hedgehogs. Like four survivors from a raft, they flung themselves on to the bottle and sucked and sucked and sucked as though they had not had a decent meal in weeks. If I had allowed it they would have drunk twice as much as was good for them. As it was, I think I tended to overfeed them, for their tiny legs could not support the weight of their fat bodies, and they would advance across the carpet with a curious swimming motion, their tummies dragging on the ground. However, they progressed very well: their legs grew stronger, their eyes opened, and they would even make daring excursions as much as six inches away from their box.

I was very proud of my prickly family, and looked forward to the day when I would be able to take them for walks in the evening and find them delicious titbits like snails or wild strawberries. Unfortunately this dream was never realized. It so happened that I had to leave home for a day, to return the following morning. It was impossible for me to take the babies with me, so I had to leave them in charge of my sister. Before I left, I emphasized the greediness of the hedgehogs and told her that on no account were they to have more than one bottle of milk each, however much they squeaked for it.

I should have known my sister better.

When I returned the following day and enquired how my hedgehogs were, she gave me a reproachful look. I had, she said, been slowly starving the poor little things to death. With a dreadful sense of foreboding, I asked her how much she had been giving them at each meal. Four bottles each, she replied, and you should just see how lovely and fat they are getting. There was no denying they were fat. Their little tummies were so bloated their tiny feet could not even touch the ground. They looked like weird, prickly footballs to which someone by mistake had attached four legs and a nose. I did the best I could, but within twenty-four hours all four of them had died of acute enteritis. No one, of course, was more sorry than my sister, but I think she could tell by the frigid way I accepted her apologies that it was the last time she would be left in charge of any of my foster-children.

Not all animals are as good as the hedgehog at looking after their babies. Some, in fact, treat the whole business with a rather casual and modern attitude. One such is the kangaroo. Baby kangaroos are born in a very unfinished condition. They are actually embryos, for a big red kangaroo squatting on its haunches may measure five feet high and yet give birth to a baby only about half an inch long. This blind and naked blob of life has to find its way up over the mother's belly and into her pouch. In its primitive condition you would think this would be hard enough, but the whole thing is made doubly difficult by the fact that as yet the baby kangaroo can use only its front legs; the hind legs are neatly crossed over its tail. During this time the mother just squats there and gives her baby no help whatever, though occasionally she has been seen to lick a kind of trail through the fur, which may act as some sort of guide. Thus the tiny, premature offspring is forced to crawl through a jungle of fur until, as much by chance as good management, it reaches the pouch, climbs inside and clamps itself on to the teat. This is a feat that makes the ascent of Everest pale into insignificance.

I have never had the privilege of trying to hand-rear a baby kangaroo, but I have had some experience with a young wallaby, which is closely related to the species and looks just like a miniature kangaroo. I was working at Whipsnade Zoo as a keeper. The wallabies there are allowed to run free in the park, and one female, carrying a well-formed youngster, was chased by a group of young lads. In her fright she did what all the kangaroo family does in moments of stress: she tossed her youngster out of her pouch. I found it some time afterwards, lying in the long grass, twitching convulsively and making faint sucking squeaks with its mouth. It was, quite frankly, the most unprepossessing baby animal I had ever seen. About a foot long, it was blind, hairless and a bright sugar-pink. It seemed to possess no control over any part of its body except its immense hind feet, which it kicked vigorously at intervals. It had been badly bruised by its fall and I had grave doubts as to whether it would live. None the less I took it back to my lodgings and, after some argument with the landlady, kept it in my bedroom.

It fed eagerly from a bottle, but the chief difficulty lay in keeping it warm enough. I wrapped it in flannel and surrounded it with hot-water bottles, but these kept growing cold, and I was afraid it would catch a chill. The obvious thing to do was to carry it close to my body, so I put it inside my shirt. It was then that I realized for the first time what a mother wallaby must suffer. Apart from the nuzzling and sucking that went on, at regular intervals the baby would lash out its hind feet, well armed with claws, and kick me accurately in the pit of the stomach. After a few hours I began to feel as though I had been in the ring with Primo Carnera for a practice bout. It was obvious I would have to think of something else, or develop stomach ulcers. I tried putting him round the back of my shirt, but he would very soon scramble his way round to the front with his long claws in a series of convulsive kicks. Sleeping with him at night was purgatory, for apart from the all-in wrestling in which he indulged, he would sometimes kick so strongly that he shot out of bed altogether, and I was constantly forced to lean out of bed and pick him up from the floor. Unfortunately he died in two days, obviously from some sort of internal haemorrhage. I am afraid I viewed his demise with mixed feelings, although it was a pity to be deprived of the opportunity of mothering such an unusual baby.

If the kangaroo is rather dilatory about her child, the pigmy marmoset is a paragon of virtue, or rather the male is. About the size of a large mouse, clad in neat brindled green fur, and with a tiny face and bright hazel eyes, the pigmy marmoset looks like something out of a fairy tale, a small furry gnome or perhaps a kelpie. As soon as the courtship is over and the female gives birth, her diminutive spouse turns into the ideal husband. The babies, generally twins, he takes over from the moment they are born and carries them slung on his hips like a couple of saddle-bags. He keeps them clean by constant grooming, hugs them to him at night to keep them warm, and only hands them over to his rather disinterested wife at feeding-time. But he is so anxious to get them back that you have the impression he would feed them himself if only he could. The pigmy marmoset is definitely a husband worth having.

Strangely enough, monkeys are generally the stupidest babies, and it takes them a long time to learn to drink out of a bottle. Having successfully induced them to do this, you have to go through the whole tedious performance again, when they are a little bit older, in an attempt to teach them to drink out of a saucer. They always seem to feel that the only way of drinking out of a saucer is to duck the face beneath the surface of the milk and stay there until you either burst for want of air or drown in your own drink.

One of the most charming baby monkeys I have ever had was a little moustached guenon. His back and tail were moss-green and his belly and whiskers a beautiful shade of buttercup yellow. Across his upper lip spread a large banana-shaped area of white, like the magnificent moustaches of some retired brigadier. Like all baby monkeys, his head seemed too big for his body, and he had long gangling limbs. He fitted very comfortably into a tea-cup.

When I first had him he refused to drink out of a bottle, plainly convinced that it was some sort of fiendish torture I had invented, but eventually, when he got the hang of it, he would go quite mad when he saw the bottle arrive, fasten his mouth on to the teat, clasp the bottle passionately in his arms and roll on his back. As the bottle was at least three times his size, he made one think of a desperate survivor clinging on to a large white airship.

When he learnt, after the normal grampus-like splutterings, to drink out of a saucer, the situation became fraught with difficulty. He would be placed on a table and then his saucer of milk produced. As soon as he saw it coming he would utter a piercing scream and start trembling all over, as if he were suffering with ague or St. Vitus dance, but it was really a form of excited rage; excitement at the sight of the milk, rage that it was never put on the table quickly enough for him. He screamed and trembled to such an extent that he bounced up in the air like a grasshopper. If you were unwise enough to put the saucer down without hanging on to his tail, he would utter one final shrill scream of triumph and dive headfirst into the centre of it, and when you had mopped the resulting tidal wave of milk from your face, you would find him sitting indignantly in the middle of an empty saucer, chattering with rage because there was nothing for him to drink.

One of the main problems when you are rearing baby animals is to keep them warm enough at night, and this, strangely enough, applies even in the tropics where the temperature drops considerably after dark. In the wild state, of course, the babies cling to the dense fur of the mother and obtain warmth and shelter in that way. Hot-water bottles, as a substitute, I have found of very little use. They grow cold so quickly and you have to get up several times during the night to refill them, an exhausting process when you have a lot of baby animals to look after, as well as a whole collection of adult ones. So in most cases the simplest way is to take the babies into bed with you. You soon learn to sleep in one position—half-waking up in the night, should you wish to move, so that you avoid crushing them as you turn over.

I have at one time or another shared my bed with a great variety of young creatures, and sometimes several different species at once. On one occasion my narrow camp-bed contained three mongooses, two baby monkeys, a squirrel and a

young chimpanzee. There was just enough room left over for me. You might think that after taking all this trouble a little gratitude would come your way, but in many cases you get the opposite. One of my most impressive scars was inflicted by a young mongoose because I was five minutes late with his bottle. When people ask me about it now, I am forced to pretend it was given me by a charging jaguar. Nobody would believe me if I told them it was really a baby mongoose under the bed-clothes.

THE BANDITS

MY first introduction to the extraordinary little animals known as kusimanses took place at the London Zoo. I had gone into the Rodent House to examine at close range some rather lovely squirrels from West Africa. I was just about to set out on my first animal-collecting expedition, and I felt that the more familiar I was with the creatures I was likely to meet in the great rain-forest, the easier my job would be.

After watching the squirrels for a time, I walked round the house peering into the other cages. On one of them hung a rather impressive label which informed me that the cage contained a creature known as a Kusimanse (*Crossarchus obscurus*) and that it came from West Africa. All I could see in the cage was a pile of straw that heaved gently and rhythmically, while a faint sound of snoring was wafted out to me. As I felt that this animal was one I was sure to meet, I felt justified in waking it up and forcing it to appear.

Every zoo has a rule I always observe, and many others should observe it too: not to disturb a sleeping animal by poking it or throwing peanuts. They have precious little privacy as it is. However, I ignored my rule on this occasion and rattled my thumbnail to and fro along the bars. I did not really think this would have any effect. But as I did so a sort of explosion took place in the depths of the straw, and the next moment a long, rubbery tip-tilted nose appeared, to be followed by a rather rat-like face with small neat ears and bright inquisitive eyes. This little face appraised me for a minute; then, noticing the lump of sugar which I held tactfully near the bars, the animal uttered a faint, spinsterish squeak and struggled madly to release itself from the cocoon of straw wound round it.

When only the head had been visible, I had the impression it was only a small creature, about the size of the average ferret, but when it eventually broke loose from its covering and waddled into view, I was astonished at its relatively large body: it was, in fact, so fat as to be almost circular. Yet it shuffled over to the bars on its short legs and fell on the lump of sugar I offered, as though that was the first piece of decent food it had received in years.

It was, I decided, a species of mongoose, but its tip-tilted, whiffling nose and the glittering, almost fanatical eyes made it look totally unlike any mongoose I had ever seen. I was convinced now that its shape was due not to Nature but to overeating. It has very short legs and fine, rather slender paws, and when it trotted about the cage these legs moved so fast that they were little more than a blur beneath the bulky body. Each time I fed it a morsel of food it gave the same faint, breathless squeak: as much as to reproach me for tempting it away from its diet.

I was so captivated by this little animal that before I realized what I was doing I had fed it all the lump-sugar in my pocket. As soon as it knew that no more titbits were forthcoming, it uttered a long-suffering sigh and trotted away to dive into the straw. Within a couple of seconds it was sound asleep once more. I decided there and then that if kusimanses were to be obtained in the area I was visiting, I would strain every nerve to find one.

Three months later I was deep in the heart of the Cameroon rain-forests and here I found I had ample opportunity for getting to know the kusimanse. Indeed, they were about the commonest members of the mongoose family, and I often saw them when I was sitting concealed in the forest waiting for some completely different animal to make its appearance.

The first one I saw appeared suddenly out of the undergrowth on the banks of a small stream. He kept me amused for a long time with a display of his crab-catching methods: he waded into the shallow water and with the aid of his long, turned-up nose (presumably holding his breath when he did so) he turned

over all the rocks he could find until he unearthed one of the large, black, freshwater crabs. Without a second's hesitation he grabbed it in his mouth and, with a quick flick of his head, tossed it on to the bank. He then chased after it, squeaking with delight and danced round it, snapping away until at last it was dead. When an exceptionally large crab succeeded in giving him a nip on the end of his *retroussé* nose, I am afraid my stifled amusement caused the kusimanse to depart hastily into the forest.

On another occasion I watched one of these little beasts using precisely the same methods to catch frogs, but this time without much success. I felt he must be young and inexperienced in the art of frog-catching. After much laborious hunting and snuffling, he would catch a frog and hurl it shorewards; but, long before he had waddled out to the bank after it, the frog would have recovered itself and leapt back into the water, and the kusimanse would be forced to start all over again.

One morning a native hunter walked into my camp carrying a small palm-leaf basket, and peering into it I saw three of the strangest little animals imaginable. They were about the size of new-born kittens, with tiny legs and somewhat moth-eaten tails. They were covered with bright gingery-red fur which stood up in spikes and tufts all over their bodies making them look almost like some weird species of hedgehog. As I gazed down at them, trying to identify them, they lifted their little faces and peered up at me. The moment I saw the long, pink, rubbery noses I knew they were kusimanses, and very young ones at that, for their eyes were only just open and they had no teeth. I was very pleased to obtain these babies, but after I had paid the hunter and set to work on the task of trying to teach them to feed, I began to wonder if I had not got more than I bargained for. Among the numerous feeding-bottles I had brought with me I could not find a teat small enough to fit their mouths, so I was forced to try the old trick of wrapping some cotton-wool round the end of a matchstick, dipping it in milk and letting them suck it. At first they took the view that I was some sort of monster endeavouring to choke them. They struggled and squeaked, and every time I pushed the cotton-wool into their mouths they frantically spat it out again. Fortunately it was not long before they discovered that the cotton-wool contained milk, and then they were no more trouble, except that they were liable to suck so hard in their enthusiasm that the cotton-wool would part company with the end of the matchstick and disappear down their throats.

At first I kept them in a small basket by my bed. This was the most convenient spot, for I had to get up in the middle of the night to feed them. For the first week or so they really behaved very well, spending most of the day sprawled on their bed of dried leaves, their stomachs bulging and their paws twitching. Only at meal-times would they grow excited, scrambling round and round inside the basket, uttering loud squeaks and treading heavily on one another.

It was not long before the baby kusimanses developed their front teeth (which gave them a firmer and more disastrous grip on the cotton-wool), and as their legs got stronger they became more and more eager to see the world that lay outside their basket. They had the first feed of the day when I drank my morning tea; and I would lift them out of their basket and put them on my bed so that they could have a walk round. I had, however, to call an abrupt halt to this habit, for one morning, while I was quietly sipping my tea, one of the baby kusimanses discovered my bare foot sticking out from under the bed-clothes, and decided that if he bit my toe hard enough it might produce milk. He laid hold with his needle-sharp teeth, and his brothers, thinking they were missing a feed, instantly joined him. When I had locked them up in their basket again and finished mopping tea off myself and the bed, I decided these morning romps would have to cease. They were too painful.

This was merely the first indication of the trouble in store for me. Very soon they had become such a nuisance that I was forced to christen them the Bandits. They grew fast, and as soon as their teeth had come through they started to eat egg and a little raw meat every day, as well as their milk. Their appetites seemed insatiable, and their lives turned into one long quest for food. They appeared to think that everything was edible unless proved otherwise. One of the things of which they made a light snack was the lid of their basket. Having demolished this they hauled themselves out and went on a tour of inspection round the camp. Unfortunately, and with unerring accuracy, they made their way to the one place where they could do the maximum damage in the minimum time: the place where the food and medical supplies were stored. Before I discovered them they had broken a dozen eggs and, to judge by the state of them, rolled in the contents. They had fought with a couple of bunches of bananas and apparently won, for the bananas looked distinctly the worse for wear. Having slaughtered the fruit, they had moved on and upset two bottles of vitamin product. Then, to their delight, they had found two large packets of boracic powder. These they had burst open and scattered far and wide, while large quantities of the white powder had stuck to their egg-soaked fur. By the time I found them they were on the point of having a quick drink from a highly pungent and poisonous bucket of disinfectant, and I grabbed them only just in time. Each of them looked like some weird Christmas-cake decoration, in a coat stiff with boracic and egg-yolk. It took me three-quarters of an hour to clean them up. Then I put them in a larger and stronger basket and hoped that this would settle them.

It took them two days to break out of *this* basket.

This time they had decided to pay a visit to all the other animals I had. They must have had a fine time round the cages, for there were always some scraps of food lying about.

Now at that time I had a large and very beautiful monkey, called Colly, in my collection. Colly was a colobus, perhaps one of the most handsome of African monkeys. Their fur is coal-black and snow-white, hanging in long silky strands round their bodies like a shawl. They have a very long plume-like tail, also black and white. Colly was a somewhat vain monkey and spent a lot of her time grooming her lovely coat and posing in various parts of the cage. On this particular afternoon she had decided to enjoy a siesta in the bottom of her box, while waiting for me to bring her some fruit. She lay there like a sunbather on a beach, her eyes closed, her hands folded neatly on her chest. Unfortunately, however, she had pushed her tail through the bars so that it lay on the ground outside like a feathery black-and-white scarf that someone had dropped. Just as Colly was drifting off into a deep sleep, the Bandits appeared on the scene.

The Bandits, as I pointed out, believed that everything in the world, no matter how curious it looked, might turn out to be edible. In their opinion it was always worth sampling everything, just in case. When he saw Colly's tail lying on the ground ahead, apparently not belonging to anyone, the eldest Bandit decided it must be a tasty morsel of something or other that Providence had placed in his path. So he rushed forward and sank his sharp little teeth into it. His two brothers, feeling that there was plenty of this meal for everyone, joined him immediately. Thus was Colly woken out of a deep and refreshing sleep by three sets of extremely sharp little teeth fastening themselves almost simultaneously in her tail. She gave a wild scream of fright and scrambled towards the top of her cage. But the Bandits were not going to be deprived of this tasty morsel without a struggle, and they hung on grimly. The higher Colly climbed in her cage, the higher she lifted the Bandits off the ground, and when eventually I got there in response to her yells, I found the Bandits, like some miniature trapeze-artists, hanging by their teeth three feet off the ground. It took me five minutes to make them let go, and then I managed it only by blowing cigarette-smoke in their faces and making them sneeze. By the time I had got them safely locked up again, poor Colly was a nervous wreck.

I decided the Bandits must have a proper cage if I did not want the rest of my animals driven hysterical by their attentions. I built them a very nice one, with every modern convenience. It had a large and spacious bedroom at one end, and an open playground and dining-room at the other. There were two doors, one to admit my hand to their bedroom, the other to put their food into their dining-room. The trouble lay in feeding them. As soon as they saw me approach with a plate they would cluster round the doorway, screaming excitedly, and the moment the door was opened they would shoot out, knock the plate from my hand and fall to the ground with it, a tangled mass of kusimanses, raw meat, raw egg and milk. Quite often when I went to pick them up they would bite me, not vindictively but simply because they would mistake my fingers for something edible. Yes, feeding the Bandits was not only a wasteful process but an extremely painful one as well. By the time I got them safely back to England they had bitten me twice as frequently as any animal I have ever kept. So it was with a real feeling of relief that I handed them over to a zoo.

The next day I went round to see how they were settling down. I found them in a huge cage, pattering about and looking, I felt, rather lost and bewildered by all the new sights and sounds. Poor little things, I thought, they have had the wind taken out of their sails. They looked so subdued and forlorn. I began to feel quite sorry to have parted with them. I stuck my finger through the wire and waggled it, calling to them. I thought it might comfort them to talk to someone they knew. I should have known better: the Bandits shot across the cage in a grim-faced bunch and fastened on to my finger like bulldogs. With a yelp of pain I at last managed to get my finger away, and as I left them, mopping the blood from my hand, I decided that perhaps, after all, I was not *so* sorry to see the back of them. Life without the Bandits might be considerably less exciting—but it would not hurt nearly so much.

WILHELMINA

Most people, when they learn for the first time that I collect wild animals for zoos, ask the same series of questions in the same order. First they ask if it is dangerous, to which the answer is no, it is not, providing you do not make any silly mistakes. Then they ask how I catch the animals—a more difficult question to answer, for there are many hundreds of ways of capturing wild animals: sometimes you have no set method, but have to improvise something on the spur of the moment. Their third question is, invariably: don't you become attached to your animals and find it difficult to part with them at the end of an expedition? The answer is, of course, that you do, and sometimes parting with a creature you have kept for eight months can be a heartbreaking process.

Occasionally you even find yourself getting attached to the strangest of beasts, some weird creature you would never in the normal way have thought you could like. One such beast as this, I remember, was Wilhelmina.

Wilhelmina was a whip-scorpion, and if anyone had told me that the day would come when I would feel even the remotest trace of affection for a whip-scorpion I would never have believed them. Of all the creatures on the face of this earth the whip-scorpion is one of the least prepossessing. To those who do not adore spiders (and I am one of those people) the whip-scorpion is a form of living nightmare. It resembles a spider with a body the size of a walnut that has been run over by a steam-roller and flattened to a wafer-thin flake. To this flake are attached what appear to be an immense number of long, fine and crooked legs which spread out to the size of a soup-plate. To cap it all, on the front (if such a creature can be said to have a front), are two enormously long slender legs like whips, about twelve inches long in a robust specimen. It possesses the ability to skim about at incredible speed and with apparently no effort—up, down or sideways—and to squeeze its revolting body into a crack that would scarcely accommodate a piece of tissue-paper.

That is a whip-scorpion, and to anyone who distrusts spiders it is the personification of the devil. Fortunately they are harmless, unless you happen to have a weak heart.

I made my first acquaintance with Wilhelmina's family when I was on a collecting trip to the tropical forest of West Africa. For many different reasons, hunting in these forests is always difficult. To begin with, the trees are enormous, some as much as a hundred and fifty feet high, with trunks as fat as a factory chimney. Their head foliage is thick, luxuriant and twined with creepers and the branches are decorated with various parasitic plants like a curious hanging garden. All this may be eighty or a hundred feet above the forest floor, and the only way to reach it is to climb a trunk as smooth as a plank which has not a single branch for the first seventy feet of its length. This, the top layer of the forest, is by far the most thickly populated, for in the comparative safety of the tree-tops live a host of creatures which rarely, if ever, descends to ground-level. Setting traps in the forest canopy is a difficult and tedious operation. It may take a whole morning to find a way up a tree, climb it and set the trap in a suitable position. Then, just as you have safely regained the forest floor, your trap goes off with a triumphant clang, and the whole laborious process has to be endured once more. Thus, although trap-setting in the tree-tops is a painful necessity, you are always on the look-out for some slightly easier method of obtaining the animals you want. Probably one of the most successful and exciting of these methods is to smoke out the giant trees.

Some of the forest trees, although apparently sound and solid, are actually hollow for part or all of their length. These are the trees to look for, though they are not so easy to find. A day of searching in the forest might end with the discovery of six of them, perhaps one of which will yield good results when finally smoked out.

Smoking out a hollow tree is quite an art. To begin with, you must, if necessary, enlarge the opening at the base of the trunk and lay a small fire of dry twigs. Then two Africans are sent up the tree with nets to cover all the holes and cracks at the upper end of the trunk, and then station themselves at convenient points to catch any animals that emerge. When all is ready, you start the fire, and as soon as it is crackling you lay on top of the flames a large bundle of fresh green leaves. Immediately the flames die away and in their place rises a column of thick and pungent smoke. The great hollow interior of the tree acts like a gigantic chimney, and the smoke is whisked up inside. You never realize, until you light the fire, quite how many holes and cracks there are in the trunk of the tree. As you watch, you see a tiny tendril of smoke appear magically on the bark perhaps twenty feet from the ground, coiling out of an almost invisible hole; a short pause and ten feet higher three more little holes puff smoke like miniature cannon-mouths. Thus, guided by the tiny streamers of smoke appearing at intervals along the trunk, you can watch the progress of the smoking. If the tree is a good one, you have only time to watch the smoke get halfway up, for it is then that the animals start to break cover and you become very busy indeed.

When one of these hollow trees is inhabited, it is really like a block of flats. In the ground-floor apartments, for example, you find things like the giant land-snails, each the size of an apple, and they come gliding out of the base of the tree with all the speed a snail is capable of mustering, even in an emergency. They may be followed by other creatures who prefer the lower apartments or else are unable to climb: the big forest toads, for example, whose backs are cleverly marked out to resemble a dead leaf, and whose cheeks and sides are a beautiful mahogany red. They come waddling out from among the tree-roots with the most ludicrously indignant expressions on their faces, and on reaching the open air suddenly squat down and stare about them in a pathetic and helpless sort of way.

Having evicted all the ground-floor tenants, you then have to wait a short time before the occupants higher up have a chance to make their way down to the opening. Almost invariably giant millipedes are among the first to appear—charming creatures that look like long brown sausages, with a fringe of legs along the underside of their bodies. They are quite harmless and rather imbecile creatures for which I have a very soft spot. One of their most ridiculous antics, when placed on a table, is to set off walking, all their legs working furiously, and on coming to the edge they never seem to notice it and continue to walk out into space until the weight of their body bends them over. Then, half on and half off the table, they pause, consider, and eventually decide that something is wrong. And so, starting with the extreme hind pair of legs, they go into reverse and get themselves on to the table again—only to crawl to the other side and repeat the performance.

Immediately after the appearance of the giant millipedes all the other top-floor tenants of the tree break cover together, some making for the top of the tree, others for the bottom. Perhaps there are squirrels with black ears, green bodies and tails of the most beautiful flame colour; giant grey dormice who gallop out of the tree, trailing their bushy tails behind them like puffs of smoke; perhaps a pair of bush-babies, with their great innocent eyes and their slender attenuated and trembly hands, like those of very old men. And then, of course, there are the bats: great fat brown bats with curious flower-like decorations on the skin of their noses and large transparent ears; others bright ginger, with black ears twisted down over their heads and pig-like snouts. And as this pageant of wild life appears the whip-scorpions are all over the place, skimming up and down the tree with a speed and silence that is un-nerving and uncanny, squeezing their revolting bodies into the thinnest crack as you make a swipe at them with the net, only to reappear suddenly ten feet lower down the tree, skimming towards you apparently with the intention of disappearing into your shirt. You step back hurriedly and the creature vanishes: only the tips of a pair of antennae, wriggling from the depths of a crevice in the bark that would hardly accommodate a visiting-card, tell you of its whereabouts. Of the many creatures in the West African forest the whip-scorpion has been respon-sible for more shocks to my system than any other. The day a particularly large and leggy specimen ran over my bare arm, as I leant against a tree, will always be one of my most vivid memories. It took at least a year off my life.

But to return to Wilhelmina. She was a well-brought-up little whip-scorpion, one of a family of ten, and I started my intimate acquaintance with her when I captured her mother. All this happened quite by chance.

I had for many days been smoking out trees in the forest in search of an elusive and rare little animal known as the pigmy scaly-tail. These little mammals, which look like mice with long feathery tails, have a curious membrane of skin stretched from ankle to wrist, with the aid of which they glide around the forest with the ease of swallows. The scaly-tails live in colonies in hollow trees, but the difficulty lay in finding a tree that contained a colony. When, after much fruitless hunting, I did discover a group of these prizes, and moreover actually managed to capture some, I felt considerably elated. I even started to take a benign interest in the numerous whip-scorpions that were scuttling about the tree. Then suddenly I noticed one which looked so extraordinary, and was behaving in such a peculiar manner, that my attention was at once arrested. To begin with, this whip-scorpion seemed to be wearing a green fur-coat that almost completely covered her chocolate body. Secondly, it was working its way slowly and carefully down the tree with none of the sudden fits and starts common to the normal whip-scorpion.

Wondering if the green fur-coat and the slow walk were symptoms of extreme age in the whip-scorpion world I moved closer to examine the creature. To my astonishment I found that the fur-coat was composed of baby whip-scorpions, each not much larger than my thumb-nail, which were obviously fairly recent additions to the family. They were, in extraordinary contrast to their dark-coloured mother, a bright and bilious green, the sort of green that confectioners are fond of using in cake decorations. The mother's slow and stately progress was due to her concern lest one of her babies lose its grip and drop off. I realized, rather ruefully, that I had never given the private life of the whip-scorpion much thought, and it had certainly never occurred to me that the female would be sufficiently maternal to carry her babies on her back. Overcome with remorse at my thoughtlessness, I decided that here was an ideal chance for me to catch up on my studies of these creatures. So I captured the female very carefully—to avoid dropping any of her progeny—and carried her back to camp.

I placed the mother and children in a large roomy box with plenty of cover in the way of bark and leaves. Every morning I had to look under these, rather gingerly I admit, to see if she was all right. At first, the moment I lifted the bark under which she was hiding, she would rush out and scuttle up the side of the box, a distressing habit which always made me jump and slam the lid down. I was very much afraid that one day I might do this and trap her legs or antennae, but fortunately after the first three days or so she settled down, and would even let me renew the leaves and bark in her box without taking any notice.

I had the female whip-scorpion and her babies for two months, and during that time the babies ceased to ride on their mother's back. They scattered and took up residence in various parts of the box, grew steadily and lost their green colouring in favour of brown. Whenever they grew too big for their skins they would split them down the back and step out of them, like spiders. Each time they did so they would emerge a little larger and a little browner. I discovered that while the mother would tackle anything from a small grasshopper to a large beetle, the babies were fussy and demanded small spiders, slugs and other easily digestible fare. They all appeared to be thriving, and I began to feel rather proud of them. Then one day I returned to camp after a few hours hunting in the forest to find that tragedy had struck.

A tame Patas monkey I kept tied up outside the tent had eaten through his rope and been on a tour of investigation. Before anyone had noticed it he had eaten a bunch of bananas, three mangos and four hard-boiled eggs, he had broken two bottles of disinfectant, and rounded the whole thing off by knocking my whip-scorpion box on to the floor. It promptly broke open and scattered the family on the ground, and the Patas monkey, a creature of depraved habits, had set to work and eaten them. When I got back he was safely tied up again, and suffering from an acute attack of hiccoughs.

I picked up my whip-scorpion nursery and peered mournfully into it, cursing myself for having left it in such an accessible place, and cursing the monkey for having such an appetite. But then, to my surprise and delight, I found, squatting in

solitary state on a piece of bark, one of the baby whip-scorpions, the sole survivor of the massacre. Tenderly I moved it to a smaller and more burglar-proof cage, showered it with slugs and other delicacies and christened it, for no reason at all, Wilhelmina.

During the time I had Wilhelmina's mother, and Wilhelmina herself, I learnt quite a lot about whip-scorpions. I discovered that though quite willing to hunt by day if hungry, they were at their most lively during the night. During the day Wilhelmina was always a little dull-witted, but in the evening she woke up and, if I may use the expression, blossomed. She would stalk to and fro in her box, her pincers at the ready, her long antennae-like legs lashing out like whips ahead of her, seeking the best route. Although these tremendously elongated legs are supposed to be merely feelers, I got the impression that they could do more than this. I have seen them wave in the direction of an insect, pause and twitch, whereupon Wilhelmina would brace herself, almost as if she had smelt or heard her prey with the aid of her long legs. Sometimes she would stalk her food like this; at other times she would simply lie in wait until the unfortunate insect walked almost into her arms, and the powerful pincers would gather it lovingly into her mouth.

As she grew older I gave her bigger and bigger things to eat, and I found her courage extraordinary. She was rather like a pugnacious terrier who, the larger the opponent, the better he likes the fight. I was so fascinated by her skill and bravery in tackling insects as big or bigger than herself that one day, rather unwisely, I put a very large locust in with her. Without a moment's hesitation, she flew at him and grasped his bulky body in her pincers. To my alarm, however, the locust gave a hearty kick with his powerful hind legs and both he and Wilhelmina soared upwards and hit the wire-gauze roof of the cage with a resounding thump, then crashed back to the floor again. This rough treatment did not deter Wilhelmina at all, and she continued to hug the locust while he leapt wildly around the cage, thumping against the roof, until eventually he was exhausted. Then she settled down and made short work of him. But after this I was always careful to give her the smaller insects, for I had visions of a leg or one of her whips being broken off in such a rough contest.

By now I had become very fond and not a little proud of Wilhelmina. She was, as far as I knew, the only whip-scorpion to have been kept in captivity. What is more, she had become very tame. I had only to rap on the side of her box with my fingers and she would appear from under her piece of bark and wave her whips at me. Then, if I put my hand inside, she would climb on to my palm and sit there quietly while I fed her with slugs, creatures for which she still retained a passion.

When the time drew near for me to transport my large collection of animals back to England, I began to grow rather worried over Wilhelmina. It was a two-week voyage, and I could not take enough insect food for that length of time. I decided therefore to try making her eat raw meat. It took me a long time to achieve it, but once I had learnt the art of waggling the bit of meat seductively enough I found that Wilhelmina would grab it, and on this unlikely diet she seemed to thrive. On the journey down to the coast by lorry Wilhelmina behaved like a veteran traveller, sitting in her box and sucking a large chunk of raw meat almost throughout the trip. For the first day on board ship the strange surroundings made her a little sulky, but after that the sea air seemed to do her good and she became positively skittish. This was her undoing.

One evening when I went to feed her, she scuttled up as far as my elbow before I knew what was happening, dropped on to a hatch-cover and was just about to squeeze her way through a crack on a tour of investigation when I recovered from my astonishment and managed to grab her. For the next few days I fed her very cautiously, and she seemed to have quietened down and regained her former self-possession.

Then one evening she waggled her whips at me so plaintively that I lifted her out of her cage on the palm of my hand and started to feed her on the few remaining slugs I had brought for her in a tin. She ate two slugs, sitting quietly and decorously on my hand, and then suddenly she jumped. She could not have chosen a worse time, for as she was in mid-air a puff of wind swept round the bulkhead and whisked her away. I had a brief glimpse of her whips waving wildly, and then she was over the rail and gone, into the vast heaving landscape of the sea. I rushed to the rail and peered over, but it was impossible to spot so small a creature in the waves and froth below. Hurriedly

I threw her box over, in the vain hope that she might find it and use it as a raft. A ridiculous hope, I know, but I did not like to think of her drowning without making some attempt to save her. I could have kicked myself for my stupidity in lifting her out of her box; I never thought I would have been so affected by the loss of such a creature. I had grown very fond of her; she in her turn had seemed to trust me. It was a tragic way for the relationship to end. But there was one slight consolation: after my association with Wilhelmina I shall never again look at a whip-scorpion with quite the same distaste.

ADOPTING AN ANTEATER

MAKING a collection of two hundred birds, mammals and reptiles is rather like having two hundred delicate babies to look after. It needs a lot of hard work and patience. You have to make sure their diet suits them, that their cages are big enough, that they get neither too hot in the tropics nor too cold when you get near England. You have to de-worm, de-tick and de-flea them; you have to keep their cages and feeding-pots spotlessly clean.

But, above all, you have to make sure that your animals are *happy*. However well looked after, a wild animal will not live in captivity unless it is happy. I am talking, of course, of the adult, wild-caught creature. But occasionally you get a baby wild animal whose mother has perhaps met with an accident, and who has been found wandering in the forest. When you capture one of these, you must be prepared for a good deal of hard work and worry, and above all you must be ready to give the animal the affection and confidence it requires; for after a day or two you will have become the parent, and the baby will trust you and depend on you completely.

This can sometimes make life rather difficult. There have been periods when I have played the adopted parent to as many as six baby animals at once, and this is no joke. Quite apart from anything else, imagine rising at three o'clock in the morning, stumbling about, half-asleep, in an effort to prepare six different bottles of milk, trying to keep your eyes open enough to put the right amount of vitamin drops and sugar in, knowing all the time that you will have to be up again in three hours to repeat the performance.

Some time ago my wife and I were on a collecting trip in Paraguay, that country shaped like a boot-box which lies almost in the exact centre of South America. Here, in a remote part of the Chaco, we assembled a lovely collection of animals. Many things quite unconnected with animals happen on a collecting trip, things that frustrate your plans or irritate you in other ways. But politics, mercifully, had never before been among them. On this occasion, however, the Paraguayans decided to have a revolution, and as a direct result we had to release nearly the whole of our collection and escape to Argentina in a tiny four-seater plane.

Just before our retreat, an Indian had wandered into our camp carrying a sack from which had come the most extraordinary noises. It sounded like a cross between a cello in pain and a donkey with laryngitis. Opening the sack, the Indian tipped out one of the most delightful baby animals I had ever seen. She was a young giant anteater, and she could not have been more than a week old. She was about the size of a corgie, with black, ash-grey and white fur, a long slender snout and a pair of tiny, rather bleary eyes. The Indian said he had found her wandering about in the forest, honking forlornly. He thought her mother might have been killed by a jaguar.

The arrival of this baby put me in a predicament. I knew that we would be leaving soon and that the plane was so tiny that most of our equipment would have to be left behind to make room for the five or six creatures we were determined to take with us. To accept, at that stage, a baby anteater who weighed a considerable amount and who would have to be fussed over and bottle-fed, would be lunatic. Quite apart from anything else, no one, as far as I knew, had ever tried to rear a baby anteater on a bottle. The whole thing was obviously out of the question. Just as I had made up my mind the baby, still blaring pathetically, suddenly discovered my leg, and with a honk of joy shinned up it, settled herself in my lap and went to sleep. Silently I paid the Indian the price he demanded, and thus became a father to one of the most charming children I have ever met.

The first difficulty cropped up almost at once. We had a baby's feeding-bottle, but we had exhausted our supply of teats. Luckily a frantic house-to-house search of the little village where we were living resulted in the discovery of one teat, of extreme age and unhygienic appearance. After one or two false starts the baby took to the bottle far better than I had dared hope, though feeding her was a painful performance.

Young anteaters, at that age, cling to their mother's back, and, since we had, so to speak, become her parents, she insisted on climbing on to one or the other of us nearly the whole time. Her claws were about three inches long, and she had a prodigious grip with them. During meals she clasped your leg affectionately with three paws, while with her remaining paw held your finger and squeezed it hard at intervals, for she was convinced that this would increase the flow of milk from the bottle. At the end of each feed you felt as though you had been mauled by a grizzly bear, while your fingers had been jammed in a door.

For the first few days I carried her about with me to give her confidence. She liked to lie across the back of my neck, her long nose hanging down one side of me and her long tail down the other, like a fur collar. Every time I moved she would tighten her grip in a panic, and this was painful. After the fourth shirt had been ruined I decided that she would have to cling to something else, so I filled a sack full of straw and introduced her to that. She accepted it without any fuss, and so between meals she would lie in her cage, clutching this substitute happily. We had already christened her "Sarah," and now that she developed this habit of sack-clutching we gave her a surname, and so she became known as "Sarah Huggersack."

Sarah was a model baby. Between feeds she lay quietly on her sack, occasionally yawning and showing a sticky, pinky-grey tongue about twelve inches long. When feeding-time came round she would suck the teat on her bottle so vigorously that it had soon changed from red to pale pink, the hole at the end of it had become about the size of a matchstick, and the whole thing drooped dismally from the neck of the bottle.

When we had to leave Paraguay in our extremely unsafe-looking four-seater plane, Sarah slept peacefully throughout the flight, lying on my wife's lap and snoring gently occasionally blowing a few bubbles of sticky saliva out of her nose.

On arriving in Buenos Aires our first thought was to give Sarah a treat. We would buy her a nice new shiny teat. We went to endless trouble selecting one exactly the right size, shape and colour, put it on the bottle and presented it to Sarah. She was scandalized. She honked wildly at the mere thought of a new teat, and sent the bottle flying with a well-directed clout from her paw. Nor did she calm down and start to feed until we had replaced the old withered teat on the bottle. She clung to it ever after; months after her arrival in England she still refused to be parted from it.

In Buenos Aires we housed our animals in an empty house on the outskirts of the city. From the centre, where we stayed, it took us half an hour in a taxi to reach it, and this journey we had to do twice and sometimes three times a day. We soon found that having a baby anteater made our social life difficult in the extreme. Have you ever tried to explain to a hostess that you must suddenly leave in the middle of dinner because you have to give a bottle to an anteater? In the end our friends gave up in despair. They used to telephone and ascertain the times of Sarah's feeds before inviting us.

By this time Sarah had become much more grown up and independent. After her evening feed she would go for a walk round the room by herself. This was a great advance, for up till then she had screamed blue murder if you moved more than a foot or so away from her. After her tour of inspection she liked to have a game. This consisted in walking past us, her nose in the air, her tail trailing temptingly. You were then supposed to grab the end of her tail and pull, whereupon she would swing round on three legs and give you a gentle clout with her paw. When this had been repeated twenty or thirty times she felt satisfied, and then you had to lay her on her back and tickle her tummy for ten minutes or so while she closed her eyes and blew bubbles of ecstasy at you. After this she would go to bed without any fuss. But try to put her to bed without giving her a game and she would kick and struggle and honk, and generally behave in a thoroughly spoilt manner.

When we eventually got on board ship, Sarah was not at all sure that she approved of sea-voyages. To begin with, the ship smelt queer; then there was a strong wind which nearly blew her over every time she went for a walk on deck; and lastly, which she hated most of all, the deck would not keep still. First it tilted one way, then it tilted another, and Sarah would go staggering about, honking plaintively, banging her nose on bulkheads and hatch-covers. When the weather improved, however, she seemed to enjoy the trip. Sometimes in the afternoon, when I had time, I would take her up to the promenade deck and we would sit in a deck-chair and sunbathe. She even paid a visit to the bridge, by special request of the captain. I thought it was because he had fallen for her charm and personality, but he confessed that it was because (having seen her only from a distance) he wanted to make sure which end of her was the front.

I must say we felt very proud of Sarah when we arrived in London Docks and she posed for the Press photographers with all the unselfconscious ease of a born celebrity. She even went so far as to lick one of the reporters—a great honour. I hastily tried to point this out to him, while helping to remove a large patch of sticky saliva from his coat. It was not everyone she would lick, I told him. His expression told me that he did not appreciate the point.

Sarah went straight from the docks to a zoo in Devonshire, and we hated to see her go. However, we were kept informed about her progress and she seemed to be doing well. She had formed a deep attachment to her keeper.

Some weeks later I was giving a lecture at the Festival Hall, and the organizer thought it would be rather a good idea if I introduced some animal on the stage at the end of my talk. I immediately thought of Sarah. Both the zoo authorities and the Festival Hall Management were willing, but, as it was now winter, I insisted that Sarah must have a dressing-room to wait in.

I met Sarah and her keeper at Paddington Station. Sarah was in a huge crate, for she had grown as big as a red setter, and she created quite a sensation on the platform. As soon as she heard my voice she flung herself at the bars of her cage and protruded twelve inches of sticky tongue in a moist and affectionate greeting. People standing near the cage leapt back hurriedly, thinking some curious form of snake was escaping and it took a lot of persuasion before we could find a porter brave enough to wheel the cage on a truck.

When we reached the Festival Hall we found that the rehearsal of a symphony concert had just come to an end. We wheeled

Sarah's big box down long corridors to the dressing-room, and just as we reached the door it was flung open and Sir Thomas Beecham strode out, smoking a large cigar. We waited for him to pass and then, very humbly, we wheeled Sarah into the dressing-room he had just vacated.

While I was on the stage, my wife kept Sarah occupied by running round and round the dressing-room with her, to the consternation and horror of one of the porters, who, hearing the noise, was convinced that Sarah had broken out of her cage and was attacking my wife. Eventually, however, the great moment arrived and amid tumultuous applause Sarah was carried on to the stage. She was very short-sighted, as all anteaters are, so to her the audience was non-existent. She looked round vaguely to see where the noise was coming from, but decided that it was not really worth worrying about. While I extolled her virtues, she wandered about the stage, oblivious, occasionally snuffling loudly in a corner, and repeatedly approaching the microphone and giving it a quick lick, which left it in a very sticky condition for the next performer. Just as I was telling the audience how well-behaved she was, she discovered the table in the middle of the stage, and with an immense sigh of satisfaction proceeded to scratch her bottom against one of the legs. She was a great success.

After the show, Sarah held court for a few select guests in her dressing-room, and became so skittish that she even galloped up and down outside in the corridor. Then we bundled her up warmly and put her on the night train for Devon with her keeper.

Apparently, on reaching the zoo again, Sarah was thoroughly spoilt. Her short spell as a celebrity had gone to her head. For three days she refused to be left alone, stamping about her cage and honking wildly, and refusing all food unless she was fed by hand.

A few months later I wanted Sarah to make an appearance on a television show I was doing, and so once again she tasted the glamour and glitter of show business. She behaved with the utmost decorum during rehearsals, except that she was dying to investigate the camera closely, and had to be restrained by force. When the show was over she resisted going back to her cage, and it took the united efforts of myself, my wife, Sarah's keeper and the studio manager to get her back into the box—for Sarah was then quite grown up, measuring six feet from nose to tail, standing three feet at the shoulder and with forearms as thick as my thigh.

We did not see Sarah again until quite recently, when we paid her a visit at her zoo. It had been six months since she had last seen us, and quite frankly I thought she would have forgotten us. Anteater fan though I am, I would be the first to admit that they are not creatures who are overburdened with brains, and six months is a long time. But the moment we called to her she came bounding out of her sleeping den and rushed to the wire to lick us. We even went into the cage and played with her, a sure sign that she really did recognize us, for no one else except her keeper dared enter.

Eventually we said good-bye to her, rather sadly, and left her sitting in the straw blowing bubbles after us. As my wife said: "It was rather as though we were leaving our child at boarding school." We are certainly her adopted parents, as far as Sarah is concerned.

Yesterday we had some good news. We heard that Sarah has got a mate. He is as yet too young to be put in with her, but soon he should be big enough. Who knows, by this time next year we may be grandparents to a fine bouncing baby anteater!

PORTRAIT OF PAVLO

It is a curious thing, but when you keep animals as pets you tend to look upon them so much as miniature human beings that you generally manage to impress some of your own characteristics on to them. This anthropomorphic attitude is awfully difficult to avoid. If you possess a golden hamster and are always watching the way he sits up and eats a nut, his little pink paws trembling with excitement, his pouches bulging as he saves in his cheeks what cannot be eaten immediately, you might one day come to the conclusion that he looks exactly like your own Uncle Amos sitting, full of port and nuts, in his favourite club. From that moment the damage is done. The hamster continues to behave like a hamster, but you regard him only as a miniature Uncle

Amos, clad in a ginger fur-coat, for ever sitting in his club, his cheeks bulging with food. There are very few animals who have characters strong and distinct enough to overcome this treatment, who display such powerful personalities that you are forced to treat them as individuals and not as miniature human beings. Of the many hundreds of animals I have collected for zoos in this country, and of the many I have kept as pets, I can remember at the most about a dozen creatures who had this strength of personality that not only made them completely different from others of their kind, but enabled them to resist all attempts on my part to turn them into something they were not.

One of the smallest of these animals was Pavlo, a black-eared marmoset, and his story really started one evening when, on a collecting trip in British Guiana, I sat quietly in the bushes near a clearing, watching a hole in a bank which I had good reason to believe contained an animal of some description. The sun was setting and the sky was a glorious salmon pink, and outlined against it were the massive trees of the forest, their branches so entwined with creepers that each tree looked as though it had been caught in a giant spider's web. There is nothing quite so soothing as a tropical forest at this time of day. I sat there absorbing sights and colours, my mind in the blank and receptive state that the Buddhists tell us is the first step towards Nirvana. Suddenly my trance was shattered by a shrill and prolonged squeak of such intensity that it felt as though someone had driven a needle into my ear. Peering above me cautiously, I tried to see where the sound had come from: it seemed the wrong sort of note for a tree-frog or an insect, and far too sharp and tuneless to be a bird. There, on a great branch about thirty feet above me, I saw the source of the noise: a diminutive marmoset was trotting along a wide branch as if it were an arterial road, picking his way in and out of the forest of orchids and other parasitic plants that grew in clumps from the bark. As I watched, he stopped, sat up on his hind legs and uttered another of his piercing cries; this time he was answered from some distance away, and within a moment or two other marmosets had joined him. Trilling and squeaking to each other, they moved among the orchids, searching diligently, occasionally uttering shrill squeaks of joy as they unearthed a cockroach or a beetle among the leaves. One of them pursued something through an orchid plant for a long time, parting the leaves and peering between them with an intense expression on his tiny face. Every time he made a grab the leaves got in the way and the insect managed to escape round the other side of the plant. Eventually, more by good luck than skill, he dived his small hands in amongst the leaves and, with a twitter of triumph, emerged with a fat cockroach clutched firmly between his fingers. The insect was a large one and its wriggling was strenuous, so, presumably in case he dropped it, he stuffed the whole thing into his mouth. He sat there munching happily, and when he had swallowed the last morsel, he carefully examined both the palms and backs of his paws to make sure there was none left.

I was so entranced by this glimpse into the private life of the marmoset that it was not until the little party had moved off into the now-gloomy forest that I realized I had an acute crick in my neck and that one of my legs had gone to sleep.

A considerable time later my attention was once again drawn to marmosets. I went down to an animal dealer's shop in London, to inquire about something quite different, and the first thing I saw on entering the shop was a cage full of marmosets, a pathetic, scruffy group of ten, crouched in a dirty cage on a perch so small that they were continuously having to jostle and squabble for a place to sit. Most of them were adults, but there was one youngster who seemed to be getting rather a rough time of it. He was thin and unkempt, so small that whenever there was a reshuffling of positions on the perch he was always the one to get knocked off. As I watched this pathetic, shivering little group, I remembered the little family party I had seen in Guiana, grubbing happily for their dinner among the orchids, and I felt that I could not leave the shop without rescuing at least one of the tiny animals. So within five minutes I had paid the price of liberation, and the smallest occupant of the cage was dragged out, screaming with alarm, and bundled into a cardboard box.

When I got him home I christened him Pavlo and introduced him to the family, who viewed him with suspicion. However, as soon as Pavlo had settled down he set about the task of winning their confidence, and in a very short time he had all of us under his minute thumb. In spite of his size (he fitted comfortably into a large teacup), he had a terrific personality, a Napoleonic air about him which was difficult to resist. His head was only the size of a large walnut, but it soon became apparent that it contained a brain of considerable power and intelligence. At first we kept him in a large cage in the drawing-room, where he would have plenty of company, but he was so obviously miserable when confined that we started letting him out for an hour or two every day. This was our undoing. Very soon Pavlo had convinced us that the cage was unnecessary, so it was consigned to the rubbish-heap, and he had the run of the house all day and every day. He became accepted as a diminutive member of the family, and he treated the house as though he owned it and we were his guests.

At first sight Pavlo resembled a curious kind of squirrel, until you noticed his very human face and his bright, shrewd, brown eyes. His fur was soft, and presented a brindled appearance because the individual hairs were banded with orange, black and grey, in that order; his tail, however, was ringed with black and white. The fur on his head and neck was chocolate brown, and hung round his shoulders and chest in a tattered fringe. His large ears were hidden by long ear-tufts of the same chocolate colour. Across his forehead, above his eyes and the aristocratic bridge of his tiny nose, was a broad white patch.

Everyone who saw him, and who had any knowledge of animals, assured me that I would not keep him long: marmosets, they said, coming from the warm tropical forests of South America, never lived more than a year in this climate. It seemed that their cheerful prophecies were right when, after six months, Pavlo developed a form of paralysis and from the waist downwards lost all power of movement. We fought hard to save his life while those who had predicted this trouble said he ought to be destroyed. But he seemed in no pain, so we persevered. Four times a day we massaged his tiny legs, his back and tail with warm cod-liver oil, and he had more cod-liver oil in his special diet, which included such delicacies as grapes and pears. He lay pathetically on a cushion, wrapped in cotton-wool for warmth, while the family took it in turn to minister to his wants. Sunshine was what he needed most and plenty of it, but the English climate provided precious little.

So the neighbours were treated to the sight of us carrying our Lilliputian invalid round the garden, carefully placing his cushion in every patch of sunlight that appeared. This went on for a month, and at the end of it Pavlo could move his feet slightly and twitch his tail; two weeks later he was hobbling round the house, almost his old self again. We were delighted, even though the house did reek of cod-liver oil for months afterwards.

Instead of making him more delicate, his illness seemed to make him tougher, and at times he appeared almost indestructible. We never pampered him, and the only concession we made was to give him a hot-water bottle in his bed during the winter. He liked this so much that he would refuse to go to bed without it, even in mid-summer. His bedroom was a drawer in a tall-boy in my mother's room, and his bed consisted of an old dressing-gown and a piece of fur-coat. Putting Pavlo to bed was quite a ritual: first the dressing-gown had to be spread in the drawer and the bottle wrapped in it so that he did not burn himself. Then the piece of fur-coat had to be made into a sort of furry cave, into which Pavlo would crawl, curl up into a ball and close his eyes blissfully. At first we used to push the drawer closed, except for a crack to allow for air, as this prevented Pavlo from getting up too early in the morning. But he very soon learned that by pushing his head into the crack he could widen it and escape.

About six in the morning he would wake up to find that his bottle had gone cold, so he would sally forth in search of alternative warmth. He would scuttle across the floor and up the leg of my mother's bed, landing on the eiderdown. Then he would make his way up the bed, uttering squeaks of welcome, and burrow under the pillow where he would stay, cosy and warm, until it was time for her to get up. When she eventually got out of bed and left him, Pavlo would be furious, and would stand on the pillow chattering and screaming with rage. When he saw, however, that she had no intention of getting back to bed to keep him warm, he would scuttle down the passage to my room and crawl in with me. Here he would remain, stretched luxuriously on my chest, until it was time for me to get up, and then he would stand on my pillow and abuse me, screwing his tiny face up into a ferocious and most human scowl. Having told me what he thought of me, he would dash off and get into bed with my brother, and when he was turned out of there he would go and join my sister for a quick nap before breakfast. This migration from bed to bed was a regular morning performance.

Downstairs he had plenty of heating at his disposal. There was a tall standard-lamp in the drawing-room which belonged to him: in the winter he would crawl inside the shade and sit next to the bulb, basking in the heat. He also had a stool and a cushion by the fire, but he preferred the lamp, and so it had to be kept on all day for his benefit, and our electricity bill went up by leaps and bounds. In the first warm days of spring Pavlo would venture out into the garden, where his favourite haunt was the fence; he would sit in the sun, or potter up and down catching spiders and other delicacies for himself. Half-way along this fence was a sort of rustic arbour made out of poles thickly overgrown with creepers, and it was into this net of creepers that Pavlo would dash if danger threatened. For many years he carried on a feud with the big white cat from next door, for this beast was obviously under the impression that Pavlo was a strange type of rat which it was her duty to kill. She would spend many painful hours stalking him, but since she was as inconspicuous as a snowball against the green leaves she never managed to catch Pavlo unawares. He would wait until she was quite close, her yellow eye glaring, her tongue flicking her lips, and then he would trot off along the fence and dive in among the creepers. Sitting there in safety, he would scream and chitter like an urchin from between the flowers, while the frustrated cat prowled about trying to find a hole among the creepers big enough for her portly body to squeeze through.

Growing by the fence, between the house and Pavlo's creeper-covered hide-out, were two young fig-trees, and round the base of their trunks we had dug deep trenches which we kept full of water during the hot weather. Pavlo was pottering along the fence one day, chattering to himself and catching spiders, when he looked up and discovered that his arch-enemy the cat, huge and white, was sitting on the fence between him and his creeper-covered arbour. His only chance of escape was to go back along the fence and into the house, so Pavlo turned and bolted, squeaking for help as he ran. The fat white cat was not such an expert tight-rope walker as Pavlo, so her progress along the fence top was slow, but even so she was catching up on him. She was uncomfortably close behind him when he reached the fig-trees, and he became so nervous that he missed his footing and with a frantic scream of fright fell off the fence and straight into the water-filled trench below. He rose to the surface, spluttering and screaming, and splashing around in circles, while the cat watched him in amazement: she had obviously never seen an aquatic marmoset before. Luckily, before she had recovered from her astonishment and hooked him out of the water, I arrived on the scene and she fled. I rescued Pavlo, gibbering with rage, and he spent the rest of the afternoon in front of the fire, wrapped in a piece of blanket, muttering darkly to himself. This episode had a bad effect on his nerves, and for a whole week he refused to go out on the fence, and if he caught so much as a glimpse of the white cat he would scream until someone put him on their shoulder and comforted him.

Pavlo lived with us for eight years, and it was rather like having a leprechaun in the house: you never knew what was going to happen next. He did not adapt himself to our ways, we had to adapt ourselves to his. He insisted, for example, on having his meals with us, and his meals had to be the same as ours. He ate on the window-sill out of a saucer. For breakfast he would have porridge or cornflakes, with warm milk and sugar; at lunch he had green vegetables, potatoes and a spoonful of whatever pudding was going. At tea-time he had to be kept off the table by force, or he would dive into the jam-pot with shrill squeaks of delight; he was under the impression that the jam was put on the table for his benefit, and would get most annoyed if you differed with him on this point. We had to be ready to put him to bed at six o'clock sharp, and if we were late he would stalk furiously up and down outside his drawer, his fur standing on end with rage. We had to learn not to slam doors shut without first looking to see if Pavlo was sitting on top, because, for some reason, he liked to sit on doors and meditate. But our worst crime, according to him, was when we went out and left him for an afternoon. When we returned he would leave us in no doubt as to his feelings on the subject; we would be in disgrace; he would turn his back on us in disgust when we tried to talk to him; he would go and sit in a corner and glower at us, his little face screwed up into a scowl. After half an hour or so he would, very reluctantly, forgive us and with regal condescension accept a lump of sugar and some warm milk before retiring to bed. Pavlo's moods were most human, for he would scowl and mutter at you when he felt bad-tempered, and, very probably, try to give you a nip. When he was feeling affectionate, however, he would approach you with a loving expression on his face, poking his tongue out and in very rapidly, and smacking his lips, climb on to your shoulder and give your ear a series of passionate nibbles.

His method of getting about the house was a source of astonishment to everyone, for he hated running on the ground, and would never descend to the floor if he could avoid it. In his native forest he would have made his way through the trees from branch to branch and from creeper to creeper, but there were no such refinements in a suburban house. So Pavlo used the picture-rails as his highways, and he would scuttle along them at incredible speeds, hanging on with one hand and one foot, humping himself along like a hairy caterpillar, until he was able to drop on to the window-sill. He could shin up the smooth edge of a door more quickly and easily than we could walk up a flight of stairs. Sometimes he would cadge a lift from the dog, leaping on to his back and clinging there like a miniature Old Man of the Sea. The dog, who had been taught that Pavlo's person was sacred, would give us mute and appealing looks until we removed the monkey from his back. He disliked Pavlo for two reasons: firstly, he did not see why such a rat-like object should be allowed the run of the house, and secondly, Pavlo used to go out of his way to be annoying. He would hang down from the arm of a chair when the dog passed and pull his eyebrows or whiskers and then leap back out of range. Or else he would wait until the dog was asleep and then make a swift attack on his unprotected tail. Occasionally, however, there would be a sort of armed truce, and the dog would lie in front of the fire while Pavlo, perched on his ribs, would diligently comb his shaggy coat.

When Pavlo died, he staged his deathbed scene in the best

Victorian traditions. He had been unwell for a couple of days, and had spent his time on the window-sill of my sister's room, lying in the sun on his bit of fur-coat. One morning he started to squeak frantically to my sister, who became alarmed and shouted out to the rest of us that she thought he was dying. The whole family at once dropped whatever they were doing and fled upstairs. We gathered round the window-sill and watched Pavlo carefully, but there seemed to be nothing very much the matter with him. He accepted a drink of milk and then lay back on his fur-coat and surveyed us all with bright eyes. We had just decided that it was a false alarm when he suddenly went limp. In a panic we forced open his clenched jaws and poured a little milk down his throat. Slowly he regained consciousness, lying limp in my cupped hands. He looked at us for a moment and then, summoning up his last remaining strength, poked his tongue out at us and smacked his lips in a last gesture of affection. Then he fell back and died quite quietly.

The house and garden seemed very empty without his minute strutting figure and fiery personality. No longer did the sight of a spider evoke cries of: "Where's Pavlo?" No longer were we woken up at six in the morning, feeling his cold feet on our faces. He had become one of the family in a way that no other pet had ever done, and we mourned his death. Even the white cat next door seemed moody and depressed, for without Pavlo in it our garden seemed to have lost its savour for her.

PART FOUR

THE
HUMAN
ANIMAL

WHEN you travel round the world collecting animals you also, of necessity, collect human beings. I am much more intolerant of a human being's shortcomings than I am of an animal's, but in this respect I have been lucky, for most of the people I have come across in my travels have been charming. In most cases, of course, the fact that you are an animal-collector helps, since people always seem delighted to meet someone with such an unusual occupation, and they go out of their way to assist you.

One of the loveliest and most sophisticated women I know has helped me cram a couple of swans into a taxi-cab boot in the middle of Buenos Aires, and anyone who has ever tried to carry livestock in a Buenos Aires taxi will know what a feat that must have been. A millionaire has let me stack cages of livestock on the front porch of his elegant town house, and even when an armadillo escaped and went through the main flower-bed like a bulldozer, he remained unruffled and calm. The madame of the local brothel once acted as our housekeeper (getting all her girls to do the housework when not otherwise employed), and she once even assaulted the local chief of police on our behalf. A man in Africa—notorious for his dislike of strangers and animals—let us stay for six weeks in his house and fill it with a weird variety of frogs, snakes, squirrels and mongooses. I have had the captain of a ship come down into the hold at eleven at night, take off his coat, roll up his sleeves and set to work helping me clean out cages and chop up food for the animals. I know an artist who, having travelled thousands of miles to paint a series of pictures of various Indian tribes, got involved in my affairs and spent his whole time catching animals and none on painting. By that time, of course, he could not paint anyway, as I had commandeered all his canvas to make snake-boxes. There was the little cockney P.W.D. man who, not having met me previously, offered to drive me a hundred-odd miles, over atrocious African roads in his brand-new Austin in order that I might follow up the rumour of a baby gorilla. All *he* got out of the trip was a hangover and a broken spring.

At times I have met such interesting and peculiar people I have been tempted to give up animals and take up anthropology.

Then I have come across the unpleasant human animal. The District Officer who drawled, "We chaps are here to help you chaps . . ." and then proceeded to be as obstructive and unpleasant as possible. The Overseer in Paraguay who, because he disliked me, did not tell me for two weeks that some local Indians had captured a rare and beautiful animal which I wanted, and were waiting for me to collect it. By the time I received the animal it was too weak to stand and died of pneumonia within forty-eight hours. The sailor who was mentally unbalanced and who, in a fit of sadistic humour, overturned a row of our cages one night, including one in which a pair of extremely rare squirrels had just had a baby. The baby died.

Fortunately these types of human are rare, and the pleasant ones I have met have more than compensated for them. But even so, I think I will stick to animals.

MacTOOTLE

When people discover my job for the first time, they always ask me for details of the many adventures they assume I have had in what they will persist in calling the "jungle".

I returned to England after my first West African trip and described with enthusiasm the hundreds of square miles of rain-forest I had lived and worked in for eight months. I said that in this forest I had spent many happy days, and during all this time I never had one experience that could, with any justification be called "hair-raising," but when I told people this they decided that I was either exceptionally modest or a charlatan.

On my way out to West Africa for the second time, I met on board ship a young Irishman called MacTootle who was going out to a job on a banana plantation in the Cameroons. He confessed to me that he had never before left England and he was quite convinced that Africa was the most dangerous place imaginable. His chief fear seemed to be that the entire snake population of the Continent was going to be assembled on the docks to meet him. In order to relieve his mind, I told him that in all the months I had spent in the forest I had seen precisely five snakes, and these had run away so fast that I had been unable to capture them. He asked me if it was a dangerous job to catch a snake, and I replied, quite truthfully, that the majority of snakes were extremely easy to capture, if you kept your head and knew your snake and its habits. All this soothed MacTootle considerably, and when he landed he swore that, before I returned to England, he would obtain some rare specimens for me; I thanked him and promptly forgot all about it.

Five months later I was ready to leave for England with a collection of about two hundred creatures, ranging from grasshoppers to chimpanzees. Very late on the night the ship was due to sail, a small van drew up with screeching brakes outside my camp and my young Irishman alighted, together with several friends of his. He explained with great glee that he had got me the specimens he had promised. Apparently he had discovered a large hole or pit, somewhere on the plantation he was working on, which had presumably been dug to act as a drainage sump. This pit, he said, was full of snakes, and they were all mine—providing I went and got them.

He was so delighted at the thought of all those specimens he had found for me that I had not the heart to point out that crawling about in a pit full of snakes at twelve o'clock at night was not my idea of a pleasurable occupation, enthusiastic naturalist though I was. Furthermore, he had obviously been boasting about my powers to his friends, and he had brought them all along to see my snake-catching methods. So, with considerable reluctance, I said I would go and catch reptiles; I have rarely regretted a decision more.

I collected a large canvas snake-bag, and a stick with a Y-shaped fork of brass at one end; then I squeezed into the van with my excited audience and we drove off. At half-past twelve we reached my friend's bungalow, and we stopped there for a drink before walking through the plantation to the pit.

"You'll be wanting some rope, will you not?" asked MacTootle.

"Rope?" I said. "What for?"

"Why, to lower yourself into the hole, of course," he said cheerfully. I began to feel an unpleasant sensation in the pit of my stomach. I asked for a description of the pit. It was apparently some twenty-five feet long, four feet wide and twelve feet deep. Everyone assured me that I could not get down there without a rope. While my friend went off to look for one which I hoped very much he would not find, I had another quick drink and wondered how I could have been foolish enough to get myself mixed up in this fantastic snake-hunt. Snakes in trees, on the ground or in shallow ditches were fairly easy to manage, but an unspecified number of them at the bottom of a pit so deep that you had to be lowered into it on the end of a rope did not sound at all inviting. I thought that I had an opportunity of backing out gracefully when the question of lighting arose, and it was dis-- covered that none of us had a torch. My friend, who had now returned with the rope, was quite determined that nothing was going to interfere with his plans: he solved the lighting question by tying a big paraffin pressure-lamp on to the end of a length of cord, and informed the company that he personally would lower it into the pit for me. I thanked him in what I hoped was a steady voice.

"That's all right," he said, "I'm determined you'll have your fun. This lamp's much better than a torch, and you'll need all the light you can get, for there's any number of the little devils down there."

We then had to wait a while for the arrival of my friend's brother and sister-in-law: he had asked them to come along, he explained, because they would probably never get another chance to see anyone capturing snakes, and he did not want them to miss it.

Eventually eight of us wended our way through the banana plantation and seven of us were laughing and chattering excitedly at the thought of the treat in store. It suddenly occurred to me that I was wearing the most inadequate clothing for snake-hunting: thin tropical trousers and a pair of plimsoll shoes. Even the most puny reptiles would have no difficulty in penetrating to my skin with one bite. However, before I could explain this we arrived at the edge of the pit, and in the lamplight it looked to me like nothing more nor less than an extremely large grave. My friend's description of it had been accurate enough, but what he had failed to tell me was that the sides of the pit consisted of dry, crumbling earth, honeycombed with cracks and holes that offered plenty of hiding-places for any number of snakes. While I crouched down on the edge of the pit, the lamp was solemnly lowered into the depths so that I might spy out the land and try to identify the snakes. Up to that moment I had cheered myself with the thought that, after all, the snakes might turn out to be a harmless variety, but when the light reached the bottom this hope was shattered, for I saw that the pit was simply crawling with young Gaboon vipers, one of the most deadly snakes in the world.

During the daytime these snakes are very sluggish and it is quite a simple job to capture them, but at night, when they wake up and hunt for their food, they can be unpleasantly quick. These young ones in the pit were each about two feet long and a couple of inches in diameter, and they were all, as far as I could judge, very much awake. They wriggled round and round the pit with great rapidity, and kept lifting their heavy, arrow-shaped heads and contemplating the lamp, flicking their tongues out and in in a most suggestive manner.

I counted eight Gaboon vipers in the pit, but their coloration matched the leaf-mould so beautifully that I could not be sure I was not counting some of them twice. Just at that moment my friend trod heavily on the edge of the pit, and a large lump of earth fell among the reptiles, who all looked up and hissed loudly. Everyone backed away hastily, and I thought it a very suitable opportunity to explain the point about my clothing. My friend, with typical Irish generosity, offered to lend me his trousers, which were of stout twill, and the strong pair of shoes he was wearing. Now the last of my excuses was gone and I had not the nerve to protest further. We went discreetly behind a bush and exchanged trousers and shoes. My friend was built on more generous lines than I, and the clothes were not exactly a snug fit; however, as he rightly pointed out, the bit of trouser-leg I had to turn up at the bottom would act as additional protection for my ankles.

Drearily I approached the pit. My audience was clustered round, twittering in delicious anticipation. I tied the rope round my waist with what I very soon discovered to be a slip-knot, and crawled to the edge. My descent had not got the airy grace of a pantomime fairy: the sides of the pit were so crumbly that every time I tried to gain a foothold I dislodged large quantities of earth, and as this fell among the snakes it was greeted with peevish hisses. I had to dangle in mid-air, being gently lowered by my companions, while the slip-knot grasped me ever tighter round the waist. Eventually I looked down and I saw that my feet

were about a yard from the ground. I shouted to my friends to stop lowering me, as I wanted to examine the ground I was to land on and make sure there were no snakes lying there. After a careful inspection I could not see any reptiles directly under me, so I shouted "Lower away" in what I sincerely hoped was an intrepid tone of voice. As I started on my descent again, two things happened at once: firstly, one of my borrowed shoes fell off and, secondly, the lamp, which none of us had remembered to pump up, died away to a faint glow of light, rather like a plump cigar-end. At that precise moment I touched ground with my bare foot, and I cannot remember ever having been so frightened, before or since.

I stood motionless, sweating with great freedom, while the lamp was hastily hauled up to the surface, pumped up, and lowered down again. I have never been so glad to see a humble pressure-lamp. Now the pit was once more flooded with lamp-light I began to feel a little braver. I retrieved my shoe and put it on, and this made me feel even better. I grasped my stick in a moist hand and approached the nearest snake. I pinned it to the ground with the forked end of the stick, picked it up and put it in the bag. This part of the procedure gave me no qualms, for it was simple enough and not dangerous provided you exercised a certain care. The idea is to pin the reptile across the head with the fork and then get a good firm grip on its neck before picking it up. What worried me was the fact that while my attention was occupied with one snake, all the others were wriggling round frantically, and I had to keep a cautious eye open in case one got behind me and I stepped back on it. They were beautifuly marked with an intricate pattern of brown, silver, pink and cream blotches, and when they remained still this coloration made them extremely hard to see; they just melted into the background. As soon as I pinned one to the ground, it would start to hiss like a kettle, and all the others would hiss in sympathy—a most unpleasant sound.

There was one nasty moment when I bent down to pick up one of the reptiles and heard a loud hissing apparently coming from somewhere horribly close to my ear. I straightened up and found myself staring into a pair of angry silver-coloured eyes approximately a foot away. After considerable juggling I managed to get this snake down on to the ground and pin him beneath my stick. On the whole, the reptiles were just as scared of me as I was of them, and they did their best to get out of my way. It was only when I had them cornered that they fought and struck viciously at the stick, but bounced off the brass fork with a reassuring ping. However, one of them must have been more experienced, for he ignored the brass fork and bit instead at the wood. He got a good grip and hung on like a bulldog; he would not let go even when I lifted him clear of the ground. Eventually I had to shake the stick really hard, and the snake sailed through the air, hit the side of the pit and fell to the ground hissing furiously. When I approached him with the stick again, he refused to bite and I had no difficulty in picking him up.

I was down in the pit for about half an hour, and during that time I caught twelve Gaboon vipers; I was not sure, even then, that I had captured all of them, but I felt it would be tempting fate to stay down there any longer. My companions hauled me out, hot, dirty and streaming with sweat, clutching in one hand a bag full of loudly hissing snakes.

"There, now," said my friend triumphantly, while I was recovering my breath, "I told you I'd get you some specimens, did I not?"

I just nodded; by that time I was beyond speech. I sat on the ground, smoking a much-needed cigarette and trying to steady my trembling hands. Now that the danger was over I began to realize for the first time how extremely stupid I had been to go into the pit in the first place, and how exceptionally lucky I was to have come out of it alive. I made a mental note that in future, if anyone asked me if animal-collecting was a dangerous occupation, I would reply that it was only as dangerous as your own stupidity allowed it to be. When I had recovered slightly, I looked about and discovered that one of my audience was missing.

"Where's your brother got to?" I asked my friend.

"Oh him," said MacTootle with fine scorn, "he couldn't watch any more—he said it made him feel sick. He's waiting over there for us. You'll have to excuse him—he couldn't take it. Sure, and it required some guts to watch you down there with all them wretched reptiles."

SEBASTIAN

Not long ago I spent some months in Argentina, and it was while there that I first met Sebastian. He was a gaucho, the South American equivalent of the North American cowboy. Like the cowboy, the gaucho is becoming rare nowadays, for most of the farms or estancias in Argentina are increasingly mechanized.

My reasons for being in Argentina were twofold: firstly, I wanted to capture live specimens of the wild animal life to bring back for zoos in this country, and, secondly, I wanted to film these same animals in their natural haunts. A friend of mine owned a large estancia about seventy miles from Buenos Aires in an area noted for its wild life, and when he invited me down there to spend a fortnight I accepted the invitation with alacrity. Unfortunately, when the time arrived my friend had some business to attend to, and all he could do was to take me down to the estancia and introduce me to the place before rushing back to the city.

He met me at the little country station, and as we jogged down the dusty road in the buggy he told me that he had got everything arranged for me.

"I'll put you in charge of Sebastian," he said, "so you should be all right."

"Who's Sebastian?" I asked.

"Oh, just one of our gauchos," said my friend vaguely. "What he doesn't know about the animal life of this district isn't worth knowing. He'll be acting host in my absence, so just ask him for anything you want."

After we had lunched on the verandah of the house, my friend suggested I should meet Sebastian, so we saddled horses and rode out across the acres of golden grass shimmering in the sun, and through the thickets of giant thistles, each plant as high as a man on horseback. In half an hour or so we came to a small wood of eucalyptus trees, and in the middle of it was a long, low, whitewashed house. A large and elderly dog, lying in the sun-drenched dust, lifted his head and gave a half-hearted bark before going back to sleep again. We dismounted and tied up the horses.

"Sebastian built this house himself," said my friend. "He's probably round the back having a siesta."

We went round the house, and there, slung between two slender eucalyptus trees, was an enormous hammock, and in it lay Sebastian.

My first impression was of a dwarf. I discovered later that he measured about five feet two inches, but lying there in that vast expanse of hammock he looked very tiny indeed. His immensely long and powerful arms dangled over the sides, and they were burnt to a rich mahogany brown, with a faint mist of white hair on them. I couldn't see his face, for it was covered by a black hat that rose and fell rhythmically, while from underneath it came the most prolonged and fearsome snores I have ever heard. My friend seized one of Sebastian's dangling hands and tugged at it vigorously, at the same time bending down and shouting in the sleeping man's ear as loudly as he could: "Sebastian—Sebastian. Wake up, you have visitors." This noisy greeting had no effect whatever; Sebastian continued to snore under his hat. My friend looked at me and shrugged.

"He's always like this when he's asleep," he explained. "Here, catch hold of his other arm and let's get him out of the hammock."

I took the other arm and we hauled him into a sitting position. The black hat rolled off and disclosed a round, brown chubby face, neatly divided into three by a great curved moustache, stained golden with nicotine, and a pair of snow-white eyebrows that curved up on to his forehead like the horns of a goat. My friend caught hold of his shoulders and shook him, repeating his name loudly, and suddenly a pair of wicked black eyes opened under the white brows and Sebastian glared at us sleepily. As soon as he recognized my friend he uttered a roar of anguish and struggled to his feet: "Señor!" he bellowed. "How nice to see you. . . . Ah, pardon me, señor, that I'm sleeping like a pig in its sty when you arrive . . . excuse me, please. I wasn't expecting you so early, otherwise I would have been prepared to welcome you properly."

He wrung my hand as my friend introduced me, and then, turning towards the house, he uttered a full-throated roar: "Maria—Maria——." In response to this nerve-shattering cry an attractive young woman of about thirty appeared, whom Sebastian introduced, with obvious pride, as his wife. Then he clasped my shoulder in one of his powerful hands and gazed earnestly into my face.

"Would you prefer coffee or maté, señor?" he asked innocently. Luckily my friend had warned me that Sebastian based his first impressions of people on whether they asked for coffee or maté, the Argentine green herb-tea, for in his opinion coffee was a disgusting drink, a liquid fit only to be consumed by city people and other depraved members of the human race. So I said I would have some maté. Sebastian turned and glared at his wife.

"Well?" he demanded. "Didn't you hear the señor say he would take maté? Are the guests to stand here dying of thirst while you gape at them like an owl in the sun?"

"The water is boiling," she replied placidly, "and they needn't stand, if you ask them to sit down."

"Don't answer me back, woman," roared Sebastian, his moustache bristling.

"You must excuse him, señor," said Maria, smiling at her husband affectionately, "he always gets excited when we have visitors."

Sebastian's face turned a deep brick-red.

"Excited?" he shouted indignantly "*Excited?* Who's excited? I'm as calm as a dead horse . . . please be seated, señors . . . excited indeed . . . you must excuse my wife, señor, she has a talent for exaggeration that would have earned her a wonderful political career if she had been born a man."

We sat down under the trees, and Sebastian lighted a small and pungent cigar while he continued to grumble good-naturedly about his wife's shortcomings.

"I should never have married again," he confided. "The trouble is that my wives never outlive me. Four times I've been married now and as I laid each woman to rest I said to myself, Sebastian, never again. Then, suddenly . . . puff! . . . I'm married again. My spirit is willing to remain single but my flesh is weak, and the trouble is that I have more flesh than spirit." He glanced down at his magnificent paunch with a rueful air, and then looked up and gave us a wide and disarming grin that displayed a great expanse of gum in which were planted two withered teeth.

"I suppose I shall always be weak, señor . . . but then a man without a wife is like a cow without an udder."

Maria brought the maté, and the little pot was handed round the circle, while we each in turn took sips from the slender silver maté pipe, and my friend explained to Sebastian exactly why I had come to the estancia. The gaucho was very enthusiastic, and when we told him that he might be required to take part in some of the film shots he stroked his moustache and shot a sly glance at his wife.

"D'you hear that, eh?" he inquired. "I shall be appearing in the cinema. Better watch that tongue of yours, my girl, for when the women in England see me on the screen they'll be flocking out here to try to get me."

"I see no reason why they should," returned his wife. "I expect they have good-for-nothings there, same as everywhere else." Sebastian contented himself with giving her a withering look, and then he turned to me.

"Don't worry, señor," he said, "I will do everything to help you in your work. I will do everything you want." He was as good as his word: that evening my friend left for Buenos Aires, and for the next two weeks Sebastian rarely left my side. His energy was prodigious, and his personality so fiery that he soon had complete control of my affairs. I simply told him just what I wanted and he did it for me, and the more extraordinary and difficult my requests the more he seemed to delight in accomplishing them for me. He could get more work out of the peons, or hired men, on the estancia than anyone I met, and, strangely enough, he did not get it by pleading or cajoling them but by insulting and ridiculing them, using a wealth of glittering similes that, instead of angering the men, convulsed them with laughter and made them work all the harder.

"Look at you," he would roar scathingly, "just look at you all . . . moving with all the speed of snails in bird-lime . . . it's a wonder to me that your horses don't take fright when you gallop, because even I can hear your eyeballs rattling in your empty skulls . . . you've not enough brain among the lot of you to make a rich soup for a bedbug. . . ." And the peons would gurgle with mirth and redouble their efforts. Apart from considering him a humorist, of course, the men knew very well that he would not ask them to do anything he could not do himself. But then there was hardly a thing that he did not know how to do, and among the peons an impossible task was always described as "something even Sebastian couldn't do." Mounted on his great black horse, his scarlet-and-blue poncho draped round his shoulders in vivid folds, Sebastian cut an impressive figure. On this horse he would gallop about the estancia, his lassoo whistling as he showed me the various methods of roping a steer. There are about six different ways of doing this, and Sebastian could perform them all with equal facility. The faster his horse travelled, the rougher the ground, the greater accuracy he seemed to obtain with his throws, until you had the impression that the steer had some sort of magnetic attraction for the rope and that it was impossible for him to miss.

If Sebastian was a master with a rope, he was a genius with his whip, a short-handled affair with a long slender thong, a deadly weapon which he was never without. I have seen him, at full gallop, pull this whip from his belt and neatly take the head off a thistle plant as he passed. Flicking cigarettes out of people's mouths was child's play to him. I was told that in the previous year a stranger to the district had cast doubts on Sebastian's abilities with a whip, and Sebastian had replied by stripping the man's shirt from his back, without once touching the skin beneath. Sebastian preferred his whip as a weapon—and he could use it like an elongated arm—yet he was very skilful with both knife and hatchet. With the latter weapon he could split a matchbox in two at about ten paces. No, Sebastian was definitely not the sort of man to get the wrong side of.

A lot of the hunting I did with Sebastian took place at night, when the nocturnal creatures came out of their burrows. Armed with torches, we would leave the estancia shortly after dark, never returning much before midnight or two in the morning, and generally bringing with us two or three specimens of one sort or another. On these hunts we were assisted by Sebastian's favourite dog, a mongrel of great age whose teeth had long since been worn down level with his gums. This animal was the perfect hunting-dog, for even when he caught a specimen it was impossible for him to hurt it with his toothless gums. Once he had chased and brought to bay some specimen, he would stand guard over it, giving one short yap every minute or so to guide us to the spot.

It was during one of these night hunts that I had a display of Sebastian's great strength. The dog had put up an armadillo, and after it had been chased for several hundred yards the creature took refuge down a hole. There were three of us that night: Sebastian, myself, and a peon. In chasing the armadillo the peon and I had far outstripped Sebastian, whose figure did not encourage running. The peon and I reached the hole just in time to see the rear end of the armadillo disappearing down it, so we flung ourselves on to the grass and while I got a grip on its tail the peon grasped its hind legs. The armadillo dug his long front claws into the sides of the hole, and though we tugged and pulled he was as immovable as though he were embedded in cement. Then the beast gave a sudden jerk and the peon lost his grip. The armadillo wriggled farther inside the hole, and I could feel his tail slipping through my fingers. Just at that moment Sebastian arrived on the scene, panting for breath. He pushed me out of the way, seized the armadillo's tail, braced his feet on either side of the hole and pulled. There was a shower of earth, and the armadillo came out of the hole like a cork out of a bottle. With one sharp tug Sebastian had accomplished what two of us had failed to do.

One of the creatures I wanted to film on the estancia was the rhea, the South American ostrich, which, like its African cousin, can run like a racehorse. I wanted to film the rheas being hunted in the old style, by men on horseback armed with boleadoras. These weapons consist of three wooden balls, about the size of cricket balls, each attached to the other by a fairly long string; they are whirled round the head and thrown so that they tangle themselves round the bird's legs and bring it to the ground. Sebastian arranged the whole hunt for me, and we spent my last day filming it. As most of the peons were to appear in these scenes, they all turned up that morning in their best clothes, each obviously trying to outdo the other by the brilliance of his costume. Sebastian surveyed them sourly from the back of his horse:

"Look at them, señor," he said, contemptuously spitting. "All done up and as shining as partridge eggs, and as excited as dogs on a bowling green, just because they think they're going to get their silly faces on the cinema screen . . . they make me sick."

But I noticed that he carefully combed his moustache before

the filming started. We were at it all day in the boiling sun, and by evening, when the last scenes had been shot, we all felt in need of a rest—all of us, that is, except Sebastian, who seemed as fresh as when he started. As we made our way home, he told me that he had organized a farewell party for me that night, and everyone on the estancia was to be present. There would be plenty of wine and singing and dancing, and his eyes gleamed as he told me about it. I had not the heart to explain that I was dead tired and would much rather go to bed, so I accepted the invitation.

The festivities took place in the great smoke-filled kitchen, with half a dozen flickering oil-lamps to light it. The band consisted of three guitars which were played with great verve. I need hardly say that the life and soul of the party was Sebastian. He drank more wine than everyone else, and yet remained sober; he played solos on the guitar; he sang a great variety of songs ranging from the vulgar to the pathetic; he consumed vast quantities of food. But, above all, he danced; danced the wild gaucho dances with their complicated steps and kicks and leaps, danced until the beams above vibrated with his steps and his spurs struck fire from the stone flags.

My friend, who had driven down from Buenos Aires to pick me up, arrived in the middle of the party and joined us. We sat in the corner, drinking a glass of wine together and watching Sebastian dance, while the peons clapped and roared applause.

"What incredible energy he's got," I remarked. "He's been working harder than anyone else today, and now he's danced us all off our feet."

"That's what a life on the pampa does for you!" replied my friend. "But, seriously, I think he's quite amazing for his age, don't you?"

"Why?" I asked casually, "how old is he?"

My friend looked at me in surprise:

"Don't you know?" he asked. "In about two months' time Sebastian will be ninety-five."